Collins | stre

EDINBURGH

CW00328158

Contents

Key to street map pages 2-3

Key to street map symbols 4

Key to route planning map symbols 5

City centre map 6-7

Street maps 8-71

Route planning maps 72-75

Index 76-112

Published by Collins
An imprint of HarperCollins*Publishers*
77-85 Fulham Palace Road, Hammersmith, London W6 8JB

www.collins.co.uk

Copyright © HarperCollins*Publishers* Ltd 2004

Collins® is a registered trademark of HarperCollins*Publishers* Limited

Mapping generated from Collins Bartholomew digital databases

Page 6 to 71 use map data licensed from Ordnance Survey ® with
the permission of the Controller of Her Majesty's Stationery Office.
© Crown copyright. Licence number 399302

The grid on mapping on pages 6 to 71 is the National Grid taken
from the Ordnance Survey map with the permission of the Controller
of Her Majesty's Stationery Office.

Printed in Hong Kong

ISBN 0 00 7170068   Imp 001   QI11607 ADM

e-mail: roadcheck@harpercollins.co.uk

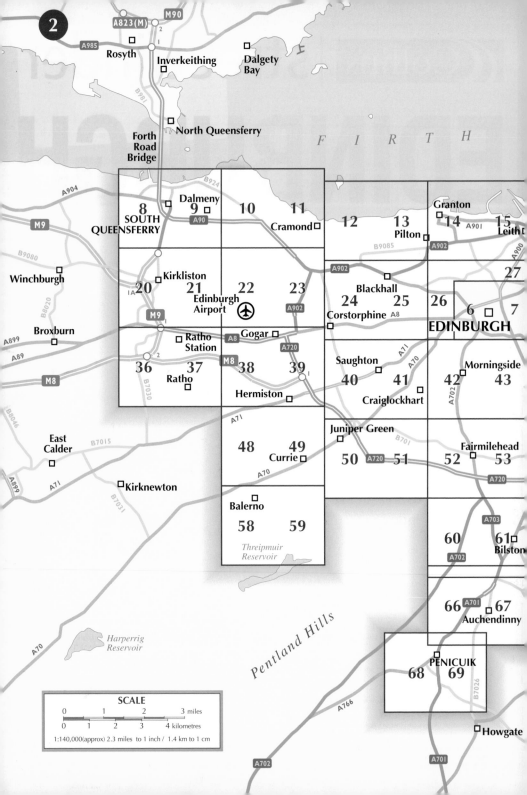

2

A823(M)
M90
A985
Rosyth
Inverkeithing
Dalgety Bay

B981

North Queensferry

Forth Road Bridge

F I R T H

A904

B924

Dalmeny

8
SOUTH QUEENSFERRY
9
A90
10
11
Cramond
12
13
Pilton
Granton
14
A901
15
Leith

M9

B9080

B9085
A902

A800

Winchburgh

Kirkliston

20
1A
21
Edinburgh Airport ✈
22
23
A902
A902
Blackhall
24
Corstorphine
25
A8
26
27
6
7
EDINBURGH

M9

B8020

Broxburn

A899

A89

M8

Ratho Station
A8
2
36
37
Ratho
B7030
M8
38
Gogar
39
1
Hermiston
A720
Saughton
40
A71
41
Craiglockhart
A70
42
A702
Morningside
43

East Calder
B7015

A71

A899

A70

Kirknewton

B7031

48
49
Currie
A70

Juniper Green
50
A720
51
B701
52
Fairmilehead
53
A720

Balerno
58
59
Threipmuir Reservoir

A703
60
A702
61
Bilston

Harperrig Reservoir

Pentland Hills

66
A701
67
Auchendinny

A70

68
PENICUIK
69
B7026

A766

A702

A701

Howgate

SCALE
0   1   2   3 miles
0   1   2   3   4 kilometres
1:140,000(approx) 2.3 miles to 1 inch / 1.4 km to 1 cm

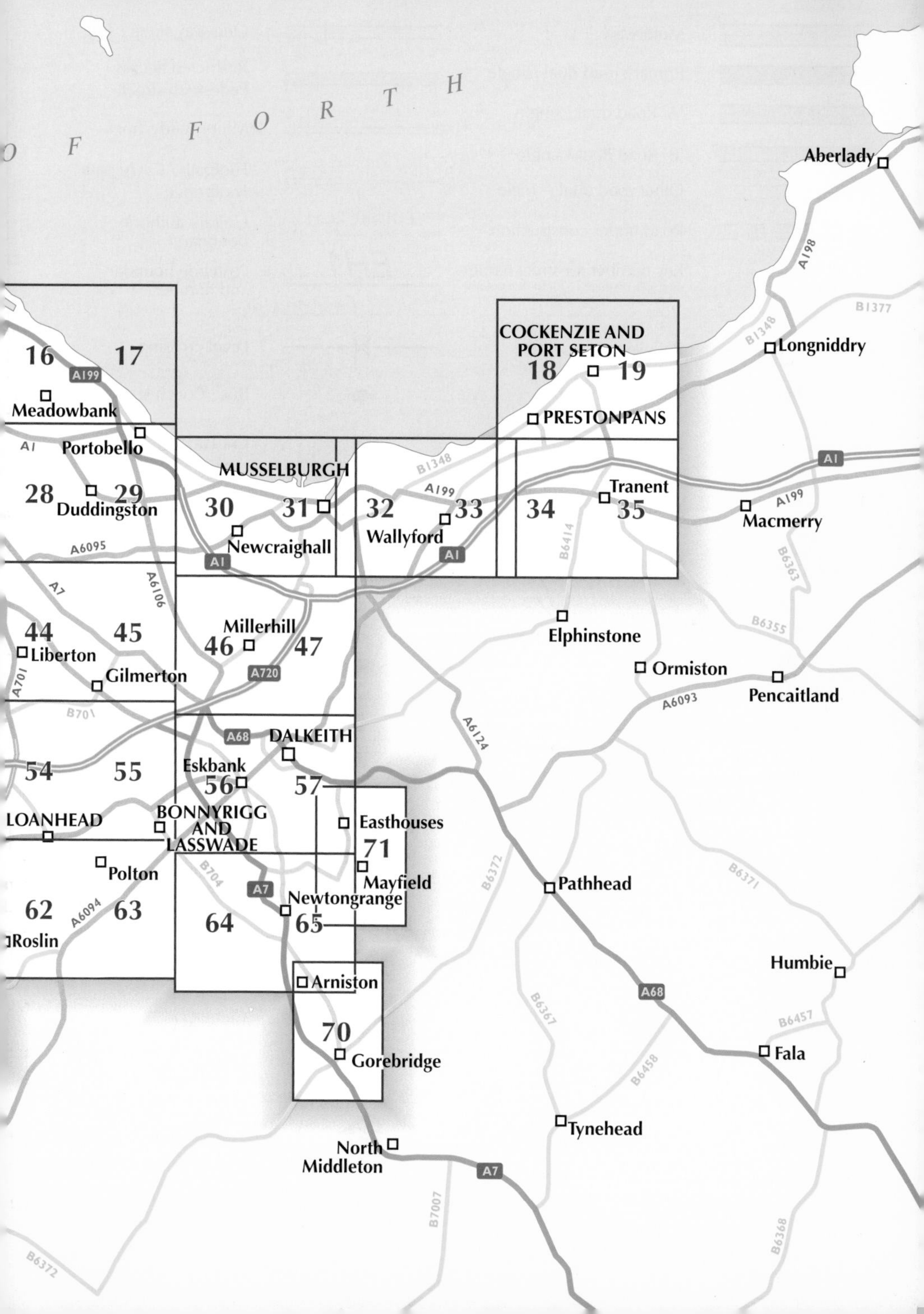

Key to street map pages 3

OF FORTH

Aberlady □

A198

B1377

16 17
A199
Meadowbank □

B1348
Longniddry □

COCKENZIE AND
PORT SETON
18 □ 19

A1

A199

A1

Portobello
A1

MUSSELBURGH

B1348

□ PRESTONPANS

28 □ 29
Duddingston

A6095

30 31 □
Newcraighall

32 33
Wallyford
A199

34 35 Tranent □

A199
Macmerry □

A7

A6106

A1

B6414

B6363

44 45
□ Liberton

Millerhill
46 □ 47

A720

Elphinstone □

□ Ormiston
A6093

Pencaitland □

B6355

A701

Gilmerton □

B701

A6124

A68

DALKEITH □

54 55
Eskbank
56 □ 57

LOANHEAD □

BONNYRIGG
AND
LASSWADE

□ Easthouses

71

B6372

□ Pathhead

B6371

Humbie □

Polton □

B704

A7

Mayfield
Newtongrange

62 63
□ Roslin
A6094

64 65 □

□ Arniston

A68

B6367

B6457

□ Fala

70
□ Gorebridge

B6458

B7007

□ Tynehead

North
Middleton □
A7

B6372

B6368

4 Key to street map symbols

Symbol	Description	Symbol	Description
M8	Motorway	Toll	One-way street / Toll
A720	Primary road dual /single		Restricted access / Pedestrian street
A70	'A' Road dual / single		Minor road / Track
B701	'B' Road dual / single	FB	Footpath / Cycle path / Footbridge
	Other road dual / single	EDINBURGH	Unitary authority boundary
	Road under construction	*EH1*	Postcode boundary and number
4	Key number for street name (See note on page 76 for further details)		
	Railway line		Level crossing
	Railway station		Bus / Coach station
	Railway tunnel	P	Car Park
	Leisure / Tourism		Hospital
	Shopping / Retail		Industry / Commerce
	Administration / Law		Other notable building
	Education		Major religious building
	Health centre		Cinema
Pol	Police station		Theatre
PO	Post Office	⊠ Hilton	Major Hotel
Lib	Library	i i	Tourist information centre (all year / seasonal)
+ ☾ ✡	Church / Mosque / Synagogue		Fire station / Ambulance station / Community centre
	Wood / Forest		Golf course
	Park / Garden / Recreation ground		Cemetery
	Public open space		Built up area
³15	National Grid reference	**15**	Page continuation number

SCALE

0	1/4	1/2	3/4	1 mile
0	0.25	0.5	0.75	1	1.25	1.5 kilometres

1 : 15,840   4 inches (10.2cm) to 1 mile / 6.3 cm to 1 km

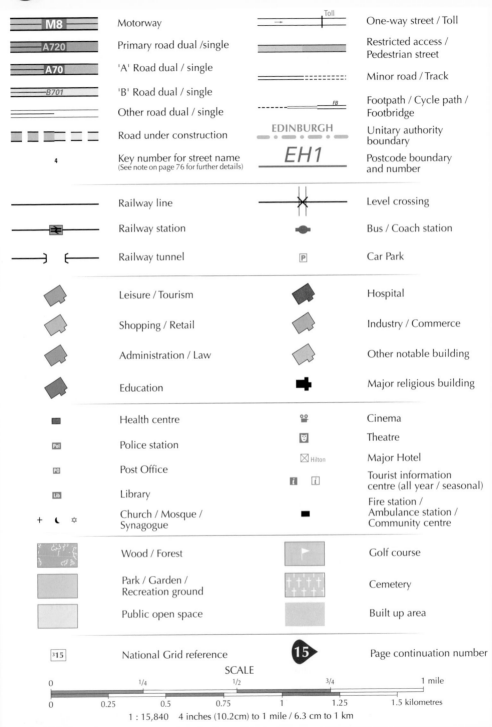

Key to route planning map symbols 5

Symbol	Description	Symbol	Description
M8	Motorway		Restricted access
8 9	Motorway junction with full / limited access		Road proposed or under construction
Stirling Harthill Hamilton	Motorway service area with off road / full / limited access		Multi-level junction
A725	Primary route dual / single carriageway		Roundabout
A73	'A' Road dual / single carriageway	6	Road distance in miles
B759	'B' Road dual / single carriageway		Road tunnel
	Minor road		Steep hill (arrows point downhill)
		Toll	Level crossing / Toll

	Railway line / station / tunnel	✈	Airport with scheduled services
	Car ferry	℗	Park and Ride site (operates at least five days a week)

	Built up area		Long distance footpath
□ □ ▫	Town / Village / Other settlement	468 ▲941	Spot / Summit height in metres
	Forest park boundary		Lake / Dam / River / Waterfall
	National / Regional park		Canal / Dry canal / Canal tunnel
	Woodland	🗼	Lighthouse

𝒊 🄸	Tourist information office (all year / seasonal)	🏟	Major sports venue
ⓜ	Ancient monument	🏁	Motor racing circuit
1738	Battlefield	🏛	Museum / Art gallery
▲ ⌗	Campsite / Caravan site		Nature reserve
🏰	Castle		Preserved railway
🕀	Country park		Racecourse
✚	Ecclesiastical building		Theme park
✿	Garden		University
⚑	Golf course		Wildlife park or Zoo
🏠	Historic house (with or without garden)	★	Other interesting feature
£	Major shopping centre / Outlet village	(NTS)	National Trust for Scotland

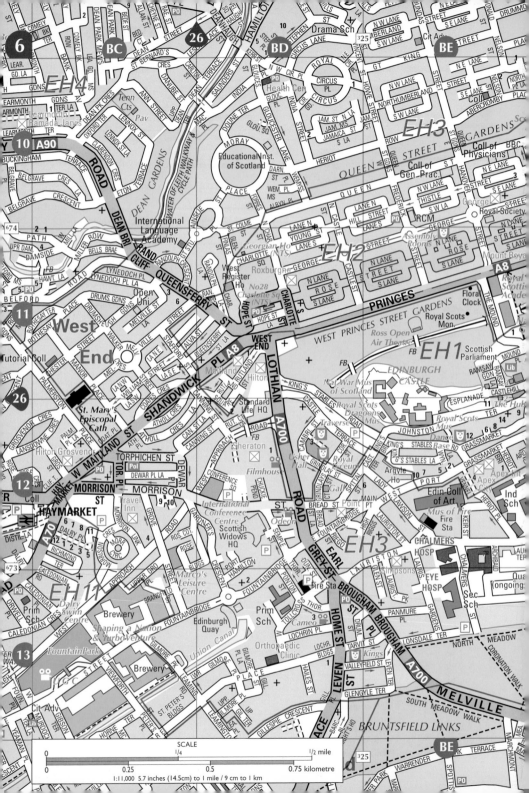

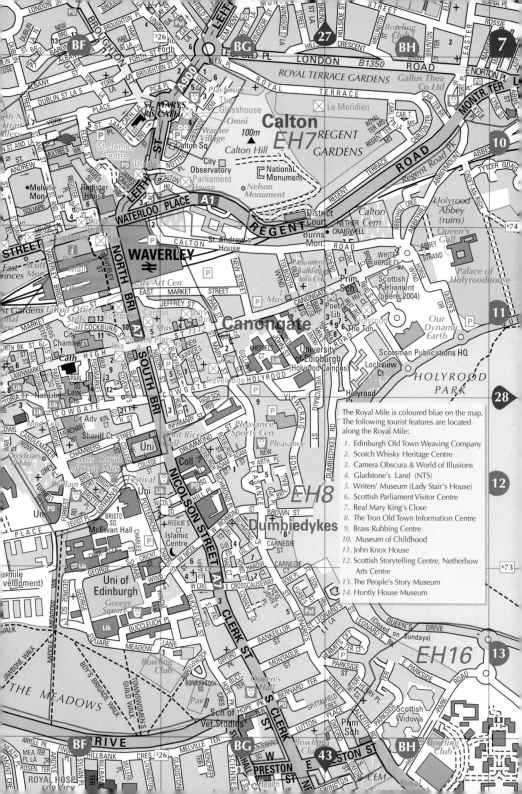

The Royal Mile is coloured blue on the map. The following tourist features are located along the Royal Mile:

1. Edinburgh Old Town Weaving Company
2. Scotch Whisky Heritage Centre
3. Camera Obscura & World of Illusions
4. Gladstone's Land (NTS)
5. Writers' Museum (Lady Stair's House)
6. Scottish Parliament Visitor Centre
7. Real Mary King's Close
8. The Tron Old Town Information Centre
9. Brass Rubbing Centre
10. Museum of Childhood
11. John Knox House
12. Scottish Storytelling Centre, Netherbow Arts Centre
13. The People's Story Museum
14. Huntly House Museum

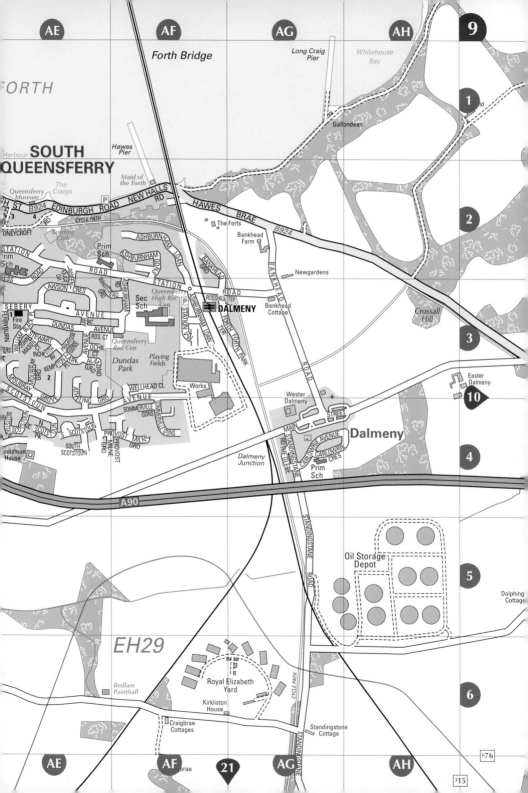

AE   **AF**   **AG**   **AH**   **9**

Forth Bridge

Long Craig Pier

Whitehouse Bay

1

FORTH

Gallondean

Harbour

Hawes Pier

SOUTH QUEENSFERRY

Queensferry Museum

The Craigs

Maid of the Forth

2

P

H ST
B924   EDINBURGH   ROAD   NEW HALLS   RD

HAWES   BRAE

B924

RD
CYCLE PATH

HONEYCROFT

Bowling Club

The Forts

Bankhead Farm

ASHBURNHAM LOAN

Newgardens

Crossall Hill

Prim Sch

STATION
Prim Sch

ASHBURNHAM GROVE

ROAD

BANKHEAD GRO

BANKHEAD

ROAD

Bankhead Cottage

3

STATION
ROAD

WHITEHEAD
ROAD

ASHBURNHAM RD

STATION
Queensferry High Rec Cen

P

ROSSHILL TER

FORTH

DALMENY

ESS

Sec Sch

QUEEN'S DR

LAWSON CRES

SEBERY

FERRYBURN

AVENUE

DUNDAS

Queensferry Rec Cen

Easter Dalmeny

10

Fire Sta

WILLIAM BLACK PL

STEWART

MASON

INCHGARVIE

PRIMROSE

AVENUE

PARK

OCHIL CT

ROS. CT

ALMOND

AVENUE

GRO

Dundas Park

Playing Fields

Wester Dalmeny

MAIN STREET

Dalmeny

MOUBRAY

MOUBRAY GRO

GROVE

CT

ATHELING GRO

WELLHEAD CL.

Works

SOMMERVILLE GDNS

STANDINGSTANE RD / THE GLEBE

CARLOWRIE AVENUE

PO

CARLOWRIE
CRES

4

SCOTSTOUN

Scotstoun House

SCOTSTOUN PK

N

SCOTSTOUN

SOUTH SCOTSTOUN

PROVOST MILNE GRO

SOMMERVILLE GDNS

AVENUE

PROVOST
MILNE
GRO

Dalmeny Junction

ROAD

Prim Sch

A90

STANDINGSTANE ROAD

Oil Storage Depot

5

Dolphing Cottage

EH29

Bedlam Paintball

Royal Elizabeth Yard

Kirkliston House

CYCLE PATH

6

Craigbrae Cottages

Standingstone Cottage

STANDINGSTANE

AE   **AF**   **21**   **AG**   **AH**

676

315

10
AJ
AK
AL
AM

1 Leuchold

LEUCHOLD
WOOD

Barnbougl
Castle

2

NEW
ENGLAND

Dalmeny
House

Crossall
Hill

Dalmeny
Stables

3

Dunter
Hill

Chapel Coppice

DALMENY PARK

MOUSE
WOOD

Easter
Dalmeny

9

MANSION HILL
WOOD

4

Dolphington Burn

Home Farm

Cock

A90

CYCLE PATH
B924

Dolphington
House

BURNSHOT
WOOD

Dolphington

5

Dolphington
Cottages

CRAIGIE
HILL

EH30

West
Craigie
Farm

Lowood

6

676

315

AJ

AK

22

AL

AM

HILLSI
TER

HILLSI   ROAD

1

2

FIRTH

OF

FORTH

DRUM SANDS

3

Tidal Ca

12

Snab Point

Long
Green

Eagle
Rock

4

eakwater

LONG GREEN
WOOD

Dalmeny
ome Farm

Linkfin Burn

Home Farm
Cottages

Cobble
Cottage
Passenger Ferry

ESPLANAD

P

Cramond
Village

P

Cramond
Tower

Cramond
House
Roman Fort
(remains)

KI

Wilderness
Wood

CRAMOND

RIVER ALMOND WALKWAY

GLEBE

Hall

MOND GDNS

5

EH4

GLEBE

THE
GLEBE

PO

CRAMOND

CRAMOND

Weir

SCHOOL BRAE

CADDELL'S
ROW

FAIR-A-FAR
COTTAGES

CRAMOND
ROAD

CRAMOND
TERRACE

CRAMOND PARK

CRAMOND

CRAMOND GN

AVENUE

ROAD

6

New
Burnshot

CYCLE PATH

FAIR-A-FAR

CRAMOND GRO

RIVER ALMOND

East
Craigie

CRAMOND VALE

WHITEHOUSE

CRAMOND
BK

CRAMOND
BK

INVER

Prim
Sch

GAMEKEEPER'S

Ind
Sch

BR

676

A90

319

12

AS AT AU AV

2

3

Cramond Island

The Knoll

Tidal Causeway

FIRTH O

4

Breakwater

ESPLANADE

SILVERKNOWES ESPLANADE

SILVERKNOWES ESPLANADE

MARINE DRIVE

MARINE

Cobble Cottage
enger Ferry

11

Cramond Tower
Cramond House
Hall
Roman Fort
(remains)

5

SILVERKNOWES
GOLF COURSE

RIVER ALMOND WALKWAY

GLEBE RD
THE GLEBE
SCHOOL BRAE
GLEBE GDNS
CRAMOND GLEBE ROAD

CRAMOND

CRAMOND ROAD NORTH

EH4

SILVERKNOWES ROAD

Clubhouse

SILVERKNOWES PARK

6

CRAMOND TERRACE
CRAMOND PARK
CRAMOND GRN
CRAMOND GDNS
CRAMOND PL
CRAMOND AVENUE
CRAMOND ROAD
CRAMOND BK

KEEPER'S ROW

BRUNTSFIELD LINKS

CRAMOND ROAD

Lauriston
Castle

Lauriston
Farm

SILVERKNOWES PARKWAY

SILVERKNOWES

676
Ind
Sch

GOLF COURSE

Clubhouse

BARNTON PARK

LAURISTON FARM ROAD

SILVERKNOWES HILL
CRESCENT

7

AVENUE WEST

CYCLE PATH

6
5
3
7
2
4
1

EASTER DRIVE

BARNTON PK
BARNTON GARDENS
BARNTON PK SOUTH

LAURISTON
SILVERKNOWES
SILVERKNOWES TER

DRIVE

ROYAL BURGESS

BARNTON AVENUE

BARNTON LOAN
BARNTON AVE
BARNTON AV

Superstore

THE GREEN

B9085

CORBIE HILL PL

AS AT

24

AU AV

319

Sec

QUALITY
SLA

BA **BB** **BC** **BD**

2

FIRTH OF

WESTERN BREAKWATER

EASTERN BREAKWATER

3

GRANTON HARBOUR

ROAD

4 **GRANTON**

WEST PIER

SEALCARR STREet

CHESTNUT ST

OXHILL ST

MIDDLE PIER

FORTH IND EST

WEST HARBOUR ROAD

NEW BROO

GRANTON PK AV

Custom House

GRAN SQ

LOWER GRANTON ROAD

A903 GRANTON

St. Columba's Hospice

MCKELVIE PARADE

ROAD A901

TRINIT CRES

13

GRANTON MS

GRANTON CRESCENT

Granton Crescent Park

GRANTON CRES

GRANTON VIEW

GRANTON SQ

WARDIE

LUFRA BANK

WARDIE SQ

BOSWALL ROAD

LOWER GRAN. RD

PRIMROSE BANK RD

ROW

RUSSELL

VICAROLINE PK

GRO

5 Bowling Club

WEST GRANTON CRESCENT

PILTON

WARDIEBURN DR

WAR DR

Comm Cen

WARDIEBURN

PL

GRANTON GDNS

GRANTON TER

WARDIEBURN PL

GRANTON PL

WARDIE CRESCENT

GRI SQ

WARDIE PL

GRIERSON AV

WARDIE

EH5 Recreation Grounds

Wardie Pavs

LENNOX

LOMOND STRING

Bowling Club Lomond Park

SPENCER PL TRINITY GRO

ZETLAND

Trinity

ROYSTON MAINS

BOSWALL

CREWE

PILTON DRIVE

PILTON PARK

Prim Sch

GRANTON

GRIERSON GDNS

BOS GDNS

GRIERSON CRES

Prim Sch

EAST

CARGIL

DENHAM GRN TER

PARKWAY

GRIERSON

AV

AFTON TER

AFTON PL

CARGIL CT

TRINITY CT

HAIG G

DENHAM GRN

BANGHO

BANGHO

Pilton

PILTON CRES

PILTON GDNS

PILTON LOAN

PILTON PLACE

PILTON PARK

AVENUE

BOSWALL GRN

BOSWALL CRES

FRASER GDNS

DARNELL RD

ROSEBANK PL

ROSE GRO

ROSE PL

Trinity Park House

CLARK

6

CREWE LOAN

CREWE TERRACE

East Pilton

BOSWALL QUAD

FRASER FRASER GDNS

FRASER AV

BANGHOLM

CREWE

PILTON

Telford Coll (North Campus)

Rec Grds

Ainslie Park Leisure Cen

BOSWAL AVENUE

BOSWALL

W FERRYFIELD

BOSWALL DRIVE

FRASER AVENUE

CYCLE PATH

Trinity Park House

WARDIE AV

ROSE

WE

76

Works

CYCLE PATH

The DuPit

Superstore

Rec Grd

INVERLEITH GDNS

Sports Centre

A902 FERRY

BOWHILL

INVERLEITH

Golden George's Sports C

EH3

Ind Sch

Sports Ground

George

7

B9085

A902

Fire Sta

Works

Playing Fields Telford Coll (South Campus)

Stewarts Melville Sports Ground

Clubhouse

Football Grd

Playing Field

Pav

FERRY ROAD

RUFC Ground Clubhouse

WARRISTON G

College of Art

WARRISTON CRE

323

ROAD

CREWE AVENUE

NORTH

ROCHEID PK

FETTES

Fettes College

WERB MS E WER

Pav

KINNEAR ROAD

Inverleith

Newfield Recreation Ground

Pav

FETTES ROW

INVERLEITH PLACE

INVERLEITH ROW

INVERLEITH TER

Glasshouse Experience

INVERLEITH

Royal Botanic Garden Edinburgh

Recreation Grounds

Pav

BA **BB** **26** **BC** **BD**

18

CG CH CJ CK

5

6

7

F I R T H   O F   F O R T H

Cockenzie
Harbour

West
Harbour

MARSHALL STREET

Cockenzie
Power
Station

EDINBURGH ROAD

WHIN PK

THORN TER

WHIN PK

WHIN
PARK

8

Whin Park
Industrial
Estate

P

EH32

9

B1348

NEW
CEMETERY

STREET

NETHERSHOT

LONGDYKES ROAD

MIDDLE

PRESTON

Playing
Fields

Football
Ground

SCHAW

SQUARE

PRESTONPANS

Infant
Sch

Town
Hall

PENNYPIT
PLAYING
FIELDS

HIGH

AVENUE

GRANGE

Community
Centre

Health
Centre

Sec
Sch

PARK
VIEW

PRESTON RD

Preston RD

THORNTREE CRES

GARDNER TERRACE

PRESTON ROAD

PRESTON AVENUE

Prestonpans
Swimming
Pool

BANKTON

10

Cuthill

CG

Bowling
Club

338

674

CH

34

Prim
Sch

ton

CJ

CK

Playing
Fields

PORT SETON

Port Seton Harbour

COCKENZIE

Seton

EH33

CL CM CN CP **19**

5

6

7

8

9

10

Seton Sands Holiday Village

Seton Collegiate Church

Seton House and Gardens

Coal Store

West Seton House

Works

Works

Open Cast Workings

Children's Resource Centre

CL CM **35** CN CP

Health Centre

Prim Sch

Bowling Club

LINKS ROAD B1348

GOSFORD ROAD

AVENUE ROAD

A198

B6371

A198

1361

674

342

THE PROM

BARRACKS STREET

WEMYSS PL

VIEWFORTH

COPSE

LINKS CT

FISHERS CRESCENT

GOLF DRIVE

LINKS VWW

LINKS VW

LONG CRAIGS

LINKS VW

FORTH GRO

THOMSON RD

PARK

CASTLE ROAD

CASTLE TER

CASTLE PARK

CASTLE VIEW

H WYND

SETON WYND

SETON VIEW

CRAIGS

SETON PARK

FISHERGATE

ROAD

LONG

LONG

JOHN'S PL

PARK VIEW

SETON TERRACE

SOUTH

NORTH

INGLIS AV

CHESTNUT

ROWANHILL PARK

SYCAMORE

ANHILL

POPLAR

ALDER

CEDAR DRIVE

ROWANHILL

ROAD

BICH

STREET

SCHOOL WYND

HARE

DOORS LANE

NEW ROW

B1348

CLAY

EARLA

INGLIS

OSBORNE CT

RESDENCE TCE

WINTON PK

SETON

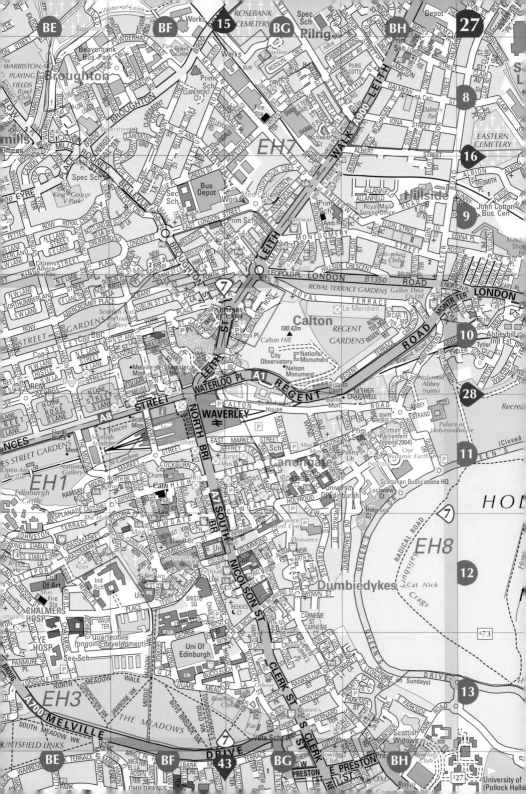

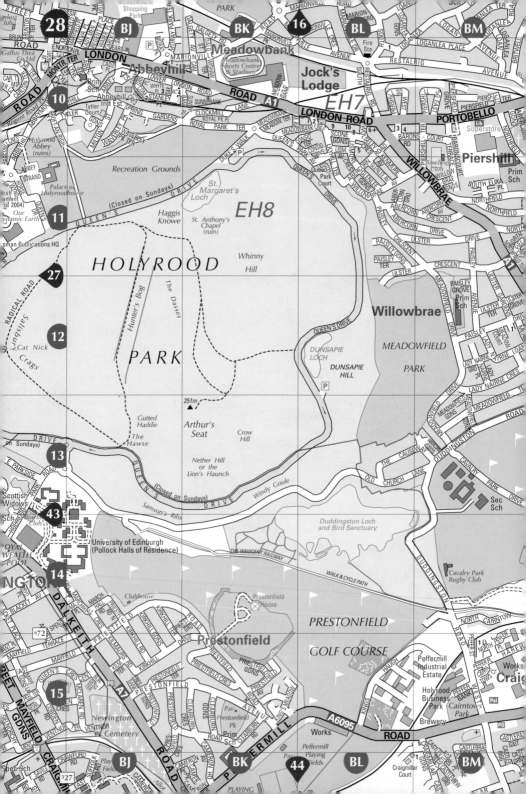

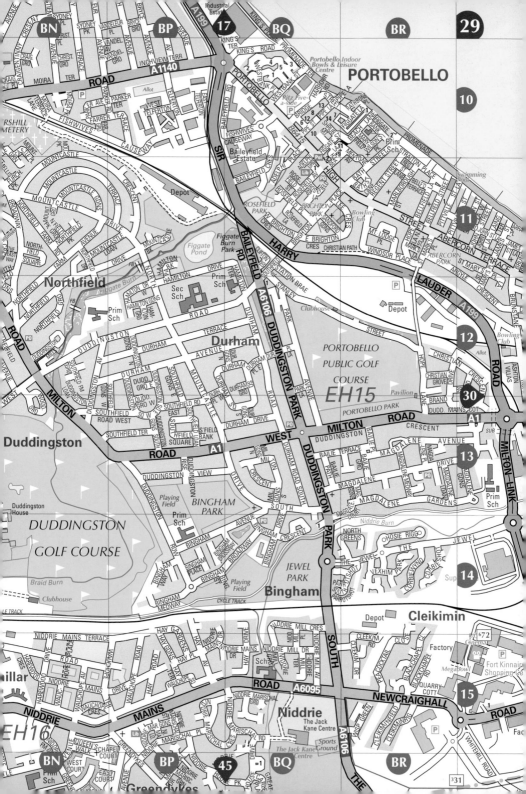

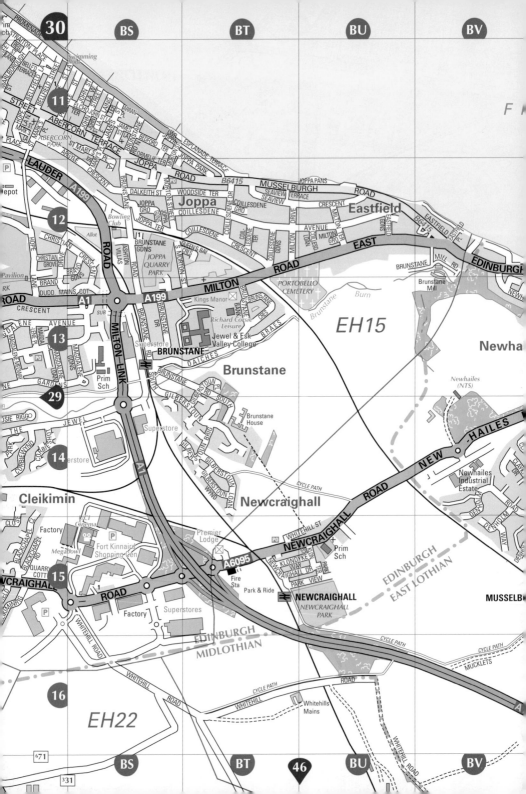

Ingliston Market

Quality Hotel Edinburgh Airport

FAIRVIEW

Port Royal Golf Range

AH

Edinburgh Exhibition & Trade Centre

Royal Highland Showground

West Ingliston

Ingliston House

Ingliston Road

East Mains of Ingliston

East Ingliston House

13

Scottish Agricultural Museum

Rec Grd

ROAD

Ingliston Cottage

GLASGOW   ROAD

A8

HALLYARDS ROAD

RATHO PK

FB

HILLWOOD GDNS

CYCLE PATH

Ratho Station Park

Ingliston Castle

Middle Norton

14

Pav

STATION

HILLWOOD RD

HILLWOOD CRES

DRIVE

HILLWOOD CR

Prim Sch

HILLWOOD AVE

HILLWOOD RISE

Ratho Station

HILLWOOD ROAD

Hillwood House

Norton House

Hillwood Cottage

Norton Mains

Easter

15

FREELAND

Pig Farm

M8

BAIRD ROAD

Hillend

Ratho Byres

ROAD

38

Freelands

Works

Ratho Cemetery

Ashley Cottage

16

EH28

FREELANDS

Manse

Ratho Hall

Kirkton Farm

Edinburgh Canal Centre

BAIRD RD

Union Canal

East Lodge

West Lodge

Clubhouse

17

RATHO GOLF CO

HALLCROFT GRN

HALLCROFT CRES

ALLCROFT GDNS

Prim Sch

WEST CROFT

EAST CROFT

ROAD

West Croft

Ratho Park Gardens

HALLCR PK

HALLCROFT

HALLCR RI

Ratho Park

Pav

RATHO PARK

CRAIGPARK

NORTH

STREET

SCHOOL WYND

STREET

RATHO RD

LIDGATE SHOT

WILKIESTON   ROAD

MAIN   STREET

DALMAHOY RD

TIMMINS CT

RATHO

LUMSDEN CT

HILLVIEW COTTAGES

Ransfield

18

Ratho Mains

Ransfield Cottages

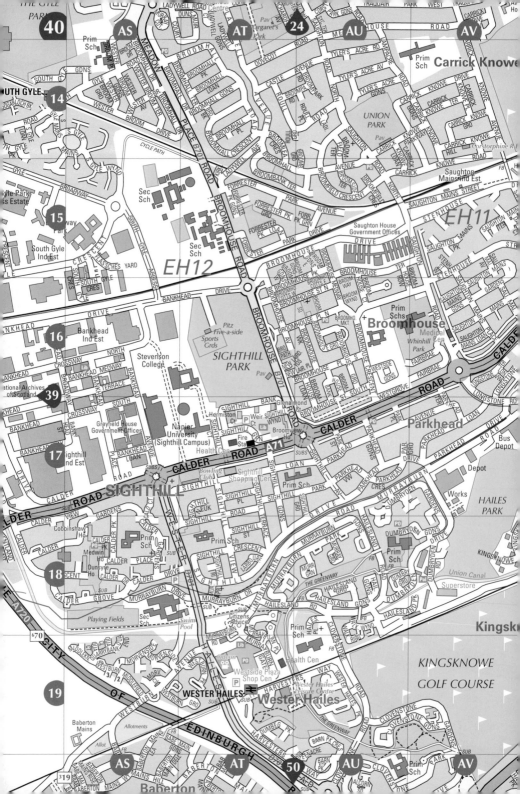

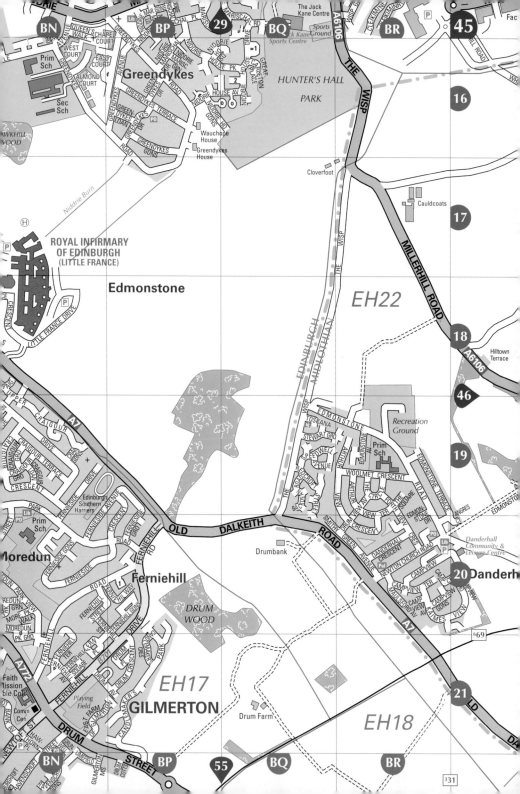

46

BS

BT

30

BU

WHITEHILL ROAD

BV

Cauldcoats

17

Shawfair

Millerhill
Marshalling
Yard

WHITEHILL ROAD

18

A6106

Hilltown
Terrace

Recreation
Ground

MILLERHILL ROAD

MOOR
COTTS

Newton
Village

Hope
Cottage

Harelaw Farm

B6415

OLD CRAIGHALL ROAD

19

EDMONSTONE TERRACE

EDMONSTONE ROAD

MILLERHILL ROAD

NEWTON VILLAGE

HARELAW

The
Scotway
Centre

Depot

45

LANGRES

Danderhall
Community &
Leisure Centre

NEWTON CHURCH ROAD

A6106

Easter
Millerhill

Millerhill

CAMPVIEW

20

Danderhall

CAMPVIEW TER

CAMPVIEW

Wester
Millerhill

A7

A720

Sheriffhall
Mains

A6106

MILLERHILL ROAD

THE CITY

21

OLD

DALKEITH

DEANHEAD
PARK

Dean Burn

22

Campend

Summerside

ROAD

MILLERHILL

A720

WESTGATE

68

BS

DINBURGH

931

BYPASS

BT

Sheriffhall
Roun

56

A68

BU

BV

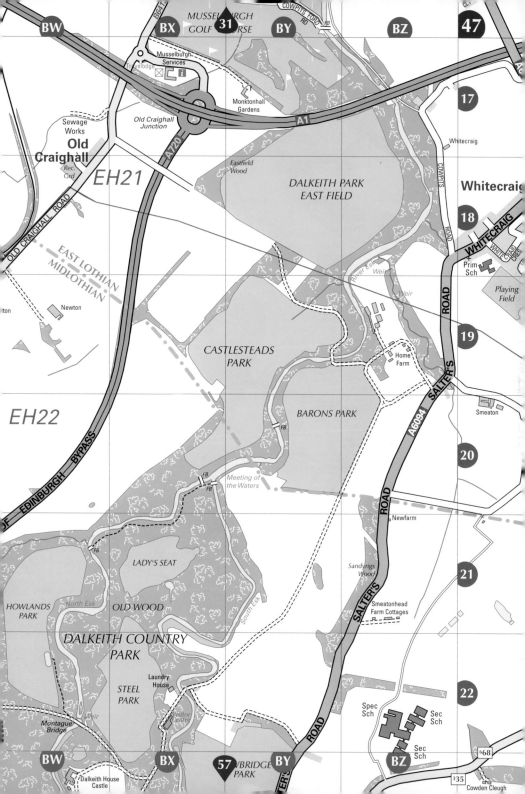

Lennox Tower

AN

AP

49

AQ

Middle Kinleith

AR

Kinleith

59

KIRKGATE

HARLAW ROAD

Carnethy

25

Wester Kinleith

BLACK WOOD

26

HARLAW ROAD

27

EH14

Reservoir (Covered)

Harlaw Farm

White

HARLAW ROAD

HARLAW ROAD

Balleny Farm

P

28

Weir

Visitor Centre

Harlaw Reservoir

29

Weir

30

Threipmuir Reservoir

⁶64

AN

AP

AQ

AR

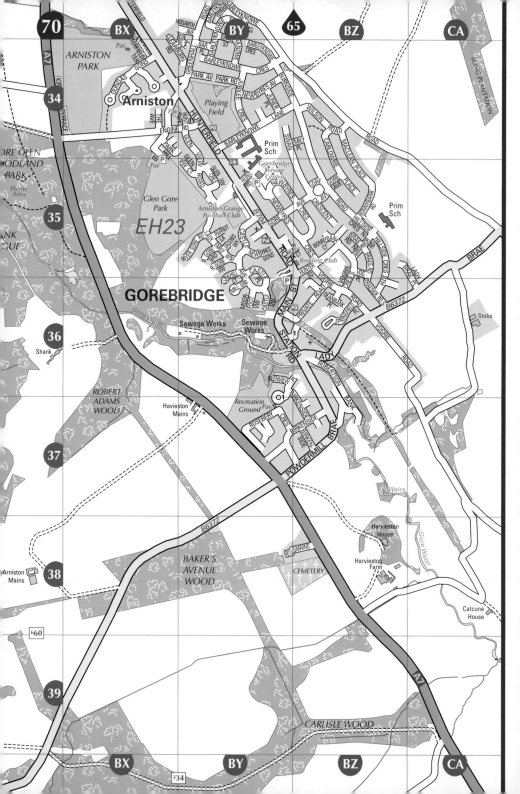

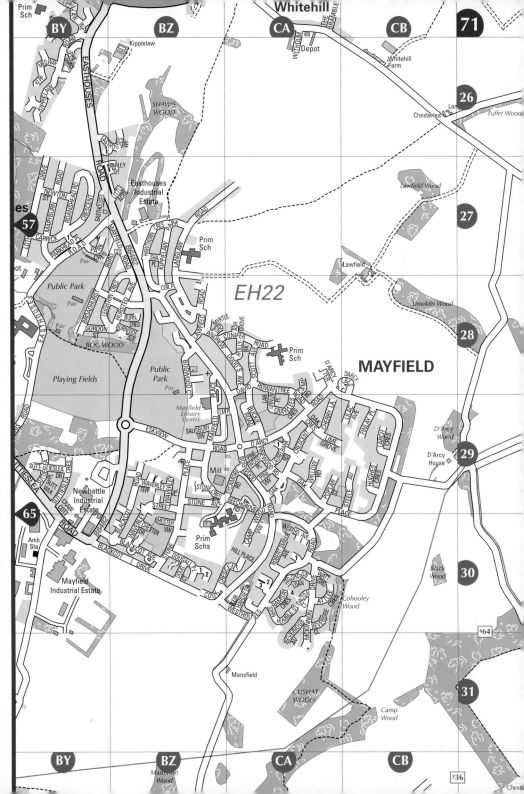

Index

General abbreviations

Acad	Academy	Est	Estate	Pas	Passage
All	Alley	Ex	Exchange	Pav	Pavilion
Allot	Allotments	Exhib	Exhibition	Pk	Park
Amb	Ambulance	FB	Footbridge	Pl	Place
App	Approach	FC	Football Club	Pol	Police
Arc	Arcade	Fld	Field	Prec	Precinct
Av	Avenue	Flds	Fields	Prim	Primary
Ave	Avenue	Fm	Farm	Prom	Promenade
Bdy	Broadway	Gall	Gallery	Pt	Point
Bk	Bank	Gar	Garage	Quad	Quadrant
Bldgs	Buildings	Gdn	Garden	RC	Roman Catholic
Boul	Boulevard	Gdns	Gardens	Rd	Road
Bowl	Bowling	Govt	Government	Rds	Roads
Br	Bridge	Gra	Grange	Rec	Recreation
Bri	Bridge	Grd	Ground	Res	Reservoir
Cath	Cathedral	Grds	Grounds	Ri	Rise
Cem	Cemetery	Grn	Green	S	South
Cen	Central, Centre	Grns	Greens	Sch	School
Cft	Croft	Gro	Grove	Sec	Secondary
Cfts	Crofts	Gros	Groves	Shop	Shopping
Ch	Church	Gt	Great	Sq	Square
Chyd	Churchyard	Ho	House	St.	Saint
Cin	Cinema	Hosp	Hospital	St	Street
Circ	Circus	Hts	Heights	Sta	Station
Cl	Close	Ind	Industrial	Sts	Streets
Clo	Close	Int	International	Sub	Subway
Co	County	Junct	Junction	Swim	Swimming
Coll	College	La	Lane	TH	Town Hall
Comm	Community	Las	Lanes	Tenn	Tennis
Conv	Convent	Lib	Library	Ter	Terrace
Cor	Corner	Ln	Loan	Thea	Theatre
Coron	Coroners	Lo	Lodge	Twr	Tower
Cors	Corners	Lwr	Lower	Twrs	Towers
Cotts	Cottages	Mag	Magistrates	Uni	University
Cov	Covered	Mans	Mansions	Vil	Villas
Crem	Crematorium	Mem	Memorial	Vil	Villa
Cres	Crescent	Mkt	Market	Vw	View
Ct	Court	Mkts	Markets	W	West
Cts	Courts	Ms	Mews	Wd	Wood
Ctyd	Courtyard	Mt	Mount	Wds	Woods
Dep	Depot	Mus	Museum	Wf	Wharf
Dev	Development	N	North	Wk	Walk
Dr	Drive	NTS	National Trust for Scotland	Wks	Works
Dws	Dwellings			Yd	Yard
E	East	Nat	National		
Ed	Education	PO	Post Office		
Embk	Embankment	Par	Parade		

Post town and locality abbreviations

Auch.	Auchendinny	Gowks.	Gowkshill	Polt.	Polton
Bal.	Balerno	Inglis.	Ingliston	Port S.	Port Seton
Bils.	Bilston	Inv.	Inveresk	Pres.	Prestonpans
Bonny.	Bonnyrigg	Jun. Grn	Juniper Green	Ratho Sta	Ratho Station
Cock.	Cockenzie	K'lis.	Kirkliston	Ricc.	Riccarton
Craig.	Craigiehall	Lass.	Lasswade	Ros.	Roslin
Cram.	Cramond	Lnhd	Loanhead	Rose.	Rosewell
Dalk.	Dalkeith	Mayf.	Mayfield	Silv.	Silverburn
Dalm.	Dalmeny	Milt.Br	Milton Bridge	S Q'fry	South Queensferry
Dand.	Danderhall	Monk.	Monktonhall		
David.M.	Davidsons Mains	Muss.	Musselburgh	Strait.	Straiton
		Newbr.	Newbridge	Tran.	Tranent
Easth.	Easthouses	Newcr.	Newcraighall	Wall.	Wallyford
Gilm.	Gilmerton	Newt.	Newtongrange	White.	Whitecraig
Gore.	Gorebridge	Pen.	Penicuik	Wool.	Woolmet

There are street names in the index which are followed by a number in **bold.** These numbers can be found on the map where there is insufficient space to show the street name in full. For example Affleck Ct (*EH12*, **1** 21 AQ11) will be found by a number **1** in the square AQ11 on page 21.

Place names are indicated in CAPITAL letters, schools and hospitals are shown in red type and other places of interest are shown by blue type.

A

Abbeygrange (Newt.),
 Dalk. *EH22* — 65 BW29
ABBEYHILL — 28 BJ10
Abbeyhill *EH8* — 7 BH11
Abbeyhill Cres *EH8* — 7 BH11
Abbeyhill Ind Est *EH8* — 28 BJ10
Abbeyhill Prim Sch *EH7* — 28 BJ10
Abbey La *EH8* — 28 BJ10
Abbeymount *EH8* — 7 BH10
Abbey Rd, Dalk. *EH22* — 56 BV25
Abbey Strand *EH8* — 7 BH11
Abbey St *EH7* — 28 BJ10
Abbotsford Ct *EH10* — 42 BC15
Abbotsford Cres *EH10* — 42 BC15
Abbotsford Pk *EH10* — 42 BC15
Abercorn Av *EH8* — 28 BM11
Abercorn Cotts *EH15* — 28 BM13
Abercorn Ct *EH8* **1** — 28 BM12
Abercorn Cres *EH8* — 28 BL11
Abercorn Dr *EH8* — 28 BL11
Abercorn Gdns *EH8* — 28 BM10
Abercorn Gro *EH8* — 28 BL11
Abercorn Rd *EH8* — 28 BL11
Abercorn Ter *EH15* — 29 BR11
Abercromby Pl *EH3* — 6 BE10
Abinger Gdns *EH12* — 25 AZ12
Academy La, Lnhd *EH20* — 54 BL27
Academy Pk *EH6* — 16 BJ7
Academy St *EH6* — 16 BJ7
Acheson Dr, Pres. *EH32* — 34 CG11
Acklam Path, Lnhd *EH20* — 61 BH28
Adams Well *EH13* — 51 AZ20
Addiston Cres, Bal. *EH14* — 48 AL24
Addistone Br (Ratho),
 Newbr. *EH28* — 48 AL19
Addiston Fm Rd (Ratho),
 Newbr. *EH28* — 38 AK18
Addiston Gro, Bal. *EH14* — 48 AL24
Addiston Pk, Bal. *EH14* — 48 AK24
Adelphi Gro *EH15* — 29 BQ11
Adelphi Pl *EH15* — 29 BQ11
Admiral Ter *EH10* — 42 BD14
Admiralty St *EH6* — 15 BH5
Adventure Centre
 Ratho *EH28* — 36 AD17
Advocates Cl *EH1* **1** — 7 BF11
Affleck Ct *EH12* **1** — 23 AQ11
Afton Pl *EH5* — 14 BC6
Afton Ter *EH5* — 14 BC6
Agnew Ter *EH6* — 15 BF6
Ainslie Pl *EH3* — 6 BC10
Aird's Cl *EH1* — 6 BE12
Airlie Pl *EH3* — 27 BE9
Aitchison's Pl *EH15* **11** — 29 BQ10
Aitkenhill *EH11* — 41 AX15
Alan Breck Gdns *EH4* — 24 AT10
Albany La *EH1* — 7 BF10
Albany St *EH1* — 7 BF10
Albany St La *EH1* — 7 BF10
Albert Cl (Wall.),
 Muss. *EH21* **2** — 33 CD14
Albert Cres (Wall.),
 Muss. *EH21* — 33 CD14
Albert Dock *EH6* — 16 BJ5
Albert Pl *EH7* — 27 BG9
Albert Pl (Wall.),
 Muss. *EH21* — 33 CD14
Albert Rd *EH6* — 16 BK6
Albert St *EH7* — 27 BH8
Albert Ter *EH10* — 42 BC15

Albert Ter, Muss. *EH21* — 32 CA13
Albion Business Cen *EH7* — 16 BJ9
Albion Gdns *EH7* — 16 BJ9
Albion Pl *EH7* — 16 BJ9
Albion Rd *EH7* — 16 BJ9
Albion Ter *EH7* — 16 BJ9
Albyn Pl *EH2* — 6 BD10
Alcorn Rigg *EH14* **1** — 50 AU20
Alcorn Sq *EH14* — 50 AU20
Alderbank, Pen. *EH26* — 68 BA39
Alderbank Gdns *EH11* — 42 BA15
Alderbank Pl *EH11* — 42 BA15
Alderbank Ter *EH11* — 42 BA15
Alder Rd (Port S.),
 Pres. *EH32* — 19 CL8
Alemoor Cres *EH7* — 16 BK8
Alemoor Pk *EH7* — 16 BK8
Alexander Dr *EH11* — 41 AZ14
Alexander Dr, Pres. *EH32* — 34 CG11
Alfred Pl *EH9* — 43 BH14
Allanfield *EH7* — 27 BH9
Allan Pk, K'lis. *EH29* — 20 AC9
Allan Pk Cres *EH14* — 41 AY16
Allan Pk Dr *EH14* — 41 AY17
Allan Pk Gdns *EH14* — 41 AY17
Allan Pk Ln *EH14* — 41 AZ17
Allan Pk Rd *EH14* — 41 AY17
Allan St *EH4* — 26 BC9
Allan Ter, Dalk. *EH22* — 57 BX24
Allermuir Av (Bils.),
 Ros. *EH25* — 61 BG30
Allermuir Ct *EH13* — 52 BB20
Allermuir Rd *EH13* — 51 AW21
Allison Pl, K'lis. *EH29* — 20 AD9
Alloway Ln *EH16* — 44 BJ19
Almond Av *EH12* — 21 AH12
Almond Bk Cotts *EH4* **1** — 11 AR5
Almondbank Ter *EH11* — 42 BA15
Almond Ct *EH16* — 45 BN16
Almond Cres, Bonny. *EH19* — 63 BR29
Almond Dr *EH12* — 21 AH12
Almond Grn *EH12* — 23 AQ11
Almond Gro, S Q'fry *EH30* — 9 AE3
Almondhill Rd, K'lis. *EH29* — 20 AD9
Almondhill Steadings,
 K'lis. *EH29* — 20 AD8
Almond Rd *EH12* — 21 AH12
Almondside, K'lis. *EH29* — 20 AD10
Almond Sq *EH12* — 23 AQ11
ALNWICKHILL — 53 BH21
Alnwickhill Ct *EH16* — 53 BH21
Alnwickhill Cres *EH16* — 53 BH21
Alnwickhill Dr *EH16* — 53 BH21
Alnwickhill Gdns *EH16* — 53 BH21
Alnwickhill Gro *EH16* — 53 BH21
Alnwickhill Ln *EH16* — 53 BH21
Alnwickhill Pk *EH16* — 44 BJ21
Alnwickhill Rd *EH16* — 44 BJ20
Alnwickhill Ter *EH16* — 53 BH21
Alnwickhill Vw *EH16* — 53 BH21
Alvanley Ter *EH9* **1** — 42 BD14
Alva Pl *EH7* — 28 BJ10
Alva St *EH2* — 6 BC11
Ambassador Ct, Muss. *EH21* — 31 BZ13
Amos Path, Lnhd *EH20* — 61 BG28
Anchor Cl *EH1* **11** — 7 BF11
Anchorfield *EH6* — 15 BF5
Ancrum Bk, Dalk. *EH22* — 56 BV26
Ancrum Rd, Dalk. *EH22* — 56 BV26
Anderson Av (Newt.),
 Dalk. *EH22* — 65 BX29

Anderson Pl *EH6* — 15 BG6
Andrew Ct, Pen. *EH26* — 68 BA36
Andrew Dodd's Av *EH22*
 (Mayf.), Dalk. — 57 BZ28
Andrew Wd Ct *EH6* — 15 BE5
Angle Pk Ter *EH11* — 42 BB14
Angres Ct (Dand.), Dalk.
 Dalk. *EH22* — 46 BS19
Annandale St *EH7* — 27 BF8
Annandale St La *EH7* — 27 BG9
Anne St, Pen. *EH26* — 68 BA36
Annfield *EH6* — 15 BF5
Annfield, Tran. *EH33* — 35 CN14
Annfield St *EH6* — 15 BF5
Ann St *EH4* — 6 BC10
Antigua St *EH1* **1** — 27 BG9
Apex City Hotel *EH1* — 6 BE12
Apex European Hotel *EH12* — 26 BB12
Apex International Hotel *EH1* — 6 BE12
Appin St *EH14* — 41 AZ16
Appin Ter *EH14* — 41 AZ15
Arboretum Av *EH4* — 26 BC9
Arboretum Pl *EH3* — 26 BC8
Arboretum Rd *EH3* — 14 BC7
Arbuthnot Rd, Lnhd *EH20* — 62 BL28
Archibald Pl *EH3* — 6 BE12
Arden St *EH9* — 43 BE14
Ardmillan Pl *EH11* — 42 BB14
Ardmillan Ter *EH11* — 42 BA14
Ardmillan Ter La *EH11* **1** — 42 BB14
Ardshiel Av *EH4* — 24 AT11
Argyle Cres *EH15* — 29 BR11
Argyle Pk Ter *EH9* — 43 BF14
Argyle Pl *EH9* — 43 BF14
Argyle Pl, Bonny. *EH19* — 63 BQ29
Argyle St *EH6* — 15 BG5
Argyll Ter *EH11* **2** — 6 BC12
Armine Pl, Pen. *EH26* — 69 BD36
ARNISTON — 70 BX34
Arniston Pl, Bonny. *EH19* **2** — 63 BR28
Arnott Gdns *EH14* — 41 AW18
Arnprior Rd, Gore. *EH23* — 70 BZ35
Arran Pl *EH15* — 30 BS11
Arras Gro, Pen. *EH26* — 66 BC35
Arrol Pl, S Q'fry *EH30* — 9 AE3
Arthur's Seat *EH8* — 28 BK13
Arthur St *EH6* — 27 BH8
Arthur St La *EH6* — 27 BH8
Arthur Vw Cres (Dand.),
 Dalk. *EH22* — 45 BR19
Arthur Vw Ter (Dand.),
 Dalk. *EH22* — 45 BR19
Ashburnham Gdns,
 S Q'fry *EH30* — 9 AF2
Ashburnham Ln,
 S Q'fry *EH30* — 9 AF2
Ashburnham Rd,
 S Q'fry *EH30* — 9 AF3
Ash Gro (Mayf.),
 Dalk. *EH22* — 71 CA28
Ashgrove, Muss. *EH21* — 32 CA13
Ashgrove Pl, Muss. *EH21* — 32 CB13
Ashgrove Vw, Muss. *EH21* — 32 CB13
Ash La, Lnhd *EH20* — 61 BG28
Ashley Dr *EH11* — 42 BA16
Ashley Gdns *EH11* — 42 BA16
Ashley Gro *EH11* — 42 BA15
Ashley Pl *EH6* — 15 BG7
Ashley Ter *EH11* — 42 BA15
Ashton Gro *EH16* — 44 BK18
Ashton Vil *EH15* — 30 BS12

Entry	Page	Ref
Ashville Ter EH6	16	BK8
Ashy Path EH10 1	42	BB19
Assembly Rooms Theatre EH2	6	BE11
Assembly St EH6	16	BJ6
Assynt Bk, Pen. EH26	69	BC37
Astley Ainslie Hosp EH9	43	BE16
Atheling Gro, S Q'fry EH30	9	AE3
Atholl Cres EH3	6	BC12
Atholl Cres La EH3	6	BC12
Atholl Pl EH3	6	BC12
Atholl Ter EH11 3	6	BC12
Attlee Cres (Mayf.), Dalk. EH22	71	CA30
AUCHENDINNY	67	BF34
Auchingane EH10	52	BA20
Auchinleck Ct EH6	15	BF5
Auchinleck's Brae EH6 1	15	BE5
Auldgate, K'lis. EH29	20	AD10
Auld Orchard, Bonny. EH19	56	BS28
Avenue, The (Ricc.), Currie EH14	49	AP20
Avenue, The, Gore. EH23	70	BX34
Avenue Rd, Dalk. EH22	56	BV25
Avenue Rd (Cock.), Pres. EH32	19	CL8
Avenue Vil EH4	26	BB9
Avondale Pl EH3	26	BD9
Avon Gro EH4	23	AQ7
Avon Gro, Pen. EH26	69	BC37
Avon Pl EH4	23	AQ7
Avon Rd EH4	23	AQ7
Ayres Wynd, Pres. EH32 3	18	CH10

B

Entry	Page	Ref
BABERTON	50	AS20
Baberton Av, Jun. Grn EH14	50	AT21
Baberton Cres, Jun. Grn EH14	50	AT21
Baberton Golf Course EH14	50	AT21
Baberton Ln, Jun. Grn EH14	50	AT22
Baberton Mains EH14	50	AT20
Baberton Mains Bk EH14	50	AT20
Baberton Mains Brae EH14	50	AS20
Baberton Mains Ct EH14	50	AT20
Baberton Mains Cres EH14	50	AT20
Baberton Mains Dell EH14	50	AS20
Baberton Mains Dr EH14	50	AS20
Baberton Mains Gdns EH14	40	AS19
Baberton Mains Grn EH14	50	AT20
Baberton Mains Gro EH14	50	AT20
Baberton Mains Hill EH14	40	AS19
Baberton Mains Lea EH14	50	AS20
Baberton Mains Ln EH14	50	AU20
Baberton Mains Pk EH14	50	AT20
Baberton Mains Pl EH14	50	AT20
Baberton Mains Ri EH14	50	AS20
Baberton Mains Row EH14	50	AT20
Baberton Mains Ter EH14	50	AT20
Baberton Mains Vw EH14	50	AT20
Baberton Mains Way EH14	50	AS20
Baberton Mains Wd EH14	50	AS20
Baberton Mains Wynd EH14	50	AT20
Baberton Pk, Jun. Grn EH14	50	AT21
Baberton Rd, Currie EH14	49	AR20
Baberton Sq, Jun. Grn EH14	50	AT21
Back Dean EH4	26	BB11
Backdean Rd, Dalk. EH22	45	BQ19
Backlee EH16	53	BH21
Back Sta Rd EH16 1	28	BM15
Baileyfield Cres EH15	29	BQ11
Baileyfield Rd EH15	29	BP10
Bailie Gro EH15	29	BR13
Bailie Path EH15	29	BQ13
Bailie Pl EH15	29	BR13
Bailie Ter EH15	29	BQ13
Baird Av EH12	25	AY13
Baird Dr EH12	41	AX14
Baird Gdns EH12	25	AY13
Baird Gro EH12	25	AY13
Baird Rd (Ratho), Newbr. EH28	37	AF15
Baird's Way, Bonny. EH19	64	BT29
Baird Ter EH12	25	AY13
Bakehouse Cl EH8	7	BG11
Baker's Pl EH3 1	26	BD9
Balbirnie Pl EH12	26	BA12
Balcarres Ct EH10	42	BC17
Balcarres Pl, Muss. EH21	31	BZ12
Balcarres Rd, Muss. EH21	31	BZ12
Balcarres St EH10	42	BC17
Balderston Gdns EH16	44	BK18
Balderston Gdns N EH16	44	BK18
Baldwin Ct, Pen. EH26	68	BA39
BALERNO	58	AM26
Balerno Community High Sch EH14	58	AL25
Balfour Pl EH6	27	BG8
Balfour Sq, Tran. EH33	35	CM13
Balfour St EH6	15	BH7
Balfour Ter, Pen. EH26	66	BD34
Balfron Ln EH4	24	AS10
Balgreen Av EH12	25	AW13
Balgreen Gdns EH12	25	AW13
Balgreen Pk EH12	25	AW13
Balgreen Prim Sch EH11	41	AY14
Balgreen Rd EH11	41	AY15
Balgreen Rd EH12	25	AX13
Ballantyne La EH6 1	15	BH6
Ballantyne Rd EH6	15	BH6
Balmoral Hotel EH2	7	BF11
Balmoral Pl EH3	26	BD9
Balm Well Av EH16	54	BK22
Balm Well Gro EH16	54	BK22
Balmwell Pk EH16 1	54	BK22
Balm Well Ter EH16	54	BJ22
Baltic St EH6	16	BJ6
Bangholm Av EH5	14	BD6
Bangholm Bower Av EH5	14	BD6
Bangholm Gro EH5	15	BE6
Bangholm Ln EH5	15	BE6
Bangholm Pk EH5	14	BD6
Bangholm Pl EH5	14	BD6
Bangholm Rd EH5	14	BD6
Bangholm Ter EH3	14	BD7
Bangholm Vw EH5	15	BE6
Bangor Rd EH6	15	BG6
Bankhead Av EH11	40	AS16
Bankhead Bdy EH11	39	AR16
Bankhead Crossway N EH11	39	AR16
Bankhead Crossway S EH11	39	AR17
Bankhead Dr EH11	40	AS16
Bankhead Gro (Dalm.), S Q'fry EH30	9	AF2
Bankhead Ind Est EH11	40	AS16
Bankhead Ln EH11	40	AS17
Bankhead Medway EH11	40	AS16
Bankhead Pl EH11	40	AS16
Bankhead Rd (Dalm.), S Q'fry EH30	9	AG2
Bankhead St EH11	40	AS17
Bankhead Ter EH11	39	AR17
Bankhead Way EH11	39	AR17
Bankmill, Pen. EH26	69	BB39
Bankmill Vw, Pen. EH26 1	69	BB39
Bankpark Brae, Tran. EH33	34	CK12
Bankpark Cres, Tran. EH33	34	CK12
Bankpark Gro, Tran. EH33	34	CK12
Bank St EH1	7	BF11
Bank St, Pen. EH26	68	BA39
Bankton Ct, Tran. EH33	35	CM13
Bankton Ter, Pres. EH32	18	CK10
Barclay Pl EH10	6	BD13
Barclay Ter EH10	42	BD14
Barley Ct (Easth.), Dalk. EH22	57	BZ27
Barleyknowe Cres, Gore. EH23	70	BY34
Barleyknowe Gdns, Gore. EH23	65	BY33
Barleyknowe La, Gore. EH23	70	BY34
Barleyknowe Pl, Gore. EH23	70	BY34
Barleyknowe Rd, Gore. EH23	65	BY33
Barleyknowe Sq, Gore. EH23	65	BY33
Barleyknowe Ter, Gore. EH23	70	BY34
Barn Pk EH14	50	AU20
Barn Pk Cres EH14	40	AU19
Barnshot Rd EH13	51	AX21
Barntalloch Ct EH12 4	23	AR12
BARNTON	23	AR9
Barnton Av EH4	12	AU7
Barnton Av W EH4	23	AR7
Barnton Brae EH4	23	AR7
Barnton Ct EH4	23	AR8
Barnton Gdns EH4	12	AU7
Barntongate Av EH4	23	AR9
Barntongate Dr EH4	23	AR9
Barntongate Ter EH4	23	AR9
Barnton Gro EH4	23	AR8
Barnton Hotel EH4	23	AR9
Barnton Ln EH4	12	AT7
Barnton Pk EH4	12	AU7
Barnton Pk Av EH4	24	AS8
Barnton Pk Cres EH4	24	AS8
Barnton Pk Dell EH4	24	AT8
Barnton Pk Dr EH4	24	AS8
Barnton Pk Gdns EH4	24	AS8
Barnton Pk Gro EH4	24	AS8
Barnton Pk Pl EH4	24	AT8
Barnton Pk Vw EH4	23	AR8
Barnton Pk Wd EH4	23	AR9
Baronscourt Rd EH8	28	BL10
Baronscourt Ter EH8	28	BM10
Barony Pl EH3 3	27	BF9
Barony St EH3	27	BF9
Barony Ter EH12	24	AT12
Barracks St (Port S.), Pres. EH32	19	CM7
Barrie's Cl EH1 14	7	BF11
Basil Paterson Coll EH3	6	BE10
Bathfield EH6	15	BG5
Bath Pl EH15 2	29	BR10
Bath Rd EH6	16	BK6
Bath St EH15	29	BR11
Bath St La EH15	29	BR11
Bavelaw Cres, Pen. EH26	68	AZ37
Bavelaw Gdns, Bal. EH14	58	AL26
Bavelaw Grn, Bal. EH14	58	AL25
Bavelaw Rd, Bal. EH14	58	AL26
Baxter's Pl EH1 1	7	BG10
Bayview (Port S.), 1 Pres. EH32	19	CM7
Beach La EH15	29	BQ11
Beach La, Muss. EH21	31	BX12
Beauchamp Gro EH16	44	BJ19
Beauchamp Rd EH16	44	BJ19
Beaufort Rd EH9	43	BF15
Beaverbank Business Pk EH7	27	BE8
Beaverbank Pl EH7	27	BF8
Beaverhall Rd EH7	27	BF8
Bedford Ct EH4	26	BC9
Bedford St EH4	26	BC9
Bedford Ter EH15	30	BS11

Name		
Bedlam Paintball EH29	9	AE6
Bedlam Theatre EH1	7	BF12
Beeches, The (Newt.), Dalk. EH22	57	BW28
Beech Gro Av, Dalk. EH22	56	BT26
Beechgrove Rd (Mayf.), Dalk. EH22	71	CA29
Beech Ln, Bonny. EH19	63	BR29
Beechmount Cres EH12	25	AX12
Beechmount Pk EH12	25	AX13
Beech Pl, Pen. EH26	69	BB39
Beechwood Mains EH12	25	AX12
Beechwood Pk (Newt.), Dalk. EH22	65	BX29
Beechwood Ter EH6	16	BK8
BEESLACK	69	BC36
Beeslack Comm High Sch EH26	69	BC36
Belford Av EH4	26	BA10
Belford Br EH4	26	BB11
Belford Gdns EH4	26	BA10
Belford Ms EH4	26	BB11
Belford Pk EH4	26	BB11
Belford Pl EH4	26	BA11
Belford Rd EH4	26	BB11
Belford Ter EH4 1	26	BB11
Belgrave Cres EH4	26	BB10
Belgrave Cres La EH4	26	BB10
Belgrave Gdns EH12	24	AU13
Belgrave Ms EH4	26	BB10
Belgrave Pl EH4	26	BB10
Belgrave Rd EH12	24	AU12
Belgrave Ter EH12	24	AU13
Belhaven Pl EH10	42	BC17
Belhaven Ter EH10	42	BC17
Bellenden Gdns EH16	44	BL18
Bellerophon Dr, Pen. EH26	69	BB39
Bellevue EH7	27	BF9
Bellevue Cres EH3	27	BF9
Bellevue Gdns EH7	27	BF8
Bellevue Gro EH7	27	BF9
Bellevue La EH7	27	BF9
Bellevue Pl EH7	27	BF9
Bellevue Rd EH7	27	BF9
Bellevue St EH7	27	BF9
Bellevue Ter EH7	27	BF8
Bellfield Av, Dalk. EH22	56	BU25
Bellfield Av, Muss. EH21	31	BX13
Bellfield Ct, Muss. EH21	31	BX14
Bellfield La EH15	29	BR11
Bellfield Sq, Pres. EH32 1	34	CG11
Bellfield St EH15	29	BR11
Bellfield Ter EH15	29	BR11
Bellfield Vw, Bonny. EH19 1	56	BT27
Bellman's Rd, Pen. EH26	68	BA37
Bell Pl EH3	26	BD9
Bells Brae EH4	6	BC11
Bellsmains, Gore. EH23	70	BY38
Bell's Mills EH4	26	BB11
Bellstane, S Q'fry EH30 1	8	AD2
Bell's Wynd EH1 2	7	BF11
Belmont Av EH12	25	AX12
Belmont Cres EH12	25	AX12
Belmont Gdns EH12	25	AX12
Belmont Pk EH12	25	AX12
Belmont Rd, Jun. Grn EH14	50	AS21
Belmont Ter EH12	25	AX12
Belmont Vw EH12	25	AX12
Belvedere Pk EH6	15	BE5
Belwood Cres (Milt.Br), Pen. EH26	66	BD34
Belwood Rd (Milt.Br), Pen. EH26	66	BA34
Beresford Av EH5	15	BE5
Beresford Gdns EH5	15	BE6
Beresford Pl EH5	14	BD6
Beresford Ter EH5	14	BD6
Bernard St EH6	16	BJ5
Bernard Ter EH8	7	BG13
Beulah, Muss. EH21	32	CA13
Bevan Lee Ct, Dalk. EH22	57	BX23
Bevan Rd (Mayf.), Dalk. EH22 2	65	BZ30
Beveridge Av (Mayf.), Dalk. EH22	71	CA31
Beveridge Cl (Mayf.), Dalk. EH22	71	CA30
Big Brae, Bonny. EH19	55	BR27
Biggar Rd EH10	52	BD22
Biggar Rd (Silv.), Pen. EH26	66	BB32
BILSTON	61	BF29
Bilston Cotts, Ros. EH25	61	BG29
Bilston Glen Ind Est, Lnhd EH20	62	BJ28
BINGHAM	29	BQ14
Bingham Av EH15	29	BP14
Bingham Bdy EH15	29	BP14
Bingham Cres EH15	29	BQ14
Bingham Crossway EH15	29	BP14
Bingham Dr EH15	29	BQ14
Bingham Medway EH15	29	BP14
Bingham Pl EH15	29	BP14
Bingham St EH15	29	BP14
Bingham Way EH15	29	BP14
Birch Ct EH4	23	AR9
Birch Cres, Lnhd EH20	61	BH28
Birkenside, Gore. EH23	70	BZ37
Birnies Ct EH4	13	AW6
Birsley Brae, Tran. EH33	34	CJ13
Birsley Rd, Tran. EH33	35	CL13
Blackadder Pl EH5	14	BA5
Blackbarony Rd EH16	44	BJ17
Blackburn Crag EH17	44	BM19
Blackchapel Cl EH15	29	BR15
Blackchapel Rd EH15	29	BR15
Blackcot Av (Mayf.), Dalk. EH22	65	BZ30
Blackcot Dr (Mayf.), Dalk. EH22	65	BY30
Blackcot Pl (Mayf.), Dalk. EH22 1	65	BZ29
Blackcot Rd (Mayf.), Dalk. EH22	65	BZ30
Blacket Av EH9	43	BH14
Blacket Pl EH9	43	BH14
BLACKFORD	43	BF17
Blackford Av EH9	43	BF16
Blackford Bk EH9	43	BF16
Blackford Gate EH9	43	BE16
Blackford Glen Cotts EH16	44	BJ18
Blackford Glen Rd EH16	43	BG18
Blackford Hill EH9	43	BF17
Blackford Hill Gro EH9	43	BF17
Blackford Hill Ri EH9	43	BF17
Blackford Hill Vw EH9	43	BF17
Blackford Rd EH9	43	BE15
Blackfriars St EH1	7	BG11
BLACKHALL	25	AW9
Blackhall Prim Sch EH4	25	AW10
Blackie Rd EH6	16	BK7
Blackthorn Ct EH4	23	AR9
Blackwood Cres EH9	43	BG14
Blaeberry Gdns EH4	23	AR9
Blair St EH1	7	BF11
Blandfield EH7	27	BF8
Blantyre Ter EH10	42	BC15
Blawearie Rd, Tran. EH33	35	CM14
Bleachfield EH6	15	BF7
Blenheim Ct, Pen. EH26	66	BC35
Blenheim Pl EH7	7	BG10
Blinkbonny Av EH4	25	AZ10
Blinkbonny Cres EH4	25	AY10
Blinkbonny Gdns EH4	25	AZ10
Blinkbonny Gro EH4	25	AZ10
Blinkbonny Gro W EH4	25	AZ10
Blinkbonny Rd EH4	25	AZ10
Blinkbonny Rd, Currie EH14	49	AR23
Blinkbonny Ter EH4	25	AY10
Boat Grn EH3	27	BE8
Boathouse Br, K'lis. EH29	21	AG10
BOGHALL	60	BC28
Bogpark Rd, Muss. EH21	31	BW13
Bog Rd, Pen. EH26	68	BA38
Bogsmill Rd EH14	41	AX18
Bogwood Ct (Mayf.), Dalk. EH22	57	BZ28
Bogwood Rd (Mayf.), Dalk. EH22	57	BZ28
BONALY	51	AW22
Bonaly Av EH13	51	AW22
Bonaly Brae EH13	51	AW22
Bonaly Cotts EH13	51	AW22
Bonaly Cres EH13	51	AX22
Bonaly Dr EH13	51	AW22
Bonaly Gdns EH13	51	AW22
Bonaly Gro EH13	51	AW22
Bonaly Prim Sch EH13	51	AW22
Bonaly Ri EH13	51	AX22
Bonaly Rd EH13	51	AW21
Bonaly Steading EH13 1	51	AW22
Bonaly Ter EH13	51	AW22
Bonaly Wester EH13	51	AW22
Bonar Pl EH6	15	BF6
Bo'ness Rd, S Q'fry EH30	8	AB2
BONNINGTON	15	BF7
Bonnington Av EH6	15	BF6
Bonnington Gait EH6 1	15	BG7
Bonnington Gro EH6	15	BF6
Bonnington Ind Est EH6	15	BG7
Bonnington Prim Sch EH6	15	BG7
Bonnington Rd EH6	15	BG7
Bonnington Rd La EH6	15	BG7
Bonnington Ter EH6	15	BF6
Bonnybank Ct, Gore. EH23	70	BZ35
Bonnybank Rd, Gore. EH23	70	BZ35
Bonnyhaugh EH6	15	BF7
Bonnyhaugh La EH6	15	BF7
BONNYRIGG & LASSWADE	56	BT28
Bonnyrigg Prim Sch EH19	64	BS29
Bonnyrigg Rd, Dalk. EH22	56	BU26
Boothacre Cotts EH6 2	16	BL7
Boothacre La EH6	16	BL7
Boroughloch EH8	7	BG13
Boroughloch Sq EH8	7	BG13
Boroughmuir High Sch EH10	42	BD14
Borthwick Pl EH12	26	BA12
Borthwick's Cl EH1 3	7	BF11
Borthwick Vw, Lnhd EH20	62	BJ28
Boswall Av EH5	14	BB6
Boswall Cres EH5	14	BB6
Boswall Dr EH5	14	BB5
Boswall Gdns EH5	14	BB6
Boswall Grn EH5	14	BC6
Boswall Gro EH5	14	BB6
Boswall Ln EH5	14	BB5
Boswall Ms EH5	14	BB5
Boswall Parkway EH5	14	BA5
Boswall Pl EH5	14	BB6
Boswall Quad EH5	14	BB6
Boswall Rd EH5	14	BC5
Boswall Sq EH5	14	BB6
Boswall Ter EH5	14	BB6
Bothwell St EH7	27	BH9

Name	Page	Grid
Boundary Rd E (Ricc.), Currie EH14	49	AP19
Boundary Rd W (Ricc.), Currie EH14	49	AN19
Bowhill Ter EH3	14	BD7
Bowie's Cl EH6 1	16	BJ6
Bowling Grn, The EH6	15	BH6
Bowling Grn Rd, K'lis. EH29	20	AC9
Bowling La EH6 8	15	BH6
Bowmont Pl EH8	7	BG13
Boyd-Orr Dr, Pen. EH26	66	BB35
Boyd's Entry EH1 2	7	BG11
Boy's Brigade Wk EH3	7	BF13
Brae, The (Auch.), Pen. EH26	67	BE34
Braeburn Dr, Currie EH14	49	AR23
Braefoot Ter EH16	44	BJ18
Braehead Av EH4	23	AQ8
Braehead Bk EH4	23	AQ8
Braehead Cres EH4	23	AQ8
Braehead Dr EH4	23	AQ8
Braehead Gro EH4	23	AQ8
Braehead Ln EH4	23	AQ8
Braehead Pk EH4	23	AQ8
Braehead Rd EH4	23	AQ8
Braehead Row EH4 1	23	AQ8
Braehead Vw EH4	23	AQ8
Brae Pk EH4	23	AQ7
Braepark Rd EH4	23	AQ7
Braeside Rd, Gore. EH23	70	BZ35
Braeside Rd, Lnhd EH20	54	BM27
Braeside Rd N, Gore. EH23	70	BZ35
Braeside Rd S, Gore. EH23	70	BZ36
Braid Av EH10	42	BD18
Braidburn Cres EH10	42	BC18
Braidburn Ter EH10	42	BC18
Braid Cres EH10	42	BC18
Braid Fm Rd EH10	42	BC18
Braid Hills App EH10	42	BD19
Braid Hills Av EH10	42	BC18
Braid Hills Cres EH10	42	BC19
Braid Hills Dr EH10	43	BE18
Braid Hills Dr EH16	43	BF19
Braid Hills Golf Course EH10	42	BD19
Braid Hills Golf Driving Range EH16	53	BG20
Braid Hills Hotel EH10	42	BC19
Braid Hills Rd EH10	42	BC19
Braidlaw Pk, Pen. EH26	68	AY38
Braid Mt EH10	42	BC19
Braid Mt Crest EH10	42	BD19
Braid Mt Ri EH10	42	BD19
Braid Mt Vw EH10	42	BD19
Braid Rd EH10	42	BC18
BRAIDS, THE	42	BD19
Bramble Dr EH4	23	AR9
Bramdean Gro EH10	42	BD19
Bramdean Pl EH10	42	BD19
Bramdean Ri EH10	42	BD19
Bramdean Vw EH10	42	BD19
Brand Dr EH15	29	BR13
Brandfield St EH3	6	BC13
Brand Gdns EH15	30	BS12
Brandon St EH3	27	BE9
Brandon Ter EH3	27	BE9
Brass Rubbing Centre EH1 9	7	BG11
Breadalbane St EH6	15	BG6
Breadalbane Ter EH11 5	6	BC12
Bread St EH3	6	BD12
Bread St La EH3	6	BD12
Breck Ter, Pen. EH26	66	BC35
Brewery Cl, S Q'fry EH30	8	AD2
Brewery La EH6 2	15	BH6
Briarbank Ter EH11	42	BA15
Brickfield EH15 12	29	BQ10
Brickworks Rd, Tran. EH33	34	CK12
Bridge End EH16	44	BK16
Bridgend, Dalk. EH22 1	56	BV23
Bridgend Ct, Dalk. EH22	56	BV23
Bridge Pl EH3	26	BC9
Bridge Rd EH13	51	AW21
Bridge Rd, Bal. EH14	58	AL25
Bridge St EH15	29	BQ10
Bridge St, Muss. EH21	31	BY13
Bridge St, Newbr. EH28	36	AB13
Bridge St, Pen. EH26	69	BB39
Bridge St, Tran. EH33	35	CL13
Bridge St La EH15 6	29	BQ10
Briery Bauks EH8	7	BG12
Brighton Pl EH15	29	BQ11
Brighton St EH1	7	BF12
Bright's Cres EH9	43	BH15
Bright Ter EH11 8	6	BC12
Bristo Pl EH1	7	BF12
Bristo Port EH1	7	BF12
Bristo Sq EH8	7	BF12
Britwell Cres EH7	28	BM10
Brixwold Bk, Bonny. EH19	64	BT29
Brixwold Dr, Bonny. EH19	64	BT29
Brixwold Neuk, Bonny. EH19	64	BT29
Brixwold Pk, Bonny. EH19	64	BT29
Brixwold Ri, Bonny. EH19	64	BT29
Brixwold Vw, Bonny. EH19	64	BT29
Broadhurst Rd (Easth.), Dalk. EH22	57	BY28
Broadway Pk EH12	39	AR15
Broad Wynd EH6 7	16	BJ6
Brockwood Av, Pen. EH26	68	AY37
Brookfield Ter (Bils.), Ros. EH25	61	BG29
Broombank Ter EH12	40	AT15
Broomburn Gro EH12	40	AU14
Broomfield Cres EH12	40	AU15
Broomfield Ter EH12	40	AU14
Broomhall Av EH12	40	AT14
Broomhall Bk EH12	40	AT14
Broomhall Cres EH12	40	AT14
Broomhall Dr EH12	40	AS14
Broomhall Gdns EH12	40	AT14
Broomhall Ln EH12	40	AT14
Broomhall Pk EH12	40	AT14
Broomhall Pl EH12	40	AT14
Broomhall Rd EH12	40	AS14
Broomhall Ter EH12	40	AS14
Broomhill Av, Pen. EH26	68	BA39
Broomhill Dr, Dalk. EH22	56	BU25
Broomhill Pk, Dalk. EH22	56	BU26
Broomhill Rd, Pen. EH26	68	BA39
BROOMHOUSE	40	AU16
Broomhouse Av EH11	40	AT16
Broomhouse Bk EH11	40	AU16
Broomhouse Cotts E EH11	40	AU16
Broomhouse Cotts W EH11	40	AT16
Broomhouse Ct EH11	40	AU16
Broomhouse Cres EH11	40	AU16
Broomhouse Dr EH11	40	AT15
Broomhouse Gdns EH11	40	AU15
Broomhouse Gdns E EH11	40	AU15
Broomhouse Gdns W EH11	40	AT15
Broomhouse Gro EH11	40	AU16
Broomhouse Ln EH11	40	AU16
Broomhouse Mkt EH11	40	AU16
Broomhouse Medway EH11	40	AU15
Broomhouse Pk EH11	40	AT16
Broomhouse Path EH11	40	AT16
Broomhouse Pl N EH11	40	AT16
Broomhouse Pl S EH11	40	AU16
Broomhouse Prim Sch EH11	40	AV16
Broomhouse Rd EH11	40	AT16
Broomhouse Rd EH12	40	AT15
Broomhouse Row EH11	40	AV15
Broomhouse Sq EH11	40	AU16
Broomhouse St N EH11	40	AT16
Broomhouse St S EH11	40	AU17
Broomhouse Ter EH11	40	AU15
Broomhouse Wk EH11	40	AU16
Broomhouse Way EH11	40	AU16
Broomhouse Wynd EH11	40	AU16
BROOMIEKNOWE	55	BQ27
Broomieknowe, Lass. EH18	55	BQ27
Broomieknowe Gdns, Bonny. EH19	55	BR27
Broomieknowe Golf Course EH19	55	BR27
Broomieknowe Pk, Bonny. EH19	55	BR26
Broomlea Cres EH12	40	AT14
Broompark Rd EH12	40	AU14
Broomside Ter EH12	40	AU15
Broomview Ho EH11	40	AT17
Broomyknowe EH14	41	AX19
Brougham Pl EH3	6	BE13
Brougham St EH3	6	BD13
BROUGHTON	27	BE8
Broughton High Sch EH4	26	BB9
Broughton Mkt EH3	27	BF9
Broughton Pl EH1	27	BF9
Broughton Pl La EH1	27	BF9
Broughton Prim Sch EH7	27	BF8
Broughton Rd EH7	27	BF8
Broughton St EH1	27	BF9
Broughton St La EH1	7	BF10
Brown's Cl EH8	7	BH11
Brown's Pl EH1 4	6	BE12
Brown St EH8	7	BG12
Brown St La EH8 8	7	BG12
Bruce Gdns, Dalk. EH22	57	BX25
Bruce St EH10	42	BC17
BRUNSTANE	30	BT13
Brunstane Bk EH15	30	BT13
Brunstane Cres EH15	30	BT13
Brunstane Dr EH15	30	BS13
Brunstane Gdns EH15	30	BS12
Brunstane Gdns, Pen. EH26	68	AZ37
Brunstane Gdns Ms EH15 1	30	BS12
Brunstane Mill Rd EH15	30	BU12
Brunstane Prim Sch EH15	30	BS13
Brunstane Rd EH15	30	BS12
Brunstane Rd N EH15	30	BS11
Brunstane Rd S EH15	30	BS13
Brunstane Sta EH15	30	BS13
Brunswick Pl EH7	27	BG9
Brunswick Rd EH7	27	BG9
Brunswick St EH7	27	BG9
Brunswick St La EH7	27	BG9
Brunswick Ter EH7 1	27	BH9
Brunton Ct, Muss. EH21	31	BY13
Brunton Gdns EH7 2	27	BH9
Brunton Pl EH7	27	BH9
Brunton's Cl, Dalk. EH22	57	BW24
Brunton Ter EH7	27	BH9
Brunton Thea EH21	31	BY13
BRUNTSFIELD	42	BD14
Bruntsfield Av EH10	42	BD14
Bruntsfield Cres EH10	42	BD14
Bruntsfield Gdns EH10	42	BD15
Bruntsfield Hotel EH10	42	BD14
Bruntsfield Links Golf Course EH4	12	AT7
Bruntsfield Pl EH10	42	BC15
Bruntsfield Prim Sch EH10	42	BC14
Bruntsfield Ter EH10	42	BD14
Bryans Av (Newt.), Dalk. EH22	65	BX29

Entry		
Bryans Prim Sch *EH22*	71	CA28
Bryans Rd (Newt.), Dalk. *EH22*	65	BW29
Bryce Av *EH7*	17	BP9
Bryce Cres, Currie *EH14*	49	AQ22
Bryce Gdns, Currie *EH14*	49	AQ22
Bryce Gro *EH7*	17	BP9
Bryce Pl, Currie *EH14*	49	AQ22
Bryce Rd, Currie *EH14*	49	AQ22
Bryson Rd *EH11*	42	BB14
Buccleuch Pl *EH8*	7	BF13
Buccleuch St *EH8*	7	BG13
Buccleuch St, Dalk. *EH22*	57	BW24
Buccleuch Ter *EH8*	7	BG13
Buchanan St *EH6*	27	BH8
Buckie Rd (Mayf.), Dalk. *EH22*	71	CA29
Buckingham Ter *EH4*	26	BB10
Buckstane Pk *EH10*	52	BC20
Buckstone Av *EH10*	52	BD21
Buckstone Bk *EH10*	52	BD20
Buckstone Circle *EH10*	53	BE21
Buckstone Cl *EH10*	53	BE21
Buckstone Ct *EH10*	52	BD21
Buckstone Cres *EH10*	52	BD20
Buckstone Crook *EH10*	53	BE22
Buckstone Dell *EH10*	52	BD20
Buckstone Dr *EH10*	52	BD20
Buckstone Gdns *EH10*	52	BD21
Buckstone Gate *EH10*	53	BE21
Buckstone Grn *EH10*	53	BE21
Buckstone Gro *EH10*	52	BD20
Buckstone Hill *EH10*	53	BE21
Buckstone Howe *EH10*	53	BE21
Buckstone Lea *EH10*	53	BE21
Buckstone Ln *EH10*	52	BD21
Buckstone Ln E *EH10*	53	BE21
Buckstone Neuk *EH10*	53	BE20
Buckstone Pl *EH10*	52	BD21
Buckstone Prim Sch *EH10*	53	BE21
Buckstone Ri *EH10*	52	BD21
Buckstone Rd *EH10*	52	BD21
Buckstone Row *EH10*	53	BE21
Buckstone Shaw *EH10*	53	BE22
Buckstone Ter *EH10*	52	BD21
Buckstone Vw *EH10*	52	BD20
Buckstone Way *EH10*	52	BD20
Buckstone Wd *EH10*	52	BD21
Buckstone Wynd *EH10*	53	BE21
BUGHTLIN	23	AR10
Bughtlin Dr *EH12*	23	AQ10
Bughtlin Gdns *EH12*	23	AQ11
Bughtlin Grn *EH12*	23	AQ10
Bughtlin Ln *EH12*	23	AQ11
Bughtlin Mkt *EH12*	23	AR11
Bughtlin Pk *EH12*	23	AR10
Bughtlin Pl *EH12*	23	AQ10
Builyeon Rd, S Q'fry *EH30*	8	AA3
Bull's Cl *EH8* 5	7	BH11
BUPA Murrayfield Hosp *EH12*	25	AW12
BURDIEHOUSE	54	BJ24
Burdiehouse Av *EH17*	54	BK23
Burdiehouse Cres *EH17*	54	BK23
Burdiehouse Crossway *EH17* 2	54	BK23
Burdiehouse Dr *EH17*	54	BK24
Burdiehouse Ln *EH17*	54	BK23
Burdiehouse Medway *EH17*	54	BK23
Burdiehouse Pl *EH17*	54	BK23
Burdiehouse Prim Sch *EH17*	54	BK23
Burdiehouse Rd *EH17*	54	BJ22
Burdiehouse Sq *EH17*	54	BJ24

Entry		
Burdiehouse St *EH17*	54	BK23
Burdiehouse Ter *EH17*	54	BK23
Burgess Rd, S Q'fry *EH30*	8	AD2
Burgess St *EH6*	16	BJ6
Burgess Ter *EH9*	28	BJ15
Burghlee Cres, Lnhd *EH20*	62	BK28
Burghlee Ter, Lnhd *EH20*	62	BL28
Burghtoft *EH17*	55	BN22
Burlington St *EH6*	15	BH6
Burnbank, Lnhd *EH20*	54	BJ27
Burnbank Cres, Lnhd *EH20*	54	BJ26
Burnbank Gro, Lnhd *EH20*	54	BJ26
Burnbank Ter (Bils.), Ros. *EH25*	61	BG29
Burnbrae *EH12*	23	AQ11
Burndene Dr (Strait.), Lnhd *EH20*	61	BH26
Burndene Pk (Strait.), Lnhd *EH20*	61	BH26
Burnhead Cres *EH16*	44	BJ20
Burnhead Gro *EH16*	44	BK21
Burnhead Ln *EH16*	44	BK21
Burnhead Path E *EH16*	44	BK21
Burnhead Path W *EH16*	44	BK21
Burnside *EH12*	23	AQ11
Burnside, Pres. *EH32* 1	18	CG10
Burnside Av (Easth.), Dalk. *EH22*	57	BZ28
Burnside Cres (Easth.), Dalk. *EH22*	57	BZ28
Burnside Pk, Bal. *EH14*	58	AL26
Burnside Rd *EH12*	22	AJ11
Burnside Rd, Gore. *EH23*	70	BY34
Burns St *EH6*	16	BJ7
BUSH	60	BD31
Bush Ln, Pen. *EH26*	67	BE32
Bush St, Muss. *EH21*	31	BX12
Bush Ter, Muss. *EH21* 1	31	BX13
Bus Sta *EH1*	7	BF10
Butlerfield, Dalk. *EH22*	64	BV30
Butlerfield Ind Est, Bonny. *EH19*	65	BW31
Butterfly & Insect World *EH18*	56	BS23

C

Entry		
Cables Wynd *EH6*	15	BH6
Cables Wynd Ho *EH6*	15	BH6
Caddell's Row *EH4*	11	AR6
Cadell Pl (Cock.), Pres. *EH32*	19	CL7
Cadell Sq,Tran. *EH33* 3	35	CM13
Cadiz St *EH6*	16	BJ6
Cadogan Rd *EH16*	44	BJ20
Cadzow Pl *EH7*	28	BJ10
Caerketton Av (Bils.), Ros. *EH25*	61	BG29
Caerketton Cotts *EH13*	42	BA19
Caerketton Ct *EH13*	52	BB20
Caerlaverock Ct *EH12* 3	23	AR12
Caesar Rd,Tran. *EH33*	35	CL13
Caesar Way,Tran. *EH33* 1	35	CL13
Caird's Row, Muss. *EH21*	31	BX12
Cairnbank Gdns, Pen. *EH26*	68	BA39
Cairnbank Rd, Pen. *EH26*	68	BA39
Cairn Hotel *EH7*	27	BG9
Cairnmuir Rd *EH12*	24	AU11
Cairnpark Sch *EH14*	41	AY18
Cairns Dr, Bal. *EH14*	58	AK27
Cairns Gdns, Bal. *EH14*	58	AK27
Cairntows Cl *EH16*	28	BM15
Caithness Pl *EH5*	14	BD6
Caiyside *EH10*	52	BC23
Caiystane Av *EH10*	52	BC22
Caiystane Cres *EH10*	52	BC21

Entry		
Caiystane Dr *EH10*	52	BB22
Caiystane Gdns *EH10*	52	BB21
Caiystane Hill *EH10*	52	BC21
Caiystane Ter *EH10*	52	BB22
Caiystane Vw *EH10*	52	BC22
Calder Ct *EH11*	40	AS18
Calder Cres *EH11*	39	AR18
Calder Dr *EH11*	40	AS18
Calder Gdns *EH11*	40	AS18
Calder Gro *EH11*	39	AR18
Calder Pk *EH11*	40	AS18
Calder Pl *EH11*	40	AS18
Calder Rd *EH11*	40	AV16
Calder Rd (Ratho), Newbr. *EH28*	48	AJ19
Calder Rd Gdns *EH11*	41	AW16
Calder Vw *EH11*	39	AR18
Caledonian Brewery Visitor Centre *EH11*	42	BA14
Caledonian Cres *EH11*	26	BB13
Caledonian Hilton Hotel *EH1*	6	BD11
Caledonian Pl *EH11*	6	BC13
Caledonian Rd *EH11*	6	BC12
CALTON	7	BG10
Calton Hill *EH1*	7	BG10
Calton Hill *EH7*	7	BG10
Calton Rd *EH8*	7	BG11
Calton Sq *EH7*	7	BG10
Cambridge Av *EH6*	27	BG8
Cambridge Gdns *EH6*	27	BG8
Cambridge St *EH1*	6	BD12
Cambridge St La *EH1* 3	6	BD12
Cambusnethan St *EH7*	28	BK10
Cameo Cinema *EH3*	6	BD13
Camera Obscura & World of Illusions *EH1* 3	6	BE11
Cameron Br *EH16*	44	BK16
Cameron Cres *EH16*	44	BK16
Cameron Cres, Bonny. *EH19*	63	BP30
Cameron Ho Av *EH16*	28	BK15
Cameron March *EH16*	44	BJ16
Cameron Pk *EH16*	44	BJ16
Cameron Smail Rd (Ricc.), Currie *EH14*	49	AN20
Cameron Ter *EH16*	44	BK16
Cameron Toll *EH16*	44	BK16
Cameron Toll Gdns *EH16*	44	BK16
Cameron Toll Shopping Centre *EH16*	44	BJ16
CAMMO	23	AP9
Cammo Bk *EH4*	23	AQ9
Cammo Brae *EH4*	23	AQ9
Cammo Cres *EH4*	23	AQ9
Cammo Gdns *EH4*	23	AQ9
Cammo Gro *EH4*	23	AP9
Cammo Hill *EH4*	23	AP9
Cammo Parkway *EH4*	23	AQ9
Cammo Pl *EH4*	23	AQ9
Cammo Rd *EH4*	23	AP9
Cammo Rd *EH12*	23	AN9
Cammo Wk *EH4*	23	AP10
Campbell Av *EH12*	25	AY12
Campbell Pk Cres *EH13*	50	AV21
Campbell Pk Dr *EH13*	50	AV21
Campbell Rd *EH12*	25	AY11
Campbell's Cl *EH8*	7	BH11
Campie Gdns, Muss. *EH21*	31	BX13
Campie Ho, Muss. *EH21*	31	BX13
Campie La, Muss. *EH21*	31	BX13
Campie Prim Sch *EH21*	31	BX13
Campie Rd, Muss. *EH21*	31	BX13
Camp Rd (Mayf.), Dalk. *EH22*	71	CA28

Name	No.	Grid
Campview (Dand.), Dalk. EH22	45	BR20
Campview Av (Dand.), Dalk. EH22	45	BR20
Campview Cres (Dand.), Dalk. EH22	45	BR20
Campview Gdns (Dand.), Dalk. EH22	45	BR20
Campview Gro (Dand.), Dalk. EH22	46	BS20
Campview Rd, Bonny. EH19	63	BR28
Campview Ter (Dand.), Dalk. EH22	45	BR20
Camp Wd Vw (Mayf.), Dalk. EH22	71	CA30
Camus Av EH10	52	BC21
Camus Pk EH10	52	BC21
Canaan La EH9	43	BE16
Canaan La EH10	43	BE16
Candlemaker Row EH1	7	BF12
Candlemaker's Cres EH17	45	BP20
Candlemaker's Pk EH17	45	BP21
Canmore St, S Q'fry EH30	8	AD3
Canning St EH3	6	BC11
Canning St La EH3	6	BC12
Cannon Wynd EH6	15	BG5
Canon Ct EH3 3	27	BE8
CANONGATE	7	BG11
Canongate EH8	7	BG11
CANONMILLS	26	BD8
Canonmills EH3	27	BE8
Canonmills Br EH3 2	27	BE8
Canonmills Sch EH7	27	BE9
Canon St EH3	27	BE9
Capelaw Ct EH13	52	BB20
Capelaw Rd EH13	51	AW22
Caplaw Way, Pen. EH26	68	AX38
Caponhall Ct, Tran. EH33	35	CL14
Caponhall Dr, Tran. EH33	34	CK14
Caponhall Rd, Tran. EH33	35	CL14
Captain's Dr EH16	44	BK21
Captain's Ln EH16	44	BK21
Captain's Rd EH17	54	BK22
Captain's Row EH16	54	BK22
Carberry Cl (Inv.), Muss. EH21	32	CA16
Carberry Gro (Inv.), Muss. EH21	31	BZ16
Carberry Pl EH12	26	BA12
Carberry Rd (Inv.), Muss. EH21	31	BZ15
Carfrae Gdns EH4	25	AW9
Carfrae Gro EH4	25	AW9
Carfrae Pk EH4	25	AW9
Carfrae Rd EH4	25	AW9
Cargil Ct EH5	14	BC6
Cargilfield Sch EH4	23	AR7
Cargil Ter EH5	14	BD6
Carlaverock Av, Tran. EH33	35	CM14
Carlaverock Cl, Tran. EH33	35	CN15
Carlaverock Ct, Tran. EH33	35	CN14
Carlaverock Cres, Tran. EH33	35	CM14
Carlaverock Dr, Tran. EH33	35	CM14
Carlaverock Gro, Tran. EH33	35	CM14
Carlaverock Ter, Tran. EH33	35	CN15
Carlaverock Vw, Tran. EH33	35	CM14
Carlaverock Wk, Tran. EH33	35	CM14
Carlops Av, Pen. EH26	68	BA37
Carlops Cres, Pen. EH26	68	BA37
Carlops Rd, Pen. EH26	68	AZ38
Carlowrie Av (Dalm.), S Q'fry EH30	9	AG4
Carlowrie Cres (Dalm.), S Q'fry EH30	9	AG4
Carlowrie Pl, Gore. EH23	70	BZ34
Carlton Hotel, The EH1	7	BF11
Carlton St EH4	6	BC10
Carlton Ter EH7	7	BH10
Carlton Ter Brae EH7	7	BH10
Carlton Ter La EH7	7	BH10
Carlton Ter Ms EH7	7	BH10
Carlyle Pl EH7	28	BJ10
Carlyle Pl, Muss. EH21	31	BY13
Carmel Av, K'lis. EH29	20	AC9
Carmelite Rd, S Q'fry EH30	8	AD3
Carmel Rd, K'lis. EH29	20	AC10
Carnbee Av EH16	44	BL21
Carnbee Cres EH16	44	BL21
Carnbee Dell EH16 1	44	BL21
Carnbee End EH16	44	BL20
Carnbee Pk EH16	44	BL21
Carnegie Ct EH8	7	BG12
Carnegie St EH8	7	BG12
Carnethie St, Rose. EH24	63	BN33
Carnethy Av EH13	51	AW21
Carnethy Av, Pen. EH26	68	BA37
Carnethy Ct, Pen. EH26	69	BB38
Caroline Gdns EH12	24	AU12
Caroline Pk Gro EH5	13	AZ5
Caroline Pl EH12	24	AU12
Caroline Ter EH12	24	AT11
Carpet La EH6	16	BJ6
Carrick Cres (Easth.), Dalk. EH22	57	BY27
CARRICK KNOWE	40	AV14
Carrick Knowe Av EH12	24	AV13
Carrick Knowe Dr EH12	40	AU14
Carrick Knowe Gdns EH12	40	AV14
Carrick Knowe Golf Course EH12	41	AX14
Carrick Knowe Gro EH12	40	AV14
Carrick Knowe Hill EH12	40	AV14
Carrick Knowe Ln EH12	40	AU14
Carrick Knowe Parkway EH12	40	AU14
Carrick Knowe Pl EH12	40	AV14
Carrick Knowe Prim Sch EH12	40	AV16
Carrick Knowe Rd EH12	40	AU15
Carrick Knowe Ter EH12	40	AV14
Carrington Rd EH4	26	BA9
Carrington Rd, Bonny. EH19	64	BT31
Carron Pl EH6	16	BK6
Carrubber's Cl EH1 5	7	BF11
Casselbank St EH6	15	BH7
Cassel's La EH6	15	BH7
Cast, The, Lass. EH18	62	BM29
Castle Av EH12	40	AT14
Castle Av, Gore. EH23	70	BY35
Castle Av (Port S.), Pres. EH32	19	CN7
Castlebrae Community High Sch EH16	45	BN16
Castlebrae Glebe EH16	28	BM15
Castlebrae Gro EH16	44	BM16
Castlebrae Pl EH16	28	BM15
Castlebrae Rigg EH16	28	BM15
Castlehill EH1	6	BE11
Castlelaw Ct, Pen. EH26	69	BB37
Castlelaw Cres (Bils.), Ros. EH25	61	BG30
Castlelaw Rd EH13	51	AW21
Castlepark Gait EH16	28	BM15
Castlepark Glade EH16	44	BM16
Castlepark Grn EH16	44	BM16
Castle Pl, Gore. EH23	70	BY35
Castle Rd (Port S.), Pres. EH32	19	CN7
Castle Rd, Tran. EH33	34	CK15
Castle St EH2	6	BD11
Castle Ter EH1	6	BD12
Castle Ter EH3	6	BE12
Castle Ter (Port S.), Pres. EH32	19	CN7
Castle Vw, Gore. EH23	70	BY36
Castle Vw (Port S.), Pres. EH32	19	CN7
Castleview Dr EH16	44	BM16
Castleview Gro EH16	44	BM16
Castleview Ho EH17	44	BM18
Castleview Prim Sch EH16	45	BN16
Castleview Ter EH16	28	BM15
Castle Wk (Port S.), Pres. EH32	19	CN7
Castle Wynd N EH1 11	6	BE12
Castle Wynd S EH1 6	6	BE12
Cathcart Pl EH11	26	BB13
Cathedral La EH1	7	BF10
Catherine Pl EH3	27	BE8
Catriona Ter, Pen. EH26	66	BD34
Causeway, The EH15	28	BL13
Causewayside EH9	43	BG16
Cavalry Pk Dr EH15	28	BM13
Cedar Dr (Port S.), Pres. EH32	19	CL8
Cedar Rd, Lnhd EH20	61	BH28
Cedars, The EH13	51	AX20
Cemetery Rd, Dalk. EH22	56	BV24
Chalmers Bldgs EH3 2	6	BD13
Chalmers Cl EH1 4	7	BG11
Chalmers Cres EH9	43	BF14
Chalmers Hosp EH3	6	BE12
Chalmers St EH3	6	BE12
Chamberlain Rd EH10	42	BD15
Chambers St EH1	7	BF12
Champigny Ct, Muss. EH21	32	CA14
Chancelot Cres EH6	15	BE6
Chancelot Gro EH5	15	BE6
Chancelot Ter EH6	15	BF6
Chapel Ct EH16	29	BN15
Chapel La EH6 2	16	BJ6
Chapel Ln, Ros. EH25	62	BJ32
Chapel St EH8	7	BG12
Chapel Wynd EH1 7	6	BE12
Chariot Dr EH28	36	AC14
Charlesfield EH8 1	7	BF12
Charles St EH8	7	BF12
Charles St, Pen. EH26	68	BA36
Charles St La EH8	7	BF12
Charlotte La EH2	6	BD11
Charlotte Sq EH2	6	BD11
Charlton Gro, Ros. EH25	67	BH32
Charterhall Gro EH9	43	BF16
Charterhall Rd EH9	43	BF17
Chatterrig EH13	52	BB20
Cherry La (Mayf.), Dalk. EH22	71	CA29
Cherry Rd, Bonny. EH19	63	BR29
Cherry Tree Av, Bal. EH14	49	AN24
Cherry Tree Cres, Bal. EH14	48	AM24
Cherry Tree Cres, Currie EH14	48	AM24
Cherry Tree Gdns, Bal. EH14	48	AM24
Cherry Tree Gro, Bal. EH14	48	AM24
Cherry Tree Ln, Bal. EH14	49	AN24
Cherry Tree Pk, Bal. EH14	48	AM24
Cherry Tree Pl, Currie EH14	49	AN24
Cherry Tree Vw, Bal. EH14	49	AN24
Chessels Ct EH8	7	BG11
Chesser Av EH14	41	AX15

Name	Page	Grid
Chesser Cotts EH11 1	41	AY15
Chesser Ct EH14	41	AX15
Chesser Cres EH14	41	AX16
Chesser Gdns EH14	41	AX15
Chesser Gro EH14	41	AX16
Chesser Ln EH14	41	AX16
Chester Ct, Bonny. EH19	63	BR29
Chester Dr (Mayf.), Dalk. EH22	65	BZ30
Chester Gro, Bonny. EH19	63	BR29
Chester St EH3	6	BC11
Chesters Vw, Bonny. EH19	63	BR29
Chester Vw (Mayf.), Dalk. EH22	65	BZ30
Chestnut Gro, Bonny. EH19	63	BR29
Chestnut Gro (Port S.), Pres. EH32	19	CM8
Chestnut St EH5	14	BA4
Cheyne St EH4	26	BC9
Chisholm Ter, Pen. EH26	69	BB36
Christian Cres EH15	29	BR12
Christian Gro EH15	29	BR12
Christian Path EH15	29	BQ11
Christiemiller Av EH7	17	BN9
Christiemiller Gro EH7	29	BN10
Christiemiller Pl EH7	17	BN9
Chuckie Pend EH3	6	BD12
CHURCH HILL	42	BD15
Church Hill EH10	42	BD15
Church Hill Dr EH10	42	BD15
Church Hill Pl EH10	42	BD15
Church Hill Theatre EH10	42	BD15
Church La, Muss. EH21	31	BY14
Church Rd, Lass. EH18	55	BP26
Church St, Lnhd EH20	62	BL28
Church St, Tran. EH33	35	CL12
Circle, The (Dand.), Dalk. EH22	45	BR19
Circus Gdns EH3	6	BD10
Circus La EH3	26	BD9
Circus Pl EH3	6	BD10
Citadel Ct EH6	15	BH5
Citadel Pl EH6	15	BH5
Citadel St EH6 2	15	BH5
City Art Centre EH1	7	BF11
City of Edinburgh Bypass, The EH10	52	BA22
City of Edinburgh Bypass, The EH12	39	AP15
City of Edinburgh Bypass, The EH13	50	AU21
City of Edinburgh Bypass, The EH14	39	AR18
City of Edinburgh Bypass, The EH17	53	BH24
City of Edinburgh Bypass, The, Dalk. EH22	46	BV21
City of Edinburgh Bypass, The, Lass. EH18	55	BQ23
City of Edinburgh Bypass, The, Muss. EH21	46	BV21
Civic Sq, Tran. EH33	35	CM13
Clackmae Gro EH16	43	BH19
Clackmae Rd EH16	43	BH19
Clan Tartan Centre EH6	15	BG6
Clapper La EH16	44	BJ17
Clarebank Cres EH6	16	BK7
Claremont Bk EH7	27	BF9
Claremont Ct EH7	27	BF8
Claremont Cres EH7	27	BF8
Claremont Gdns EH6	16	BK7
Claremont Gro EH7	27	BF8
Claremont Pk EH6	16	BK7
Claremont Rd EH6	16	BK7
Clarence St EH3	26	BD9
Clarendon Cres EH4	6	BC10
Clarinda Gdns, Dalk. EH22	57	BZ24
Clarinda Ter EH16	44	BJ18
Clark Av EH5	15	BE6
Clark Pl EH5	14	BD6
Clark Rd EH5	14	BD6
Claverhouse Dr EH16	44	BJ19
Clayhills Gro, Bal. EH14	58	AK26
Clayhills Pk, Bal. EH14	58	AK26
Clayknowes Av, Muss. EH21	31	BW14
Clayknowes Ct, Muss. EH21	31	BW15
Clayknowes Dr, Muss. EH21	30	BV14
Clayknowes Pl, Muss. EH21	30	BV14
Clayknowes Rd, Muss. EH21	31	BW14
Clayknowes Way, Muss. EH21	31	BW14
Clearburn Cres EH16	28	BK15
Clearburn Gdns EH16	28	BK15
Clearburn Rd EH16	28	BK15
Clearburn Rd, Gore. EH23	65	BX33
Cleekim Dr EH15	29	BR15
Cleekim Rd EH15	29	BR15
CLEIKIMIN	29	BR14
Cleikiminfield EH15	29	BR15
Cleikiminrig EH15	29	BR15
Cleric's Hill, K'lis. EH29	20	AC10
Clerk Rd, Pen. EH26	68	AZ38
Clerk St EH8	7	BG13
Clerk St, Lnhd EH20	54	BL27
CLERMISTON	24	AS9
Clermiston Av EH4	24	AT9
Clermiston Cres EH4	24	AT9
Clermiston Dr EH4	24	AT9
Clermiston Gdns EH4	24	AT10
Clermiston Grn EH4	24	AT9
Clermiston Gro EH4	24	AT10
Clermiston Hill EH4	24	AT9
Clermiston Ln EH4	24	AT9
Clermiston Medway EH4	24	AT9
Clermiston Pk EH4	24	AT9
Clermiston Pl EH4	24	AT10
Clermiston Prim Sch EH4	24	AT9
Clermiston Rd EH12	24	AU13
Clermiston Rd N EH4	24	AU9
Clermiston Ter EH12 1	24	AU12
Clermiston Vw EH4	24	AU10
Clerwood Bk EH12	24	AT11
Clerwood Gdns EH12	24	AT11
Clerwood Gro EH12	24	AU11
Clerwood Ln EH12	24	AT11
Clerwood Pk EH12	24	AT11
Clerwood Pl EH12	24	AU11
Clerwood Row EH12	24	AT11
Clerwood Ter EH12	24	AU11
Clerwood Vw EH12	24	AU11
Clerwood Way EH12	24	AT11
Cliftonhall Rd, Newbr. EH28	36	AB15
Clifton Rd, Newbr. EH28	36	AA16
Clifton Sq EH15	29	BQ11
Clifton Ter EH12	6	BC12
Clifton Trd Est, Newbr. EH28	36	AB15
Clinton Rd EH9	42	BD15
Clockmill La EH8	28	BK10
Clovenstone Dr EH14	50	AU20
Clovenstone Gdns EH14	40	AU18
Clovenstone Pk EH14	50	AU20
Clovenstone Prim Sch EH14	50	AU20
Clovenstone Rd EH14	40	AU18
Cloverfoot EH16	45	BQ17
Clufflat, S Q'fry EH30	8	AB1
Clufflat Brae, S Q'fry EH30	8	AB1
Cluny Av EH10	42	BD17
Cluny Dr EH10	42	BD17
Cluny Gdns EH10	42	BD17
Cluny Pl EH10	43	BE17
Cluny Ter EH10	42	BD16
Coalgate Av, Tran. EH33	35	CN12
Coalgate Rd, Tran. EH33	35	CM12
Coalhill EH6	15	BH6
Coal Neuk, Tran. EH33	35	CL13
Coal Neuk Cor, Tran. EH33 7	35	CL13
Coal Neuk Ct, Tran. EH33	35	CL13
COATES	26	BA11
Coates Cres EH3	6	BC12
Coates Gdns EH12	26	BB12
Coates Pl EH3	6	BC12
Coatfield La EH6	16	BJ6
Cobbinshaw Ho EH11	40	AS18
Cobden Cres EH9	43	BH15
Cobden Rd EH9	43	BH15
Cobden Ter EH11 7	6	BC12
Coburg St EH6	15	BH6
Cochrane Pl EH6 1	16	BJ7
Cochran Pl EH7	27	BF9
Cochran Ter EH7	27	BF9
Cochrina Pl, Rose. EH24	62	BM33
Cockburn Cres, Bal. EH14	58	AL28
Cockburnhill Rd, Bal. EH14	58	AK27
Cockburn St EH1	7	BF11
COCKENZIE	19	CM8
Cockenzie Prim Sch EH32	19	CL8
Cockmylane EH10	52	BB21
Cockpen Av, Bonny. EH19	63	BQ30
Cockpen Cres, Bonny. EH19	63	BQ30
Cockpen Dr, Bonny. EH19	63	BQ30
Cockpen Pl, Bonny. EH19 1	63	BQ30
Cockpen Rd, Bonny. EH19	64	BS29
Cockpen Ter, Bonny. EH19	63	BQ30
Cockpen Vw, Bonny. EH19	63	BQ30
Coffin La EH11	26	BB13
Coillesdene Av EH15	30	BS12
Coillesdene Cres EH15	30	BT12
Coillesdene Dr EH15	30	BT12
Coillesdene Gdns EH15	30	BT12
Coillesdene Gro EH15	30	BT12
Coillesdene Ln EH15	30	BU12
Coillesdene Ter EH15	30	BT12
Coinyie Ho Cl EH1 1	7	BG11
COLINTON	51	AW21
Colinton Gro EH14	41	AZ17
Colinton Gro W EH14	41	AZ17
Colinton Mains Cres EH13	51	AZ21
Colinton Mains Dr EH13	41	AZ19
Colinton Mains Gdns EH13	41	AZ19
Colinton Mains Grn EH13	51	AZ20
Colinton Mains Gro EH13	52	BA20
Colinton Mains Ln EH13	51	AZ20
Colinton Mains Pl EH13	52	BA20
Colinton Mains Rd EH13	52	BA20
Colinton Mains Ter EH13	52	BA20
Colinton Prim Sch EH13	51	AZ20
Colinton Rd EH10	42	BB16
Colinton Rd EH13	41	AY19
Colinton Rd EH14	42	BA16
College Wynd EH1 2	7	BF12
Colliery Cres (Newt.), Dalk. EH22	65	BW31
Colliery Vw (Newt.), Dalk. EH22	65	BX31
Collins Pl EH3	26	BD9
Colmestone Gate EH10	52	BC21
Coltbridge Av EH12	25	AZ12
Coltbridge Gdns EH12	26	BA12
Coltbridge Millside EH12	26	BA12
Coltbridge Ter EH12	25	AZ12
Coltbridge Vale EH12	26	BA12
Columba Av EH4	25	AX9
Columba Rd EH4	25	AX9
Colville Pl EH3	26	BD9
COMELY BANK	26	BB9

Name	Page	Grid
Comely Bk *EH4*	26	BB9
Comely Bk Av *EH4*	26	BC9
Comely Bk Gro *EH4*	26	BB10
Comely Bk Pl *EH4*	26	BC9
Comely Bk Pl Ms *EH4* 2	26	BC9
Comely Bk Rd *EH4*	26	BC9
Comely Bk Row *EH4*	26	BC9
Comely Bk St *EH4*	26	BB9
Comely Bk Ter *EH4*	26	BB9
Comely Grn Cres *EH7*	28	BJ10
Comely Grn Pl *EH7*	28	BJ10
COMISTON	52	BC21
Comiston Dr *EH10*	42	BB18
Comiston Gdns *EH10*	42	BC17
Comiston Gro *EH10*	52	BC20
Comiston Pl *EH10*	42	BC17
Comiston Prim Sch *EH13*	52	BB21
Comiston Ri *EH10*	52	BC20
Comiston Rd *EH10*	42	BC18
Comiston Springs Av *EH10*	52	BC20
Comiston Ter *EH10*	42	BC17
Comiston Vw *EH10*	52	BC20
Commercial St *EH6*	15	BH5
Commercial Wf *EH6* 1	16	BJ5
Conference Sq *EH3*	6	BD12
Conifer Rd (Mayf.), Dalk. *EH22*	71	CA28
Connaught Pl *EH6*	15	BF6
Considine Gdns *EH8*	28	BL10
Considine Ter *EH8*	28	BL10
Constitution Pl *EH6*	16	BJ5
Constitution St *EH6*	15	BH7
Convening Ct *EH4* 1	6	BC11
Cook Cres (Mayf.), Dalk. *EH22*	65	BZ30
Cookies Wynd, Pres. *EH32* 2	18	CG10
Cooper's Cl *EH8* 3	7	BH11
Cope La (Port S.), Pres. *EH32*	19	CM7
Corbiehill Av *EH4*	25	AW8
Corbiehill Cres *EH4*	24	AV8
Corbiehill Gdns *EH4*	25	AW8
Corbiehill Gro *EH4*	25	AW8
Corbiehill Pk *EH4*	24	AV8
Corbiehill Pl *EH4*	24	AV8
Corbiehill Rd *EH4*	24	AV8
Corbiehill Ter *EH4*	24	AV8
Corbieshot *EH15*	29	BR14
Corbiewynd *EH15*	29	BR14
CORNBANK	68	AZ38
Cornbank St. James' Prim Sch *EH26*	68	AZ38
Cornhill Ter *EH6*	16	BK7
Cornwallis Pl *EH3*	27	BE9
Cornwall St *EH1*	6	BD12
Coronation Pl (Mayf.), Dalk. *EH22*	57	BZ28
Coronation Pl, Tran. *EH33*	35	CL13
Coronation Wk *EH3*	6	BE13
Corrennie Dr *EH10*	42	BD17
Corrennie Gdns *EH10*	42	BD18
Corrie Ct (Newt.), Dalk. *EH22*	65	BX31
Corslet Cres, Currie *EH14*	49	AR22
Corslet Pl, Currie *EH14*	49	AQ22
Corslet Rd, Currie *EH14*	49	AQ22
CORSTORPHINE	24	AT12
Corstorphine Bk Av *EH12*	24	AS12
Corstorphine Bk Dr *EH12*	24	AS12
Corstorphine Bk Ter *EH12*	24	AS12
Corstorphine High St *EH12*	24	AT13
Corstorphine Hill Av *EH12*	24	AU12
Corstorphine Hill Cres *EH12*	24	AU12
Corstorphine Hill Gdns *EH12*	24	AU12
Corstorphine Hill Rd *EH12*	24	AU12
Corstorphine Hosp *EH12*	24	AV13
Corstorphine Ho Av *EH12*	24	AU13
Corstorphine Ho Ter *EH12*	24	AU13
Corstorphine Pk Gdns *EH12*	24	AU13
Corstorphine Prim Sch *EH12*	24	AT13
Corstorphine Rd *EH12*	23	AY12
Cortleferry Dr, Dalk. *EH22*	56	BU26
Cortleferry Gro, Dalk. *EH22*	56	BU26
Cortleferry Pk, Dalk. *EH22*	56	BU26
Cortleferry Ter, Dalk. *EH22*	56	BU26
Corunna Pl *EH6*	15	BH6
Corunna Ter, Pen. *EH26*	66	BC35
Costkea Way, Lnhd *EH20*	54	BJ27
Cotlaws, K'lis. *EH29*	20	AB10
Cottage Grn *EH4*	23	AR7
Cottage Homes *EH13*	51	AX21
Cottage La, Muss. *EH21*	32	CA14
Cottage Pk *EH4*	25	AW10
County Hotel *EH22*	57	BW24
County Rd, Pres. *EH32*	18	CG10
County Sq, Pres. *EH32*	18	CG10
Couperfield *EH6*	15	BH6
Couper St *EH6*	15	BH5
Covenanters La, S Q'fry *EH30*	8	AD2
Cowan Rd *EH11*	42	BA15
Cowan's Cl *EH8*	7	BG13
Cowan Ter, Pen. *EH26*	69	BB36
Cowden Cres, Dalk. *EH22*	57	BZ24
Cowden Gro, Dalk. *EH22*	57	BZ24
Cowden La, Dalk. *EH22*	57	BZ24
Cowden Pk, Dalk. *EH22*	57	BY24
Cowden Ter, Dalk. *EH22*	57	BZ24
Cowden Vw, Dalk. *EH22*	57	BZ24
Cowgate *EH1*	7	BF12
Cowgatehead *EH1*	7	BF12
Cowpits Ford Rd, Muss. *EH21*	31	BY16
Cowpits Rd (White.), Muss. *EH21*	47	BZ18
Coxfield *EH11*	41	AY15
Craigcrook Av *EH4*	25	AW9
Craigcrook Gdns *EH4*	25	AX10
Craigcrook Gro *EH4*	25	AW10
Craigcrook Pk *EH4*	25	AW10
Craigcrook Pl *EH4* 1	25	AY9
Craigcrook Rd *EH4*	25	AX10
Craigcrook Sq *EH4*	25	AW9
Craigcrook Ter *EH4*	25	AX9
Craigend Pk *EH16*	44	BL18
CRAIGENTINNY	16	BM8
Craigentinny Av *EH7*	29	BN10
Craigentinny Av N *EH6*	16	BM7
Craigentinny Cres *EH7*	29	BN10
Craigentinny Golf Course *EH7*	17	BN8
Craigentinny Gro *EH7*	29	BN10
Craigentinny Pl *EH7*	29	BN10
Craigentinny Prim Sch *EH7*	16	BM9
Craigentinny Rd *EH7*	16	BM9
Craighall Av *EH6*	15	BE5
Craighall Bk *EH6*	15	BE5
Craighall Cres *EH6*	15	BE5
Craighall Gdns *EH6*	15	BE6
Craighall Rd *EH6*	15	BE5
Craighall Ter *EH6*	15	BE6
Craighall Ter, Muss. *EH21*	32	CB13
Craighill Gdns *EH10*	42	BB18
Craighouse Av *EH10*	42	BB17
Craighouse Gdns *EH10*	42	BB17
Craighouse Pk *EH10*	42	BB17
Craighouse Rd *EH10*	42	BB17
Craighouse Ter *EH10*	42	BB17
Craigiebield Cres, Pen. *EH26*	68	BA39
Craigievar Sq *EH12*	23	AR11
Craigievar Wynd *EH12*	23	AQ12
Craiglea Dr *EH10*	42	BB18
Craiglea Pl *EH10*	42	BB17
CRAIGLEITH	25	AZ9
Craigleith Av N *EH4*	25	AY11
Craigleith Av S *EH4*	25	AY11
Craigleith Bk *EH4*	25	AY10
Craigleith Cres *EH4*	25	AY10
Craigleith Dr *EH4*	25	AY10
Craigleith Gdns *EH4*	25	AY10
Craigleith Gro *EH4*	25	AY10
Craigleith Hill *EH4*	25	AZ10
Craigleith Hill Av *EH4*	25	AY9
Craigleith Hill Cres *EH4*	25	AZ9
Craigleith Hill Gdns *EH4*	25	AZ9
Craigleith Hill Grn *EH4*	25	AZ9
Craigleith Hill Gro *EH4*	25	AZ9
Craigleith Hill Ln *EH4*	25	AZ9
Craigleith Hill Pk *EH4*	25	AZ9
Craigleith Hill Row *EH4*	25	AZ9
Craigleith Retail Pk *EH4*	25	AZ9
Craigleith Retail Pk *EH4*	25	AZ9
Craigleith Ri *EH4*	25	AY11
Craigleith Rd *EH4*	25	AZ10
Craigleith Vw *EH4*	25	AY11
CRAIGLOCKHART	41	AZ17
Craiglockhart Av *EH14*	41	AY17
Craiglockhart Bk *EH14*	41	AY18
Craiglockhart Cres *EH14*	41	AY18
Craiglockhart Dell Rd *EH14*	41	AY17
Craiglockhart Dr N *EH14*	41	AY17
Craiglockhart Dr S *EH14*	41	AY19
Craiglockhart Gdns *EH14*	41	AY17
Craiglockhart Gro *EH14*	41	AY19
Craiglockhart Ln *EH14*	41	AY18
Craiglockhart Pk *EH14*	41	AY18
Craiglockhart Pl *EH14*	41	AZ17
Craiglockhart Prim Sch *EH11*	42	BA15
Craiglockhart Quad *EH14*	41	AY18
Craiglockhart Rd *EH14*	41	AY19
Craiglockhart Rd N *EH14*	41	AZ17
Craiglockhart Ter *EH14*	42	BA17
Craiglockhart Vw *EH14*	41	AZ17
CRAIGMILLAR	28	BM15
Craigmillar Castle *EH1*	44	BM17
Craigmillar Castle Av *EH16*	44	BM16
Craigmillar Castle Gdns *EH16*	28	BM15
Craigmillar Castle Ln *EH16*	28	BM15
Craigmillar Castle Rd *EH16*	44	BM17
Craigmillar Ct *EH16*	44	BL16
Craigmillar Pk *EH16*	43	BH16
Craigmillar Park Golf Course *EH9*	43	BG17
Craigmount App *EH12*	24	AS12
Craigmount Av *EH12*	24	AS12
Craigmount Av N *EH4*	23	AR10
Craigmount Av N *EH12*	24	AS10
Craigmount Bk *EH4*	23	AR10
Craigmount Bk W *EH4*	23	AR10
Craigmount Brae *EH12*	23	AR10
Craigmount Ct *EH4*	23	AR10
Craigmount Cres *EH12*	23	AR11
Craigmount Dr *EH12*	23	AR11
Craigmount Gdns *EH12*	23	AR12
Craigmount Gro *EH12*	23	AR11
Craigmount Gro N *EH12*	23	AR11
Craigmount High Sch *EH12*	23	AR12
Craigmount Hill *EH4*	23	AR10
Craigmount Ln *EH12*	23	AR11
Craigmount Pk *EH12*	23	AR11
Craigmount Pl *EH12*	23	AR11
Craigmount Ter *EH12*	23	AR12
Craigmount Vw *EH12*	23	AR11

Name	Page	Grid
Craigmount Way EH12	24	AS10
Craigour Av EH17	45	BN19
Craigour Cres EH17	45	BN19
Craigour Dr EH17	44	BM18
Craigour Gdns EH17	45	BN19
Craigour Grn EH17	44	BM19
Craigour Gro EH17	45	BN19
Craigour Ln EH17	45	BN19
Craigour Park Prim Sch EH17	45	BN20
Craigour Pl EH17	44	BM19
Craigour Ter EH17	45	BN19
Craigpark Av (Ratho), Newbr. EH28	37	AE17
Craigpark Cres (Ratho), Newbr. EH28	37	AE17
Craigroyston Community High Sch EH4	13	AX7
Craigroyston Gro EH4	13	AW7
Craigroyston Pl EH4	13	AW6
Craigroyston Prim Sch EH4	13	AX7
Craigs Av EH12	39	AR13
Craigs Bk EH12	23	AR12
Craigs Cres EH12	23	AR12
Craigs Dr EH12	23	AR12
Craigs Gdns EH12	23	AR12
Craigs Gro EH12	24	AS12
Craigs Ln EH12	24	AS12
Craigs Pk EH12	23	AR12
Craigs Rd EH12	23	AR12
Crame Ter, Dalk. EH22	56	BU25
CRAMOND	11	AQ5
Cramond Av EH4	11	AR5
Cramond Bk EH4	11	AR6
CRAMOND BRIDGE	23	AP8
Cramond Br Cotts EH4	23	AP7
Cramond Brig Toll EH4	23	AP7
Cramond Cres EH4	11	AR6
Cramond Gdns EH4	11	AR6
Cramond Glebe Gdns EH4	12	AS5
Cramond Glebe Rd EH4	11	AR5
Cramond Glebe Ter EH4	11	AR5
Cramond Grn EH4	11	AR5
Cramond Gro EH4	11	AR6
Cramond New Br EH4	23	AP8
Cramond Pk EH4	11	AR6
Cramond Pl EH4	12	AS6
Cramond Prim Sch EH4	11	AR6
Cramond Regis EH4	23	AR7
Cramond Rd N EH4	12	AS5
Cramond Rd S EH4	12	AT6
Cramond Ter EH4	11	AR6
Cramond Vale EH4	11	AQ6
Cramond Village EH4	11	AR5
Cranston St EH8	7	BG11
Cranston St, Pen. EH26	68	BA38
Crarae Av EH4	25	AZ11
Craufurdland EH4	23	AQ8
Crawford Br EH7 1	16	BJ9
Crawfurd Rd EH16	43	BH16
Crawlees Cotts (Newt.), Dalk. EH22	65	BY29
Crawlees Cres (Mayf.), Dalk. EH22	71	CA29
Crescent, The EH10	42	BC17
Crescent, The (Gowks.), Gore. EH23	65	BY32
Crewe Bk EH5	14	BA6
Crewe Cres EH5	13	AZ6
Crewe Gro EH5	14	BA6
Crewe Ln EH5	13	AZ6
Crewe Path EH5	13	AZ6
Crewe Pl EH5	13	AZ6
Crewe Rd Gdns EH5	13	AZ6
Crewe Rd N EH5	13	AZ6
Crewe Rd S EH4	13	AZ7
Crewe Rd W EH5	13	AZ6
Crewe Ter EH5	13	AZ6
Crewe Toll EH4	13	AZ7
Crichton's Cl EH8 4	7	BH11
Crichton St EH8	7	BF12
Crighton Pl EH7	27	BH8
Croall Pl EH7	27	BG9
Crockett Gdns, Pen. EH26	68	AZ38
Croft-an-righ EH8	7	BH10
Croft St, Dalk. EH22	57	BW24
Croft St, Pen. EH26	68	BA39
Cromwell Pl EH6	15	BH5
Crookston Ct (Inv.), Muss. EH21	32	CA15
Crookston Dr (Inv.), Muss. EH21	31	BZ15
Cross Cotts, Pres. EH32 2	18	CJ10
Cross Rd, Lnhd EH20	61	BH27
Crosswood Av, Bal. EH14	58	AK27
Crosswood Cres, Bal. EH14	58	AK27
Crown Ct, Tran. EH33	35	CM13
Crowne Plaza Edinburgh Hotel EH1	7	BG11
Crown Pl EH6	15	BH7
Crown St EH6	15	BH7
Cruachan Ct, Pen. EH26	69	BC37
Crusader Dr, Ros. EH25	67	BH32
Cuddies Ln EH13 1	51	AW21
Cuddy La EH10	42	BC16
Cuguen Pl, Lass. EH18	55	BR26
CUIKEN	68	BA37
Cuiken Av, Pen. EH26	68	BA37
Cuiken Bk, Pen. EH26	68	AZ37
Cuiken Br, Pen. EH26	69	BB37
Cuikenburn, Pen. EH26	68	BA36
Cuiken Prim Sch EH26	68	AZ37
Cuiken Ter, Pen. EH26	68	AZ37
Cultins Rd EH11	39	AR16
Cumberland St EH3	27	BE9
Cumberland St N E La EH3	27	BE9
Cumberland St N W La EH3	27	BE9
Cumberland St S E La EH3	27	BE9
Cumberland St S W La EH3	27	BE9
Cumin Pl EH9	43	BG14
Cumlodden Av EH12	25	AY11
Cumnor Cres EH16	44	BJ18
Cunningham Pl EH6 1	15	BH7
CURRIE	49	AN23
Currie Community High Sch EH14	49	AP23
Curriehill Castle Dr, Bal. EH14	48	AM23
Curriehill Prim Sch EH14	49	AQ23
Curriehill Rd, Currie EH14	49	AP22
Curriehill Sta EH14	49	AP22
Currievale Dr, Currie EH14	49	AP22
Currievale Pk, Currie EH14	49	AN23
Currievale Pk Gro, Currie EH14	49	AN23
CUTHILL	34	CG11

D

Name	Page	Grid
Daiches Braes EH15	30	BT13
Daisy Ter EH11 3	42	BA15
Dalgety Av EH7	16	BK9
Dalgety Rd EH7	16	BK9
Dalgety St EH7	28	BK10
Dalhousie Av, Bonny. EH19	63	BQ29
Dalhousie Av W, Bonny. EH19	63	BP29
Dalhousie Castle Hotel EH19	64	BU31
Dalhousie Courte Hotel EH19	64	BT30
Dalhousie Cres, Dalk. EH22	56	BV26
Dalhousie Dr, Bonny. EH19	63	BQ29
Dalhousie Gdns, Bonny. EH19	63	BQ29
Dalhousie Pl, Bonny. EH19	63	BP29
Dalhousie Rd, Dalk. EH22	56	BV25
Dalhousie Rd E, Bonny. EH19	63	BQ29
Dalhousie Rd W, Bonny. EH19	63	BQ29
Dalhousie Ter EH10	42	BC17
DALKEITH	57	BX25
Dalkeith Country Park Visitor Centre EH22	47	BX22
Dalkeith High Sch EH22	57	BZ23
Dalkeith Rd EH16	7	BH13
Dalkeith St EH15	30	BS12
Dalkeith Western Bypass, Dalk. EH22	56	BT26
Dalkeith Western Bypass, Lass. EH18	56	BT24
Dalmahoy Cres, Bal. EH14	48	AK24
Dalmahoy Rd (Ratho), Newbr. EH28	37	AF17
DALMENY	9	AH4
Dalmeny House EH30	58	AM25
Dalmeny Prim Sch EH30	9	AG4
Dalmeny Rd EH6	15	BF6
Dalmeny Sta EH30	9	AF3
Dalmeny St EH6	27	BH8
DALRY	26	BA13
Dalrymple Cres EH9	43	BG15
Dalrymple Cres, Muss. EH21	31	BW13
Dalrymple Ln, Muss. EH21	31	BY13
Dalry Pl EH11	6	BC12
Dalry Prim Sch EH11	26	BB13
Dalry Rd EH11	26	BB12
Dalton Ct (Mayf.), Dalk. EH22	71	CA30
Dalum Ct, Lnhd EH20	54	BJ27
Dalum Dr, Lnhd EH20	54	BJ27
Dalum Gro, Lnhd EH20	54	BJ27
Dalum Ln, Lnhd EH20	54	BJ27
Dalziel Pl EH7 1	28	BJ10
Dambrae, Muss. EH21 1	31	BZ13
Damhead Holdings EH10	61	BF26
Damside EH4	26	BB11
Dance Base EH1	6	BE12
DANDERHALL	46	BS20
Danderhall Cres (Dand.), Dalk. EH22	45	BR20
Danderhall Prim Sch EH22	45	BR19
Dania Ct EH11	40	AV15
Danube St EH4	6	BC10
D'Arcy Cres (Mayf.), Dalk. EH22	71	CB28
D'Arcy Rd (Mayf.), Dalk. EH22	71	CA29
D'Arcy Ter (Mayf.), Dalk. EH22	71	CA28
Darnaway St EH3	6	BD10
Darnell Rd EH5	14	BC6
David Scott Av (Mayf.), Dalk. EH22	71	CA28
Davidson Gdns EH4	25	AW8
Davidson Pk EH4	25	AZ8
Davidson Rd EH4	25	AZ8
DAVIDSONS MAINS	24	AU8
Davidson's Mains Prim Sch EH4	24	AV8
Davies Row EH12	24	AT13
Davie St EH8	7	BG12

Name	Page	Grid
Dean Bk La EH3	26	BD9
Deanbank Pl, Gore. EH23	70	BZ36
Dean Br EH3	6	BC10
Dean Br EH4	6	BC10
DEANBURN	68	BA36
Deanburn, Pen. EH26	68	BA36
Deanery Cl EH7 1	28	BL10
Dean Gall EH4	26	BB11
Deanhaugh St EH4	26	BD9
Dean Pk (Newt.), Dalk. EH22	65	BW30
Deanpark Av, Bal. EH14	58	AK26
Deanpark Bk, Bal. EH14	58	AL26
Deanpark Brae, Bal. EH14	58	AL26
Deanpark Ct, Bal. EH14	58	AK27
Deanpark Ct (Newt.), Dalk. EH22 1	65	BW30
Dean Pk Cres EH4	6	BC10
Deanpark Cres, Bal. EH14	58	AL26
Deanpark Gdns, Bal. EH14	58	AL26
Deanpark Gro, Bal. EH14	58	AL26
Dean Pk Ms EH4	26	BC9
Deanpark Pl, Bal. EH14	58	AL26
Dean Pk Pl (Newt.), Dalk. EH22	65	BW30
Dean Park Prim Sch EH14	58	AL27
Deanpark Sq, Bal. EH14	58	AL26
Dean Pk St EH4	26	BC9
Dean Path EH4	26	BB10
Dean Path Bldgs EH4 2	6	BC11
Dean Pl, Pen. EH26	68	AZ37
Dean Rd, Pen. EH26	68	AZ37
Dean St EH4	26	BC9
Dean Ter EH4	6	BC10
DEAN VILLAGE	26	BB11
Dechmont Rd EH12	23	AQ12
Delhaig EH11	41	AY15
Dell Rd EH13	51	AX20
Delta Av, Muss. EH21	32	CC14
Delta Cres, Muss. EH21	32	CC14
Delta Dr, Muss. EH21	32	CC13
Delta Gdns, Muss. EH21	32	CC14
Delta Pl (Inv.), Muss. EH21	31	BZ15
Delta Rd, Muss. EH21	32	CC14
Delta Vw, Muss. EH21	32	CC13
Denham Grn Av EH5	14	BD6
Denham Grn Pl EH5	14	BD6
Denham Grn Ter EH5	14	BD6
Denholm Av, Muss. EH21	30	BV15
Denholm Dr, Muss. EH21	31	BW15
Denholm Rd, Muss. EH21	30	BV14
Denholm Way, Muss. EH21	30	BV15
De Quincey Path, Lass. EH18	63	BN29
De Quincey Rd, Lass. EH18	63	BN29
Dequincey Wk, Tran. EH33 1	35	CL14
Derby St EH6	15	BF5
Devon Pl EH12	26	BB12
Dewar Pl EH3	6	BC12
Dewar Pl La EH3	6	BC12
Dick Pl EH9	43	BF15
Dicksonfield EH7	27	BG9
Dickson Gro, Bonny. EH19 1	64	BS29
Dickson's Cl EH1 5	7	BG11
Dickson St EH6	27	BH8
Dick Ter, Pen. EH26	69	BB37
Dinmont Dr EH16	44	BK18
Distillery La EH11	26	BB12
Dobbie's Rd, Bonny. EH19	63	BQ28
Dobbie's Rd, Lass. EH18	63	BQ28
Dochart Dr EH4	24	AS10
Dock Pl EH6	15	BH5
Dock St EH6	15	BH5
Dolphin Av, Currie EH14	49	AP23
Dolphin Gdns E, Currie EH14	49	AP23
Dolphin Gdns W, Currie EH14	49	AP23
Dolphin Rd, Currie EH14	49	AN24
Dominion Cinema EH10	42	BD15
Donaldson's Coll EH12	26	BB12
Doo'Cot Pl, Pres. EH32 1	34	CJ11
Dorset Pl EH11	42	BC14
Double Dykes (Inv.), Muss. EH21	31	BZ15
Double Hedges Pk EH16	44	BJ18
Double Hedges Rd EH16	44	BJ18
Dougall Ct (Mayf.), Dalk. EH22	65	BZ30
Dougall Pl (Mayf.), Dalk. EH22	65	BZ30
Dougall Rd (Mayf.), Dalk. EH22 1	65	BZ30
Douglas Cres EH12	26	BB11
Douglas Cres, Bonny. EH19	63	BR28
Douglas Gdns EH4	26	BB11
Douglas Gdns Ms EH4 3	26	BB11
Douglas Ter EH11 1	6	BC12
Doune Ter EH3	6	BD10
Dovecot Brae, Tran. EH33	35	CL12
Dovecot Gro EH14	41	AW18
Dovecot Ln EH14	41	AW18
Dovecot Pk EH14	41	AW19
Dovecot Rd EH12	40	AT14
Dowie's Mill Cotts EH4	23	AP7
Dowie's Mill La EH4	23	AP7
Downfield Pl EH11	26	BB13
Downie Gro EH12	24	AV13
Downie Pl, Muss. EH21	31	BY13
Downie Ter EH12	24	AV13
Downing Ct, Ros. EH25	62	BJ32
DREGHORN	51	AY22
Dreghorn Av EH13	52	BA22
Dreghorn Cotts EH13	51	AZ22
Dreghorn Dr EH13	52	BA22
Dreghorn Gdns EH13	52	BA21
Dreghorn Gro EH13	52	BA22
Dreghorn Junct EH10	52	BA23
Dreghorn Junct EH13	52	BA23
Dreghorn Link EH13	52	BA22
Dreghorn Ln EH13	51	AX21
Dreghorn Pk EH13	51	AZ21
Dreghorn Pl EH13	52	BA22
Drum Av EH17	45	BN21
DRUMBRAE	24	AS10
Drum Brae Av EH12	24	AS11
Drum Brae Cres EH4	24	AS10
Drum Brae Dr EH4	24	AT10
Drum Brae Gdns EH4	24	AS11
Drum Brae Gro EH4	24	AS10
Drum Brae Neuk EH12	24	AS11
Drum Brae N EH4	23	AR9
Drum Brae Pk EH12	24	AS11
Drum Brae Pk App EH12	24	AS11
Drum Brae Pl EH12	24	AS11
Drumbrae Prim Sch EH4	24	AS11
Drum Brae S EH12	24	AS10
Drum Brae Ter EH4	24	AS10
Drum Brae Wk EH4	24	AS10
Drum Cotts EH17	55	BP22
Drum Cres EH17	45	BP21
Drumdryan St EH3	6	BD13
Drummohr Av (Wall.), Muss. EH21	32	CC14
Drummohr Gdns (Wall.), Muss. EH21	33	CD14
Drummond Comm High Sch EH7	27	BF9
Drummond Pl EH3	27	BE9
Drummond St EH8	7	BG12
Drummore Dr, Pres. EH32	34	CG11
Drum Pl EH17	45	BP21
Drumsheugh Gdns EH3	6	BC11
Drumsheugh Pl EH3 3	6	BC11
Drum St EH17	45	BN21
Drum Ter EH7	16	BJ9
Drum Vw Av (Dand.), Dalk. EH22	45	BR20
Dryden Av, Lnhd EH20	62	BJ28
Dryden Cres, Lnhd EH20	62	BJ28
Dryden Gait EH7	27	BG8
Dryden Gdns EH7	27	BG8
Dryden Glen, Lnhd EH20	61	BH28
Dryden Gro, Ros. EH25	62	BJ31
Dryden Ln, Lnhd EH20	61	BH29
Dryden Pl EH9	43	BH14
Dryden Pl, Lnhd EH20	61	BH28
Dryden Rd, Lnhd EH20	61	BH28
Dryden St EH7	27	BG8
Dryden Ter EH7	27	BG8
Dryden Ter, Lnhd EH20	62	BJ28
Dryden Vale, Lnhd EH20	61	BH28
Dryden Vw, Lnhd EH20	62	BJ28
DRYLAW	25	AX8
Drylaw Av EH4	25	AY9
Drylaw Cres EH4	25	AX9
Drylaw Gdns EH4	25	AX8
Drylaw Grn EH4	25	AX9
Drylaw Gro EH4	25	AX9
Drylaw Ho Gdns EH4	25	AX8
Drylaw Ho Paddock EH4	25	AX8
Duart Cres EH4	24	AS10
Dublin Meuse EH3	7	BF10
Dublin St EH1	27	BF9
Dublin St EH3	27	BF9
Dublin St La N EH3	27	BF9
Dublin St La S EH1	7	BF10
DUDDINGSTON	29	BN13
Duddingston Av EH15	29	BN13
Duddingston Cres EH15	29	BQ13
Duddingston Gdns N EH15	29	BP12
Duddingston Gdns S EH15	29	BP13
Duddingston Golf Course EH15	29	BN14
Duddingston Gro E EH15	29	BP12
Duddingston Gro W EH15	29	BP13
Duddingston Ln EH15	29	BN12
Duddingston Mains Cotts EH15	29	BR13
Duddingston Mills EH8	29	BN12
Duddingston Pk EH15	29	BQ12
Duddingston Pk S EH15	29	BQ13
Duddingston Prim Sch EH15	29	BN12
Duddingston Ri EH15	29	BP13
Duddingston Rd EH15	29	BN12
Duddingston Rd W EH15	28	BM13
Duddingston Rd W EH16	28	BM14
Duddingston Row EH15	29	BP13
Duddingston Sq E EH15	29	BP12
Duddingston Sq W EH15	29	BP12
Duddingston Vw EH15	29	BP13
Duddingston Yards EH15 1	29	BQ14
Dudgeon Pl, K'lis. EH29	20	AD9
Dudley Av EH6	15	BF5
Dudley Av S EH6	15	BG6
Dudley Bk EH6	15	BF5
Dudley Cres EH6	15	BF5
Dudley Gdns EH6	15	BF5
Dudley Gro EH6	15	BF5
Dudley Ter EH6	15	BF5
Duff Rd EH11	26	BB13
Duff St EH11	26	BB13
Duff St La EH11	26	BB13
Duke Pl EH6	16	BJ7
Duke St EH6	16	BJ7

Name	Page	Grid
Duke St, Dalk. EH22	57	BW24
Duke's Wk EH8	28	BK11
Dumbeg Pk EH14	40	AT19
DUMBIEDYKES	7	BG12
Dumbiedykes Rd EH8	7	BH12
Dumbryden Dr EH14	40	AU18
Dumbryden Gdns EH14	40	AU17
Dumbryden Gro EH14	40	AU18
Dumbryden Prim Sch EH14	40	AU18
Dumbryden Rd EH14	40	AV18
Dun-ard Gdn EH9	43	BF16
Dunbar St EH3	6	BD12
Duncan Gdns, Tran. EH33	35	CL12
Duncan Pl EH6	16	BJ7
Duncans Gait EH14	40	AV17
Duncan St EH9	43	BG15
Dundas Av, S Q'fry EH30	9	AE3
Dundas Cres, Dalk. EH22	56	BU26
Dundas Gdns, Gore. EH23	70	BX34
Dundas Gro, Dalk. EH22	56	BU25
Dundas Pk, Bonny. EH19	56	BS28
Dundas Parks Golf Course EH30	8	AC5
Dundas Pl, K'lis. EH29	20	AD9
Dundas Rd, Dalk. EH22	56	BU25
Dundas St EH3	27	BE9
Dundas St, Bonny. EH19	63	BR28
Dundee St EH11	26	BB13
Dundee Ter EH11	42	BB14
Dundonald St EH3	27	BE9
Dundrennan Cotts EH16	44	BL17
Dunedin St EH7	27	BF8
Dunlop's Ct EH1 12	6	BE12
Dunlop Ter, Pen. EH26	69	BC38
Dunollie Ct EH12 2	23	AR12
Dunrobin Pl EH3	26	BD9
Dunsmuir Ct EH12	24	AS13
Dunsyre Ho EH11	40	AS18
Dunvegan Ct EH4	23	AR7
Durar Dr EH4	24	AS11
DURHAM	29	BP12
Durham Av EH15	29	BP12
Durham Bk, Bonny. EH19	64	BS29
Durham Dr EH15	29	BQ13
Durham Gdns N EH15	29	BQ12
Durham Gdns S EH15	29	BQ13
Durham Gro EH15	29	BQ12
Durham Gro, Bonny. EH19	64	BS29
Durham Pl, Bonny. EH19	63	BR29
Durham Pl E EH15	29	BQ12
Durham Pl La EH15	29	BQ12
Durham Pl W EH15	29	BP12
Durham Rd EH15	29	BQ12
Durham Rd S EH15	29	BQ13
Durham Sq EH15	29	BP12
Durham Ter EH15	29	BP12
Durward Gro EH16	44	BK17
Dykes Rd, Pen. EH26	68	BA36

E

Name	Page	Grid
Earl Grey St EH3	6	BD12
Earl Haig Gdns EH5	14	BD6
Earl Haig Homes EH11	41	AW15
Earlston Pl EH7	28	BJ10
East Adam St EH8	7	BG12
East Barnton Av EH4	12	AU7
East Barnton Gdns EH4	24	AU8
East Brighton Cres EH15	29	BQ11
East Broughton Pl EH1 1	27	BF9
East Caiystane Pl EH10	52	BC22
East Caiystane Rd EH10	52	BD22
East Camus Pl EH10	52	BC21
East Camus Rd EH10	52	BC21
East Castle Rd EH10	42	BC14

Name	Page	Grid
East Champanyie EH9	43	BG16
East Clapperfield EH16	44	BJ18
East Claremont St EH7	27	BF9
East Comiston EH10	52	BC21
East Ct EH4 2	25	AY10
East Ct EH16	45	BP16
EAST CRAIGS	23	AR11
East Craigs Prim Sch EH12	23	AR11
East Craigs Rigg EH12	23	AQ12
East Cft (Ratho), Newbr. EH28	37	AG17
East Cromwell St EH6	15	BH5
East Crosscauseway EH8	7	BG13
Easter Auchendinny Br, Pen. EH26	67	BE35
Easter Belmont Rd EH12	25	AX12
Easter Currie Ct, Currie EH14	49	AQ23
Easter Currie Cres, Currie EH14	49	AQ22
Easter Currie Pl, Currie EH14	49	AQ22
Easter Currie Ter, Currie EH14	49	AQ23
Easter Dalry Dr EH11	26	BB13
Easter Dalry Pl EH11 1	26	BB12
Easter Dalry Rigg EH11 3	26	BB13
Easter Dalry Rd EH11	26	BB12
Easter Dalry Wynd EH11	26	BB12
Easter Drylaw Av EH4	25	AY8
Easter Drylaw Bk EH4	13	AY7
Easter Drylaw Dr EH4	25	AZ8
Easter Drylaw Gdns EH4	25	AY8
Easter Drylaw Gro EH4	25	AY8
Easter Drylaw Ln EH4	13	AY7
Easter Drylaw Pl EH4	25	AY8
Easter Drylaw Vw EH4	13	AY7
Easter Drylaw Way EH4	25	AY8
Easter Haugh EH13	52	BA20
Easter Hermitage EH6	16	BK8
EASTER HOWGATE	60	BC30
Eastern General Hosp EH6	44	BM18
Easter Pk Dr EH4	12	AU7
Easter Pk Ho EH4 5	12	AU7
Easter Rd EH6	16	BJ8
Easter Rd EH7	27	BH9
Easter Road Stadium (Hibernian FC) EH7	16	BJ9
Easter Steil EH10	42	BB18
Easter Warriston EH7	15	BE7
East Fm of Gilmerton EH17	45	BN21
East Fettes Av EH4	26	BB8
EASTFIELD, Penicuik	69	BB36
EASTFIELD, Portobello	30	BU12
Eastfield EH15	30	BV12
Eastfield Dr, Pen. EH26	69	BB37
Eastfield Fm Rd, Pen. EH26	69	BB36
Eastfield Gdns EH15	30	BU12
Eastfield Ind Est, Pen. EH26	69	BB37
Eastfield Ln, Tran. EH33	35	CM12
Eastfield Pk Rd, Pen. EH26	69	BB37
Eastfield Pl EH15	30	BV12
Eastfield Prim Sch EH26	69	BB37
Eastfield Rd, Newbr. EH28	22	AJ12
East Fountainbridge EH3	6	BD12
East Hannahfield, Bal. EH14	58	AJ25
East Hermitage Pl EH6	16	BJ7
EASTHOUSES	57	BX27
Easthouses Ct, Dalk. EH22	57	BY27
Easthouses Ind Est (Easth.), Dalk. EH22	57	BZ27
Easthouses Pl (Easth.), Dalk. EH22 1	57	BY26
Easthouses Rd (Easth.), Dalk. EH22	57	BY26

Name	Page	Grid
Easthouses Way (Easth.), Dalk. EH22	57	BY26
East Kilngate Pl EH17	54	BM22
East Kilngate Rigg EH17	54	BM22
East Kilngate Wynd EH17	54	BM22
East Lillypot EH5	14	BD6
East Ln, Pres. EH32	18	CH9
East London St EH7	27	BF9
East Lorimer Pl (Cock.), Pres. EH32 3	19	CL7
EAST MAINS OF INGLISTON	37	AH13
East Mkt St EH8	7	BF11
East Mayfield EH9	43	BH15
East Montgomery Pl EH7	27	BH9
East Newington Pl EH9	43	BG14
East Norton Pl EH7	7	BH10
East Parkside EH16	7	BH13
EAST PILTON	14	BA6
East Preston St EH8	43	BG14
East Preston St La EH8 3	43	BG14
East Queensway, Pen. EH26	69	BB36
East Restalrig Ter EH6	16	BK7
East Savile Rd EH16	43	BH16
East Sciennes St EH9	43	BG14
East Scotland St La EH3	27	BF9
East Sea Side, Pres. EH32 2	18	CH9
East Silvermills La EH3	26	BD9
East Suffolk Rd EH16	44	BJ16
East Telferton EH7	29	BP10
East Ter, S Q'fry EH30 4	9	AE2
East Trinity Rd EH5	14	BD6
East Way, The EH8	29	BN11
East Werberside EH4	14	BA7
East Werberside Pl EH4	14	BA7
Echline, S Q'fry EH30	8	AB3
Echline Av, S Q'fry EH30	8	AB2
Echline Dr, S Q'fry EH30	8	AB3
Echline Gdns, S Q'fry EH30	8	AB2
Echline Grn, S Q'fry EH30	8	AB2
Echline Gro, S Q'fry EH30	8	AC2
Echline Pk, S Q'fry EH30	8	AB3
Echline Pl, S Q'fry EH30	8	AC3
Echline Prim Sch EH30	8	AC2
Echline Rigg, S Q'fry EH30	8	AC2
Echline Steadings, S Q'fry EH30 1	8	AB3
Echline Ter, S Q'fry EH30	8	AC3
Echline Vw, S Q'fry EH30	8	AC3
Edenhall Bk, Muss. EH21	32	CA14
Edenhall Cres, Muss. EH21	32	CA14
Edenhall Hosp EH21	32	CA15
Edenhall Rd, Muss. EH21	32	CA14
Eden La EH10	42	BD16
Eden Ter EH10 1	42	BD16
Edgefield Ind Est, Lnhd EH20	54	BL26
Edgefield Pl, Lnhd EH20	54	BL27
Edgefield Rd, Lnhd EH20	54	BL27
Edina Pl EH7	27	BH9
Edina St EH7	27	BH9
Edinburgh Academy EH3	26	BD9
Edinburgh Academy Jun Sch EH3	14	BC7
Edinburgh Airport EH12	22	AJ11
Edinburgh Birds of Prey Centre EH18	56	BS24
Edinburgh Canal Centre EH28	37	AF17
Edinburgh Castle EH1	6	BE11
Edinburgh Coll of Art EH3	6	BE12
Edinburgh Coll of Art (Inverleith) EH3	14	BD7
Edinburgh Crystal Visitor Centre EH26	69	BB37
Edinburgh Dock EH6	16	BK5
Edinburgh Dungeon EH1	7	BF11

Edinburgh International Conference Centre *EH3* — 6 BD12
Edinburgh Old Town Weaving Company *EH1* **1** — 6 BE11
Edinburgh Pk *EH12* — 39 AP14
Edinburgh Pk Business Cen *EH12* — 39 AP15
Edinburgh Park Sta *EH12* — 39 AQ16
Edinburgh Rd, Dalk. *EH22* — 57 BW24
Edinburgh Rd, Muss. *EH21* — 30 BV12
Edinburgh Rd, Newbr. *EH28* — 36 AB13
Edinburgh Rd, Pen. *EH26* — 69 BB36
Edinburgh Rd (Cock.), Pres. *EH32* — 18 CK8
Edinburgh Rd, S Q'fry *EH30* — 9 AE2
Edinburgh Rd, Tran. *EH33* — 34 CK13
Edinburgh Sch of Shiatsu *EH10* — 42 BD14
Edinburgh Tutorial Coll *EH3* — 6 BC11
Edinburgh Zoo *EH12* — 24 AV12
EDMONSTONE — 45 BP18
Edmonstone Av (Dand.), Dalk. *EH22* — 45 BR19
Edmonstone Dr (Dand.), Dalk. *EH22* — 45 BR19
Edmonstone Rd (Dand.), Dalk. *EH22* — 45 BQ19
Edmonstone Ter (Dand.), Dalk. *EH22* — 45 BR19
Eglinton Cres *EH12* — 26 BB12
Eglinton St *EH12* **3** — 26 BA12
Egypt Ms *EH10* — 43 BE16
Eighth St (Newt.), Dalk. *EH22* — 65 BX30
Eildon St *EH3* — 27 BE8
Eildon Ter *EH3* — 26 BD8
Elbe St *EH6* — 16 BJ6
Elcho Pl (Port S.), Pres. *EH32* **2** — 19 CL7
Elcho Ter *EH15* — 30 BS11
Elder St *EH1* — 7 BF10
Elder St, Tran. *EH33* — 35 CL12
Elder St E *EH1* **5** — 7 BF10
ELDINDEAN — 56 BS27
Eldindean Pl, Bonny. *EH19* — 55 BR27
Eldindean Rd, Bonny. *EH19* — 55 BR27
Eldindean Ter, Bonny. *EH19* — 55 BR27
Eldin Ind Est, Lnhd *EH20* — 54 BL25
Electra Pl *EH15* **2** — 29 BQ10
Elgin Pl *EH12* — 26 BB12
Elgin St *EH7* — 27 BH9
Elgin St N *EH7* — 27 BH9
Elgin Ter *EH7* — 27 BH9
Elizafield *EH6* — 15 BG7
Ellangowan Ter *EH16* — 44 BL18
Ellen's Glen Ln *EH17* — 44 BL20
Ellen's Glen Rd *EH17* — 44 BL20
Ellersly Rd *EH12* — 25 AX12
Elliot Gdns *EH14* — 41 AY19
Elliot Pk *EH14* — 41 AY19
Elliot Pl *EH14* — 41 AY19
Elliot Rd *EH14* — 41 AY19
Elliot St *EH7* — 27 BH9
Elmfield Ct, Dalk. *EH22* — 57 BW24
Elmfield Pk, Dalk. *EH22* — 57 BW24
Elmfield Rd, Dalk. *EH22* — 57 BW24
Elm Pl *EH6* **2** — 16 BK7
Elm Pl (Mayf.), Dalk. *EH22* — 65 BZ29
Elm Row *EH7* — 27 BG9
Elm Row, Lass. *EH18* — 55 BQ26
Elmwood Ter *EH6* — 16 BK7
Elphinstone Ct, Tran. *EH33* **3** — 35 CL13
Elphinstone Rd, Tran. *EH33* — 34 CK15

Elphinstone Wk *EH33* **6** — 35 CL14
Eltringham Gdns *EH14* — 41 AY15
Eltringham Gro *EH14* — 41 AY15
Eltringham Ter *EH14* — 41 AY15
Emily Ct, Gore. *EH23* **1** — 70 BY34
Emily Pl, Gore. *EH23* — 70 BY34
Engine Rd, Gore. *EH23* — 70 BX34
Engine Rd, Lnhd *EH20* — 54 BL27
Esdaile Bk *EH9* — 43 BF15
Esdaile Gdns *EH9* — 43 BF15
Esdaile Pk *EH9* **1** — 43 BF15
ESKBANK — 56 BV25
Eskbank Ct, Dalk. *EH22* **2** — 56 BU25
Eskbank Rd, Bonny. *EH19* — 56 BS27
Eskbank Rd, Dalk. *EH22* — 56 BV25
Eskbank Ter, Dalk. *EH22* — 56 BV25
Eskbank Toll, Dalk. *EH22* — 56 BV25
Esk Br, Pen. *EH26* — 69 BD38
Eskdaill Ct, Dalk. *EH22* **4** — 57 BW24
Eskdaill St, Dalk. *EH22* — 57 BW24
Eskdale Ct, Bonny. *EH19* — 63 BQ28
Eskdale Dr, Bonny. *EH19* — 63 BQ28
Eskdale Ms, Muss. *EH21* — 31 BY13
Eskdale Ter, Bonny. *EH19* — 63 BQ28
Eskfield Gro, Dalk. *EH22* — 56 BT25
Esk Glades, Dalk. *EH22* — 57 BX23
ESKGROVE — 55 BP27
Eskgrove Dr (Bils.), Ros. *EH25* — 61 BG29
Eskhill, Pen. *EH26* — 69 BB38
Eskmill Ind Est, Pen. *EH26* — 69 BC38
Eskmill Rd, Pen. *EH26* — 69 BC38
Eskmills Pk, Muss. *EH21* — 31 BX14
Esk Pl, Dalk. *EH22* — 56 BV24
Eskside Ct, Dalk. *EH22* — 56 BV23
Eskside E, Muss. *EH21* — 31 BY13
Eskside W, Muss. *EH21* — 31 BX13
Eskvale Ct, Pen. *EH26* — 69 BC38
Eskvale Cres, Pen. *EH26* — 69 BC38
Eskvale Dr, Pen. *EH26* — 69 BC37
Eskvale Vw, Pen. *EH26* — 69 BC37
Eskview Av, Muss. *EH21* — 31 BX14
Eskview Cres, Muss. *EH21* — 31 BX14
Eskview Gro, Dalk. *EH22* — 56 BV24
Eskview Gro, Muss. *EH21* — 31 BX14
Eskview Rd (Mayf.), Dalk. *EH22* — 65 BZ29
Eskview Rd, Muss. *EH21* — 31 BX14
Eskview Ter, Muss. *EH21* — 31 BX14
Eskview Vil, Dalk. *EH22* — 56 BU25
Esplanade *EH1* — 6 BE12
Esplanade *EH4* — 12 AS4
Esplanade Ter *EH15* — 30 BT11
Essendean Pl *EH4* — 24 AT10
Essendean Ter *EH4* — 24 AT10
Essex Brae *EH4* — 23 AQ7
Essex Pk *EH4* — 23 AQ7
Essex Rd *EH4* — 23 AQ7
Esslemont Rd *EH16* — 43 BH17
Ethel Ter *EH10* — 42 BC17
Eton Ter *EH4* — 6 BC10
Ettrickdale Pl *EH3* — 26 BD8
Ettrick Gro *EH10* — 42 BC14
Ettrick Ln *EH10* — 42 BB15
Ettrick Rd *EH10* — 42 BB15
Evans Gdns, Bonny. *EH19* — 56 BT27
Eva Pl *EH9* — 43 BG17
Evelyn Ter (Auch.), Pen. *EH26* — 67 BE34
Ewerland *EH4* — 23 AQ7
Ewing St, Pen. *EH26* — 69 BB36
Eyre Cres *EH3* — 27 BE9
Eyre Pl *EH3* — 27 BE9
Eyre Ter *EH3* — 27 BE9

F

Fair-a-Far *EH4* — 11 AR6
Fair-a-Far Cotts *EH4* — 11 AR6
Fair-a-Far Shot *EH4* — 11 AR6
Fairbrae *EH11* — 40 AV16
Fairford Gdns *EH16* — 44 BK18
Fairhaven Vil, Dalk. *EH22* **1** — 56 BU26
Fairmile Av *EH10* — 52 BD21
FAIRMILEHEAD — 52 BD22
Fairview Rd, Newbr. *EH28* — 21 AH12
Fairways (Monk.), Muss. *EH21* — 31 BX16
Faith Mission Bible Coll *EH17* — 45 BN21
Fala Ct *EH16* — 44 BK21
Falcon Av *EH10* — 42 BD16
Falcon Ct *EH10* — 42 BD16
Falcon Gdns *EH10* — 42 BD15
Falcon Rd *EH10* — 42 BD16
Falcon Rd W *EH10* — 42 BD16
Falkland Gdns *EH12* — 24 AU10
Farm Av, Lass. *EH18* — 63 BP29
Farquhar Ter, S Q'fry *EH30* — 8 AC2
Farrer Gro *EH7* — 29 BN10
Farrer Ter *EH7* — 29 BN10
Fa'side Av, Tran. *EH33* **1** — 35 CM14
Fa'side Av Ct (Wall.), Muss. *EH21* — 33 CD15
Fa'side Av N (Wall.), Muss. *EH21* — 33 CD15
Fa'side Av S (Wall.), Muss. *EH21* — 33 CD15
Fa'side Bldgs (Wall.), Muss. *EH21* — 33 CD15
Fa'side Cres (Wall.), Muss. *EH21* — 33 CD15
Fa'side Cres, Tran. *EH33* **2** — 35 CM14
Fa'side Dr (Wall.), Muss. *EH21* — 33 CD15
Fa'side Gdns (Wall.), Muss. *EH21* — 33 CD15
Fa'side Rd, Tran. *EH33* — 35 CM14
Fa'side Ter (Wall.), Muss. *EH21* — 33 CD15
Fa'side Vw, Tran. *EH33* — 34 CK15
Fauldburn *EH12* — 23 AR10
Fauldburn Pk *EH12* — 23 AR10
Featherhall Av *EH12* — 24 AT13
Featherhall Cres *EH12* **1** — 24 AS13
Featherhall Cres N *EH12* — 24 AS13
Featherhall Cres S *EH12* — 24 AS13
Featherhall Gro *EH12* — 24 AT13
Featherhall Pl *EH12* — 24 AT13
Featherhall Rd *EH12* — 24 AT13
Featherhall Ter *EH12* — 24 AT13
Ferguson Ct, Muss. *EH21* — 31 BY16
Ferguson Dr, Muss. *EH21* — 31 BX16
Ferguson Gdns, Muss. *EH21* — 31 BX16
Ferguson Grn, Muss. *EH21* — 31 BX16
Ferguson Vw, Muss. *EH21* — 31 BX16
Ferguson Way (Newt.), Dalk. *EH22* — 65 BX31
FERNIEHILL — 45 BP20
Ferniehill Av *EH17* — 45 BN21
Ferniehill Dr *EH17* — 45 BN21
Ferniehill Gdns *EH17* — 45 BP20
Ferniehill Gro *EH17* **1** — 45 BP20
Ferniehill Pl *EH17* — 45 BN21
Ferniehill Rd *EH17* — 45 BP20
Ferniehill Sq *EH17* — 45 BN21
Ferniehill St *EH17* — 45 BN20
Ferniehill Ter *EH17* — 45 BN21
Ferniehill Way *EH17* — 45 BP20
Fernielaw Av *EH13* — 51 AW22

Fernieside Av *EH17*	45	BN20
Fernieside Cres *EH17*	45	BN20
Fernieside Dr *EH17*	45	BN20
Fernieside Gdns *EH17*	45	BN20
Fernieside Gro *EH17*	45	BP20
Ferryburn, S Q'fry *EH30* 1	9	AE3
Ferryburn Grn, S Q'fry *EH30*	9	AE3
Ferryfield *EH5*	14	BB7
Ferryhill Prim Sch *EH4*	25	AY8
Ferrymuir, S Q'fry *EH30*	8	AD3
Ferrymuir Gait, S Q'fry *EH30*	8	AD3
Ferrymuir La, S Q'fry *EH30*	8	AD3
Ferrymuir Rd, S Q'fry *EH30*	8	AD3
Ferry Rd *EH3*	13	AY7
Ferry Rd *EH5*	14	BD6
Ferry Rd *EH6*	15	BF6
Ferry Rd Av *EH4*	13	AZ7
Ferry Rd Dr *EH4*	13	AZ6
Ferry Rd Gdns *EH4*	13	AY7
Ferry Rd Gro *EH4*	13	AY7
Ferry Rd Pl *EH4*	13	AY7
Festival Sq *EH3* 1	6	BD12
Festival Theatre *EH8*	7	BG12
Fetteresk Cotts, Pen. *EH26*	68	BA39
Fettes Av *EH4*	26	BB9
Fettes Coll *EH4*	26	BB8
Fettes Ri *EH4*	14	BB7
Fettes Row *EH3*	27	BE9
Fidra Ct *EH4*	13	AW6
Fifth St (Newt.), Dalk. *EH22*	65	BW30
Figgate Bk *EH15*	29	BR10
Figgate La *EH15*	29	BR10
Figgate St *EH15*	29	BQ10
Fillyside Av *EH7*	17	BN9
Fillyside Rd *EH7*	17	BN8
Fillyside Ter *EH7*	17	BN8
Filmhouse Cinema *EH3*	6	BD12
Findhorn Pl *EH9*	43	BG14
Findlay Av *EH7*	16	BL8
Findlay Cotts *EH7*	16	BL8
Findlay Gdns *EH7*	16	BL8
Findlay Gro *EH7*	16	BL8
Findlay Medway *EH7*	16	BL8
Fingal Pl *EH9*	43	BF14
Fingzies Pl *EH6* 3	16	BK7
Finlaggan Ct *EH12* 2	23	AQ11
Finlay Pl (Mayf.), Dalk. *EH22*	71	CB29
FIRRHILL	42	BA19
Firrhill Cres *EH13*	41	AZ19
Firrhill Dr *EH13*	52	BA20
Firrhill High Sch *EH14*	41	AZ19
Firrhill Ln *EH13*	52	BA20
First Gait (Ricc.), Currie *EH14*	49	AN19
First St (Newt.), Dalk. *EH22*	65	BX31
Firth Br, Ros. *EH25*	67	BF35
Firth Cres (Auch.), Pen. *EH26*	67	BF34
Firth Rd (Auch.), Pen. *EH26*	67	BF34
Fir Vw, Lnhd *EH20* 1	61	BH28
Fishergate Rd (Port S.), Pres. *EH32*	19	CN8
FISHERROW	31	BY12
Fisherrow Ind Pk, Muss. *EH21*	31	BW13
Fishers Rd (Port S.), Pres. *EH32*	19	CM7
Fishers Wynd, Muss. *EH21*	31	BX13
Fishmarket Sq *EH6* 2	15	BF4
Fishwives' Causeway *EH7*	29	BN10
Fishwives' Causeway *EH15*	29	BQ10
Flassches Yd *EH12*	40	AS15
Fleets Gro, Tran. *EH33*	35	CM15
Fleets Ind Est, Tran. *EH33*	35	CL16
Fleets Rd, Tran. *EH33*	35	CL14
Fleets Vw, Tran. *EH33*	35	CM15
Fleshmarket Cl *EH1* 13	7	BF11
Fletcher Gro, Pen. *EH26*	66	BB35
Flora Stevenson Prim Sch *EH4*	26	BB9
Flotterstone Br, Pen. *EH26*	66	BA33
Forbes Rd *EH10*	42	BD15
Forbes St *EH8*	7	BG13
Ford's Rd *EH11*	41	AX15
Forester's Vw, Tran. *EH33*	35	CM13
Forres St *EH3*	6	BD10
Forrester High Sch *EH12*	40	AT15
Forrester Pk Av *EH12*	40	AT15
Forrester Pk Dr *EH12*	40	AT15
Forrester Pk Gdns *EH12*	40	AT15
Forrester Pk Grn *EH12*	40	AU15
Forrester Pk Gro *EH12*	40	AT15
Forrester Pk Ln *EH12*	40	AT15
Forrester Rd *EH12*	24	AT12
Forrest Hill *EH1*	7	BF12
Forrest Rd *EH1*	7	BF12
Forteviot Ho *EH17*	44	BM19
Forth Ct (Port S.), Pres. *EH32*	19	CN7
Forth Gdns (Port S.), Pres. *EH32*	19	CN7
Forth Gro (Port S.), Pres. *EH32*	19	CN7
Forth Ind Est *EH5*	14	BA4
Forth Ho *EH6*	15	BG5
Forth Pk (Dalm.), S Q'fry *EH30*	9	AG3
Forth Pl, S Q'fry *EH30*	8	AB2
Forth St *EH1*	7	BF10
Forth Ter (Dalm.), S Q'fry *EH30*	9	AF3
Forth Vw Av, Currie *EH14*	49	AP23
Forthview Av (Wall.), Muss. *EH21*	32	CC14
Forth Vw Cres, Currie *EH14*	49	AP22
Forth Vw Cres (Dand.), Dalk. *EH22*	45	BR19
Forthview Cres (Wall.), Muss. *EH21*	32	CC14
Forthview Dr (Wall.), Muss. *EH21* 1	33	CD14
Forthview Prim Sch *EH4*	13	AZ7
Forthview Rd *EH4*	25	AY9
Forth Vw Rd, Currie *EH14*	49	AP23
Forthview Ter *EH4*	25	AX9
Forthview Ter (Wall.), Muss. *EH21*	33	CD14
Forth Wynd (Port S.), Pres. *EH32*	19	CN7
Fort Kinnaird Shopping Centre *EH15*	30	BS15
Fort Prim Sch *EH6*	15	BG5
Foulis Cres, Jun. Grn *EH14*	50	AT21
Foundry La, Lnhd *EH20*	54	BM26
Fountainbridge *EH3*	6	BD13
Fountainhall Rd *EH9*	43	BG16
Fountain Park *EH11*	6	BC13
Fountain Pl, Lnhd *EH20*	54	BK27
Fourth Gait (Ricc.), Currie *EH14*	49	AN20
Fourth St (Newt.), Dalk. *EH22*	65	BX30
Fowler Cres, Lnhd *EH20* 1	54	BM27
Fowlers Ct, Pres. *EH32* 3	18	CH9
Fowler Sq, Lnhd *EH20* 2	54	BM27
Fowler St, Tran. *EH33*	35	CL12
Fowler Ter *EH11*	42	BB14
Fox Covert Av *EH12*	24	AU10
Fox Covert Gro *EH12*	24	AU10
Fox Covert Prim Sch *EH12*	24	AU11
Fox Covert RC Prim Sch *EH12*	24	AU11
Fox Spring Cres *EH10*	52	BB20
Fox Spring Ri *EH10*	52	BC20
Fox St *EH6*	16	BK6
Fraser Av *EH5*	14	BC6
Fraser Cres *EH5*	14	BC6
Fraser Gdns *EH5*	14	BC6
Fraser Gro *EH5*	14	BC6
Frederick St *EH2*	6	BE10
Freelands Rd (Ratho), Newbr. *EH28*	38	AJ15
Friarton Gdns, Pen. *EH26*	68	AY38
Frogston Av *EH10*	52	BD22
Frogston Brae *EH17*	53	BG23
Frogston Gdns *EH10*	52	BD22
Frogston Gro *EH10*	53	BE22
Frogston Rd E *EH17*	53	BG23
Frogston Rd W *EH10*	52	BD22
Frogston Ter *EH10*	53	BE22
Furcheons Pk *EH8*	29	BN11

G

Gabriel's Rd *EH2* 6	7	BF10
Gabriel's Rd *EH3* 6	26	BD9
Galachlawshot *EH10*	53	BE21
Galachlawside *EH10*	53	BE22
Galadale (Newt.), Dalk. *EH22*	65	BW29
Galadale Cres (Newt.), Dalk. *EH22*	65	BW29
Galadale Dr (Newt.), Dalk. *EH22*	65	BW29
Gallolee, The *EH13*	51	AZ21
Galt Av, Muss. *EH21*	32	CC14
Galt Cres, Muss. *EH21*	32	CC14
Galt Dr, Muss. *EH21*	32	CC14
Galt Rd, Muss. *EH21*	32	CC14
Galt Ter, Muss. *EH21*	32	CC14
Gamekeeper's Ln *EH4*	11	AR6
Gamekeeper's Pk *EH4*	11	AR6
Gamekeeper's Rd *EH4*	11	AR6
Gardener's Cl (Cock.), Pres. *EH32*	19	CL7
Gardeners Pl, Tran. *EH33* 2	35	CL12
Gardeners' Wk, Pen. *EH26*	68	AY37
Garden Ter *EH4*	12	AT7
Gardiner Cres, Pres. *EH32*	18	CK10
Gardiner Gro *EH4*	25	AX9
Gardiner Pl (Newt.), Dalk. *EH22*	65	BW29
Gardiner Rd *EH4*	25	AX9
Gardiner Rd, Pres. *EH32*	18	CJ10
Gardiner Ter *EH4*	25	AX10
Gardiner Ter, Pres. *EH32*	34	CJ11
Gardner's Cres *EH3*	6	BC12
Garscube Ter *EH12*	25	AZ11
Garvald Ct *EH16*	44	BK15
Gateside Rd, K'lis. *EH29*	20	AC10
Gateway Theatre *EH7*	27	BG9
Gayfield Cl *EH1*	27	BG9
Gayfield Pl *EH7*	27	BG9
Gayfield Pl La *EH1*	27	BG9
Gayfield Sq *EH1*	27	BG9
Gayfield St *EH1*	27	BF9
Gayfield St La *EH1*	27	BF9
Gaynor Av, Lnhd *EH20*	54	BJ27
Gentle's Entry *EH8* 8	7	BH11
George Av, Lnhd *EH20*	54	BK27
George Cres, Lnhd *EH20* 1	54	BL27
George Dr, Lnhd *EH20*	54	BK27

Name	Page	Grid
George IV Br EH1	7	BF11
George Heriot's Sch EH3	6	BE12
George Intercontinental Hotel EH2	6	BE10
George Sq EH8	7	BF13
George Sq La EH8	7	BF13
George Square Theatre EH8	7	BF13
George St EH2	6	BD11
George Ter, Lnhd EH20	54	BK27
George Wk, Tran. EH33	35	CL13
George Watson's Coll EH10	42	BB16
George Way, Tran. EH33 3	35	CL13
Georgian House (NTS) EH2	6	BD11
Gibbs Entry EH8	7	BG12
Gibraltar Ct, Dalk. EH22	57	BX24
Gibraltar Gdns, Dalk. EH22	57	BW24
Gibraltar Rd, Dalk. EH22	57	BW24
Gibraltar Ter, Dalk. EH22	57	BX24
Gibson Dr, Dalk. EH22	57	BY24
Gibson St EH7	15	BG7
Gibson Ter EH11	6	BC13
Gifford Pk EH8	7	BG13
Gilberstoun EH15	30	BS13
Gilberstoun Brig EH15	30	BT14
Gilberstoun Ln EH15	30	BT14
Gilberstoun Pl EH15	30	BT14
Gilberstoun Wynd EH15	30	BT14
Giles St EH6	15	BH6
Gillespie Cres EH10	6	BD13
Gillespie Pl EH10	6	BD13
Gillespie Rd EH13	50	AV21
Gillespie St EH3	6	BD13
Gillsland Pk EH10	42	BB15
Gillsland Rd EH10	42	BB15
GILMERTON	45	BP21
Gilmerton Dykes Av EH17	44	BM21
Gilmerton Dykes Cres EH17	44	BL21
Gilmerton Dykes Dr EH17	44	BM21
Gilmerton Dykes Gdns EH17	44	BL21
Gilmerton Dykes Gro EH17	44	BL21
Gilmerton Dykes Ln EH17	54	BL22
Gilmerton Dykes Pl EH17	44	BL21
Gilmerton Dykes Rd EH17	54	BM22
Gilmerton Dykes St EH17	44	BM21
Gilmerton Dykes Ter EH17	54	BM22
Gilmerton Dykes Vw EH17	54	BM22
Gilmerton Ms EH17	55	BN22
Gilmerton Pl EH17	54	BM22
Gilmerton Prim Sch EH17	44	BM21
Gilmerton Rd EH16	44	BJ17
Gilmerton Rd EH17	44	BL19
Gilmerton Rd (Gilm.) EH17	55	BP22
Gilmerton Rd, Dalk. EH22	56	BU24
Gilmerton Rd, Lass. EH18	56	BS23
Gilmerton Sta Rd EH17	55	BN24
Gilmore Pk EH3	6	BC13
Gilmore Pl EH3	42	BC14
Gilmore Pl La EH3	6	BD13
Gilmour Rd EH16	43	BH16
Gilmour's Entry EH8 7	7	BG12
Gilmour St EH8	7	BG12
Gladstone Pl EH6	16	BK7
Gladstone's Land (NTS) EH1 4	7	BF11
Gladstone Ter EH9	43	BG14
Glanville Pl EH3 5	26	BD9
Glasgow Rd EH12	39	AQ13
Glasgow Rd, Newbr. EH28	37	AG13
Glaskhill Ter, Pen. EH26	68	BA37
Glasshouse Experience EH3	14	BD7
Glasshouse Hotel, The EH1	7	BG10
Glebe, The EH4	11	AR5
Glebe, The, K'lis. EH29	20	AC10
Glebe, The (Dalm.), S Q'fry EH30	9	AG4
Glebe Gdns EH12	24	AU13
Glebe Gdns, Pres. EH32 4	18	CH10
Glebe Gro EH12	24	AT13
Glebe Pl, Lass. EH18	55	BP26
Glebe Rd EH12	24	AT13
Glebe St, Dalk. EH22	57	BW24
Glebe Ter EH12	24	AU13
Glenallan Dr EH16	44	BK17
Glenallan Ln EH16	44	BK17
Glenalmond Ct EH11	40	AT17
Glenbrook Rd, Bal. EH14	58	AJ26
Glencairn Cres EH12	26	BB12
GLENCORSE	66	BD35
Glencorse Golf Course EH26	66	BD34
Glencorse Pk (Milt.Br), Pen. EH26	67	BE35
Glencorse Prim Sch EH26	66	BD34
Glencross Gdns, Pen. EH26	68	AY38
Glendevon Av EH12	25	AX13
Glendevon Gdns EH12	25	AX13
Glendevon Gro EH12	25	AX13
Glendevon Pk EH12	41	AX14
Glendevon Pl EH12	25	AX13
Glendevon Rd EH12	41	AX14
Glendevon Ter EH12	25	AX13
Glendinning Cres EH16	44	BJ19
Glendinning Dr, K'lis. EH29	20	AB9
Glendinning Pl, K'lis. EH29	20	AB9
Glendinning Rd, K'lis. EH29	20	AB9
Glendinning Way, K'lis. EH29	20	AB9
Glenesk Cres, Dalk. EH22	56	BV25
Glenfinlas St EH3	6	BD11
Glengyle Ter EH3	6	BD13
Glenisla Gdns EH9	43	BF16
Glenisla Gdns La EH9 1	43	BF16
Glenlea Cotts EH11	41	AY15
Glenlee Av EH8	28	BL11
Glenlee Gdns EH8	28	BL11
Glenlockhart Bk EH14	41	AZ18
Glenlockhart Rd EH10	42	BA18
Glenlockhart Rd EH14	41	AZ18
Glenlockhart Valley EH14	41	AZ17
Glennie Gdns, Tran. EH33	35	CM13
Glenogle Ct EH3	26	BD8
Glenogle Pl EH3 7	26	BD9
Glenogle Rd EH3	26	BD9
Glenogle Ter EH3	26	BD8
Glenorchy Pl EH1 4	7	BG10
Glenorchy Ter EH9	43	BH15
Glen Pl, Pen. EH26	68	BA37
Glen St EH3	6	BE12
Glenure Ln EH4	24	AT10
Glenvarloch Cres EH16	44	BJ18
Glenview, Pen. EH26	68	BA37
Glen Vw Ct, Gore. EH23	70	BY34
Glen Vw Cres, Gore. EH23	70	BY35
Glenview Pl, Gore. EH23	70	BY36
Glen Vw Rd, Gore. EH23	70	BY34
Gloucester La EH3	6	BD10
Gloucester Pl EH3	6	BD10
Gloucester Sq EH3	6	BD10
Gloucester St EH3	6	BD10
Goff Av EH7	17	BP9
Gogarbank EH12	39	AN17
Gogar Br Rd EH12	22	AJ11
Gogarburn Golf Course EH12	38	AK15
Gogarloch Bk EH12	39	AR14
Gogarloch Haugh EH12	39	AR14
Gogarloch Muir EH12	39	AR14
Gogarloch Rd EH12	39	AQ14
Gogarloch Syke EH12	39	AQ14
Gogar Mains Fm Rd EH12	38	AL13
Gogar Roundabout EH12	39	AN13
Gogar Sta Rd EH12	39	AQ17
Gogarstone Rd EH12	38	AK14
GOLDENACRE	14	BD7
Goldenacre Ter EH3	14	BD7
Goldie Ter, Lnhd EH20	62	BJ28
Golf Course Rd, Bonny. EH19	55	BR27
Golf Dr (Port S.), Pres. EH32	19	CM7
GOOSE GREEN	31	BZ12
Goose Grn Av, Muss. EH21	31	BZ12
Goose Grn Br, Muss. EH21	31	BZ12
Goose Grn Cres, Muss. EH21	31	BZ12
Goose Grn Pl, Muss. EH21	31	BZ12
Goose Grn Rd, Muss. EH21	31	BZ12
Gordon Av, Bonny. EH19	63	BP29
Gordon Ln EH12	24	AU12
Gordon Rd EH12	24	AU12
Gordon St EH6	16	BJ7
Gordon St (Easth.), Dalk. EH22	57	BY28
Gordon Ter EH16	44	BJ17
Gore Av, Gore. EH23	70	BZ35
GOREBRIDGE	70	BX36
Gorebridge Prim Sch EH23	70	BY34
GORGIE	41	AZ15
Gorgie Cotts EH11	41	AY15
Gorgie Pk Cl EH14	41	AZ15
Gorgie Pk Rd EH11	41	AZ14
Gorgie Pk Rd EH14	41	AZ15
Gorgie Rd EH11	41	AZ14
Gorton Ln, Rose. EH24	62	BM33
Gorton Pl, Rose. EH24	62	BM33
Gorton Rd, Rose. EH24	62	BM33
Gosford Pl EH6	15	BF6
Gosford Rd (Port S.), Pres. EH32	19	CL7
Gosford Wk (Port S.), Pres. EH32	19	CL7
Gote La, S Q'fry EH30	8	AD2
Gowanhill Rd, Currie EH14	48	AK22
GOWKSHILL	65	BY32
Gracefield Ct, Muss. EH21	31	BX13
GRACEMOUNT	44	BK21
Gracemount Av EH16	44	BK20
Gracemount Dr EH16	44	BK21
Gracemount High Sch EH16	54	BL22
Gracemount Pl EH16	44	BK21
Gracemount Prim Sch EH16	44	BK21
Gracemount Rd EH16	54	BJ22
Gracemount Sq EH16	44	BK20
Graham's Rd (Milt.Br), Pen. EH26	66	BD34
Graham St EH6	15	BG6
Granby Rd EH16	43	BH16
Grandfield EH6	15	BE6
Grandville EH6	15	BE5
GRANGE	43	BF15
Grange Ct EH9	43	BG14
Grange Cres EH9	43	BF15
Grange Cres E, Pres. EH32	18	CH10
Grange Cres W, Pres. EH32	18	CH10
Grange Gro, Pres. EH32	18	CH10
Grange Ln EH9	43	BE15
Grange Ln Gdns EH9	43	BF15
Grange Rd EH9	43	BF14
Grange Rd, Pres. EH32	18	CH10
Grange Ter EH9	43	BF16
Grannies Pk Ind Est, Dalk. EH22	57	BW23
Grannus Ms (Inv.), Muss. EH21 1	31	BZ14
Grant Av EH13	51	AW21

Name	Page	Grid
GRANTON	14	BA4
Granton Cres *EH5*	14	BB5
Granton Gdns *EH5*	14	BB5
Granton Gro *EH5*	14	BB5
Granton Harbour *EH5*	14	BB3
Granton Mains Av *EH4*	13	AY5
Granton Mains Bk *EH4* 1	13	AY5
Granton Mains Brae *EH4*	13	AY5
Granton Mains Ct *EH4*	13	AZ5
Granton Mains E *EH4*	13	AZ5
Granton Mains Gait *EH4*	13	AY5
Granton Mains Vale *EH4*	13	AY5
Granton Mains Wynd *EH4*	13	AY5
Granton Medway *EH5*	14	BA5
Granton Mill Cres *EH4*	13	AY5
Granton Mill Dr *EH4*	13	AY5
Granton Mill March *EH4*	13	AX6
Granton Mill Pk *EH4*	13	AX6
Granton Mill Pl *EH4*	13	AX5
Granton Mill Rd *EH4*	13	AX5
Granton Mill W *EH4* 1	13	AX5
Granton Pk Av *EH5*	14	BA4
Granton Pl *EH5*	14	BB5
Granton Prim Sch *EH5*	14	BB5
Granton Rd *EH5*	14	BB5
Granton Sq *EH5*	14	BB4
Granton Ter *EH5*	14	BB5
Granton Vw *EH5*	14	BB4
Grantully Pl *EH9*	43	BH15
Granville Ter *EH10*	42	BC14
Grassmarket *EH1*	6	BE12
Grays Ct *EH8* 6	7	BG12
Graysknowe *EH14* 1	41	AX17
Gray's Ln *EH10*	42	BA15
Graysmill Sch *EH14*	41	AX18
Great Cannon Bk *EH15* 3	29	BQ10
Great Carleton Pl *EH16*	45	BQ16
Great Carleton Sq *EH16* 1	45	BQ16
Great Junct St *EH6*	15	BH6
Great King St *EH3*	6	BE10
Great Michael Cl *EH6* 4	15	BF4
Great Michael Ri *EH6*	15	BF5
Great Michael Sq *EH4* 1	15	BF4
Great Stuart St *EH3*	6	BC11
Green, The *EH4*	12	AV7
Green, The, Bal. *EH14*	58	AM27
Green, The, Lnhd *EH20* 1	54	BL26
Greenacre *EH14*	50	AU20
GREENBANK	42	BB19
Greenbank Av *EH10*	42	BC18
Greenbank Cres *EH10*	42	BB19
Greenbank Dr *EH10*	42	BB18
Greenbank Gdns *EH10*	42	BB19
Greenbank Gro *EH10*	42	BB19
Greenbank La *EH10*	42	BB18
Greenbank Ln *EH10*	42	BB19
Greenbank Pk *EH10*	42	BB19
Greenbank Pl *EH10*	42	BC18
Greenbank Ri *EH10*	42	BB19
Greenbank Rd *EH10*	42	BB19
Greenbank Row *EH10*	42	BB19
Greenbank Ter *EH10*	42	BC18
Greendale Pk *EH4*	13	AW7
GREENDYKES	45	BP16
Greendykes Av *EH16*	45	BP16
Greendykes Dr *EH16*	45	BP16
Greendykes Gdns *EH16*	45	BP16
Greendykes Ho *EH16*	45	BP16
Greendykes Ln *EH16*	45	BP16
Greendykes Rd *EH16*	45	BN16
Greendykes Ter *EH16*	45	BP16
GREENEND	44	BL19
Greenend Dr *EH17*	44	BL20
Greenend Gdns *EH17*	44	BL19
Greenend Gro *EH17*	44	BL19
Greenfield Cres, Bal. *EH14*	58	AL27
Greenfield Pk (Monk.), Muss. *EH21*	31	BX16
Greenfield Rd, Bal. *EH14*	58	AL27
Greenhall Cres, Gore. *EH23* 1	70	BX34
Greenhall Rd, Gore. *EH23*	70	BY34
Greenhill Ct *EH9*	42	BD14
Greenhill Gdns *EH10*	42	BD14
Greenhill Pk *EH10*	42	BD15
Greenhill Pk, Pen. *EH26*	68	AZ38
Greenhill Pl *EH10*	42	BD15
Greenhill Ter *EH10*	42	BD14
Green La, Lass. *EH18*	55	BP27
Greenlaw Gro (Milt.Br), Pen. *EH26*	66	BC34
Greenlaw Hedge *EH13*	52	BA20
GREENLAW MAINS	66	BC35
Greenlaw Rig *EH13*	52	BA20
Greenmantle Ln *EH16*	44	BK18
Greenpark *EH17*	44	BL19
Greens Hotel *EH12*	26	BB11
Greenside End *EH1* 6	7	BG10
Greenside La *EH1*	7	BG10
Greenside Pl *EH1* 5	7	BG10
Greenside Pl, Rose. *EH24*	62	BM33
Greenside Row *EH1*	7	BG10
Green St *EH7*	27	BF9
Greenway, The *EH14*	40	AU18
Greyfriars Bobby *EH1*	7	BF12
Greyfriars Pl *EH1*	7	BF12
Grey Sch Cor, Pres. *EH32*	18	CH10
Grierson Av *EH5*	14	BC5
Grierson Cres *EH5*	14	BC5
Grierson Gdns *EH5*	14	BC5
Grierson Rd *EH5*	14	BB5
Grierson Sq *EH5*	14	BC5
Grierson Vil *EH5*	14	BC5
Grieve Ct, Pen. *EH26*	69	BB36
Grigor Av *EH4*	25	AZ8
Grigor Dr *EH4*	25	AZ8
Grigor Gdns *EH4*	25	AZ8
Grigor Ter *EH4*	25	AZ8
Grindlay St *EH3*	6	BD12
Grindlay St Ct *EH3*	6	BD12
Groathill Av *EH4*	25	AY9
Groathill Gdns E *EH4*	25	AY9
Groathill Gdns W *EH4*	25	AY9
Groathill Rd N *EH4*	25	AY8
Groathill Rd S *EH4*	25	AY9
Grosvenor Cres *EH12*	26	BB12
Grosvenor Gdns *EH12*	26	BB12
Grosvenor St *EH12*	6	BC12
Grotto Br, S Q'fry *EH30*	23	AN8
Grove, The, Muss. *EH21*	32	CA14
Grove End, Lass. *EH18*	55	BR27
Grove Pl, Jun. Grn *EH14*	50	AT21
Grove St *EH3*	6	BC12
Grove St, Muss. *EH21*	31	BZ14
Grove Ter *EH3* 4	6	BC12
Grundie's Well Rd *EH17*	45	BN21
Guardianswood *EH12*	25	AY12
Guardwell Cres *EH17*	44	BL20
Gullan's Cl *EH8*	7	BG11
Gunnet Ct *EH4*	13	AW6
Guthrie St *EH1*	7	BF12
GYLE, THE	39	AR13
Gyle Av *EH12* 1	39	AP14
Gylemuir Prim Sch *EH12*	40	AS14
Gylemuir Rd *EH12*	24	AS13
Gyle Pk Gdns *EH12*	39	AQ13
Gyle Service La *EH12*	39	AQ14
Gyle Shopping Centre *EH12*	39	AQ14
Gypsy Brae *EH5*	13	AX5

H

Name	Page	Grid
Haddington Pl *EH7*	27	BG9
Haddington Rd, Muss. *EH21*	32	CC13
Haddington Rd, Tran. *EH33*	35	CN13
Haddon's Ct *EH8*	7	BG12
HAILES	51	AW20
Hailes App *EH13*	51	AW20
Hailes Av *EH13*	41	AW19
Hailes Bk *EH13*	51	AW20
Hailes Cres *EH13*	51	AW20
Hailes Gdns *EH13*	50	AV20
Hailes Gro *EH13*	51	AW20
Hailesland Gdns *EH14*	40	AU18
Hailesland Gro *EH14*	40	AU18
Hailesland Pk *EH14*	40	AU18
Hailesland Pl *EH14*	40	AU18
Hailesland Prim Sch *EH14*	40	AU19
Hailesland Rd *EH14*	40	AU18
Hailes Pk *EH13*	50	AV20
Hailes St *EH3*	6	BD13
Hailes Ter *EH13*	51	AW20
Hainburn Pk *EH10*	52	BB22
Hallcroft Cl (Ratho), Newbr. *EH28*	37	AE17
Hallcroft Cres (Ratho), Newbr. *EH28*	37	AE17
Hallcroft Gdns (Ratho), Newbr. *EH28*	37	AE17
Hallcroft Grn (Ratho), Newbr. *EH28*	37	AE17
Hallcroft Neuk (Ratho), Newbr. *EH28*	37	AE17
Hallcroft Pk (Ratho), Newbr. *EH28*	37	AE17
Hallcroft Ri (Ratho), Newbr. *EH28*	37	AE17
Hallhead Rd *EH16*	43	BH17
Hall Ter *EH12*	24	AU13
Hallyards Rd, K'lis. *EH29*	20	AD11
Hallyards Rd, Newbr. *EH28*	37	AF13
Halmyre St *EH6*	27	BH8
Hamburgh Pl *EH6* 1	15	BG5
Hamilton Cres (Newt.), Dalk. *EH22*	65	BX29
Hamilton Dr *EH15*	29	BP12
Hamilton Dr W *EH15*	29	BP12
Hamilton Gdns *EH15*	29	BP12
Hamilton Gro *EH15*	29	BP11
Hamilton Pk *EH15*	29	BP11
Hamilton Pl *EH3*	26	BD9
Hamilton's Cl, S Q'fry *EH30* 1	9	AE2
Hamilton's Folly Ms *EH8* 5	7	BG13
Hamilton Ter *EH15*	29	BQ11
Hamilton Wynd *EH6*	15	BG5
Hammermen's Entry *EH8*	7	BG11
Hampton Pl *EH12* 4	26	BA12
Hampton Ter *EH12*	26	BA12
Hanover St *EH2*	6	BE10
Harbour La, S Q'fry *EH30* 5	8	AD2
Harbour Pl *EH15* 13	29	BQ10
Harbour Rd *EH15*	29	BQ10
Harbour Rd, Muss. *EH21*	31	BW13
Hardengreen Business Pk, Dalk. *EH22*	56	BU26
Hardengreen Ind Est, Dalk. *EH22*	56	BU26
Hardengreen La, Dalk. *EH22*	56	BU27
Harden Pl *EH11*	42	BB14
Hardwell Cl *EH8*	7	BG13
Harelaw, Dalk. *EH22*	46	BT19

Name	Page	Ref
Harelaw Rd *EH13*	51	AX21
Hares Cl (Cock.), Pres. *EH32*	19	CL7
Harewood Cres *EH16*	29	BN15
Harewood Dr *EH16*	29	BN15
Harewood Rd *EH16*	28	BM15
Harkenburn Gdns, Pen. *EH26*	68	AY37
Harkness Cres, Tran. *EH33*	35	CM13
Harlaw Gait, Bal. *EH14*	58	AM26
Harlaw Gro, Pen. *EH26*	68	AZ38
Harlaw Hill, Pres. *EH32*	18	CH9
Harlawhill Gdns, Pres. *EH32*	18	CH10
Harlaw March, Bal. *EH14*	58	AM27
Harlaw Rd, Bal. *EH14*	59	AR25
Harmeny Sch *EH14*	58	AM27
Harmony Ct, Bonny. *EH19*	56	BT28
Harmony Cres, Bonny. *EH19*	56	BT28
Harmony St, Bonny. *EH19*	56	BT28
Harmony Wk, Bonny. *EH19*	56	BT28
Harnes Ct, Lnhd *EH20* **2**	62	BL28
Harper's Brae, Pen. *EH26*	69	BD37
Harrismith Pl *EH7*	16	BJ9
Harrison Gdns *EH11*	42	BA15
Harrison La *EH11*	42	BB14
Harrison Pl *EH11*	42	BA15
Harrison Rd *EH11*	42	BA14
Hartington Gdns *EH10*	42	BD14
Hartington Pl *EH10*	42	BC14
Hart St *EH1*	27	BF9
Hart St La *EH1*	27	BF9
Harvest Dr, Newbr. *EH28*	36	AD14
Harvesters Way *EH14*	40	AT19
Harvest Rd, Newbr. *EH28*	36	AD14
Harvieston Vil, Gore. *EH23* **1**	70	BZ36
Hatton Pl *EH9*	43	BF14
Haugh Pk *EH14*	41	AW17
Haugh St *EH4*	26	BD9
Hawes Brae, S Q'fry *EH30*	9	AF2
Hawes Pier, S Q'fry *EH30*	9	AF1
Hawkhead Cres *EH16*	44	BJ19
Hawkhead Gro *EH16*	44	BJ19
Hawkhill *EH7*	16	BK8
Hawkhill Av *EH7*	16	BJ8
Hawkhill Ct *EH7*	16	BK8
Hawkins Ter, Pen. *EH26*	66	BD34
Hawthornbank (Cock.), Pres. *EH32* **1**	18	CK7
Hawthorn Bk, S Q'fry *EH30*	8	AD2
Hawthornbank La *EH4*	6	BC11
Hawthornbank Pl *EH6*	15	BG5
Hawthornbank Ter *EH6* **2**	15	BG5
Hawthorn Bldgs *EH4* **2**	26	BB11
Hawthorn Cres (Mayf.), Dalk. *EH22*	57	BZ27
Hawthornden Av, Bonny. *EH19*	63	BQ29
Hawthornden Gdns, Bonny. *EH19*	63	BQ28
Hawthornden Pl *EH7*	27	BG8
Hawthornden Prim Sch *EH19*	63	BP29
Hawthorn Gdns, Lnhd *EH20*	54	BK26
Hawthorn Pl *EH17*	45	BN21
Hawthorn Rd, Pres. *EH32*	18	CK10
Hawthorn Ter *EH4* **5**	6	BC11
Hawthorn Ter (Cock.), Pres. *EH32*	18	CK8
Hawthornvale *EH6*	15	BF5
Hay Av *EH16*	29	BP15
Hay Dr *EH16*	29	BQ15
Hayfield *EH12*	23	AQ11
Hay Gdns *EH16*	29	BP14
Haymarket *EH12*	6	BC12
Haymarket Sta *EH12*	26	BB12
Haymarket Ter *EH12*	26	BB12
Haymarket Yards *EH12*	26	BB12
Hay Rd *EH16*	29	BP15
Hay Ter *EH16*	29	BP15
Hazelbank Ter *EH11*	42	BA15
Hazeldean Ter *EH16*	44	BK18
Hazel Dr, Bonny. *EH19*	63	BR29
Hazel La, Lnhd *EH20*	61	BG28
Hazelwood Gro *EH16*	44	BL17
Headrigg Row *EH16*	44	BK18
Hedge Row, Lnhd *EH20*	61	BG28
Henderland Rd *EH12*	25	AZ12
Henderson Gdns *EH6* **4**	15	BH6
Henderson Gdns, Tran. *EH33*	35	CM13
Henderson Pl *EH3*	27	BE9
Henderson Pl La *EH3*	26	BD9
Henderson Row *EH3*	26	BD9
Henderson St *EH6*	15	BH6
Henderson Ter *EH11*	42	BB14
Henry Pl *EH8*	7	BH13
Henry Ross Pl, S Q'fry *EH30*	8	AD2
Henry St *EH8*	7	BH13
Hepburn Dr, Dalk. *EH22*	57	BY25
Hercus Ln, Muss. *EH21*	31	BX13
Herd Ter, Lnhd *EH20*	62	BJ28
Heriot Br *EH1*	6	BE12
Heriot Cross *EH1* **1**	6	BE12
Heriot Hill Ter *EH7*	27	BE8
Heriot Pl *EH3*	6	BE12
Heriot Row *EH3*	6	BD10
Heriot-Watt Research Pk (Ricc.), Currie *EH14*	49	AN19
Heriot-Watt Uni (Edinburgh Campus) *EH14*	49	AP20
Hermand Cres *EH11*	42	BA15
Hermand St *EH11*	41	AZ15
Hermand Ter *EH11*	41	AZ15
Hermiston Ct *EH11*	40	AT17
Hermiston Gait Retail Pk *EH11*	39	AQ17
Hermiston Gait Retail Pk *EH11*	39	AQ17
Hermiston Ho Rd *EH12*	38	AM17
Hermiston Ho Rd, Currie *EH14*	39	AN18
Hermitage Dr *EH10*	42	BD18
Hermitage Gdns *EH10*	42	BD18
Hermitage Pk *EH6*	16	BK8
Hermitage Pk Gro *EH6*	16	BK8
Hermitage Pk Lea *EH6*	16	BK8
Hermitage Park Prim Sch *EH6*	16	BK8
Hermitage Pk S *EH6*	16	BK8
Hermitage Pl *EH6*	16	BJ7
Hermitage Ter *EH10*	42	BD17
Hermits Cft *EH8*	7	BH13
Heugh, The, Tran. *EH33*	35	CL12
Higginson Ln (Mayf.), Dalk. *EH22*	71	CA30
High Buckstone *EH10*	53	BE21
Highlea Circle, Bal. *EH14*	58	AK28
Highlea Gro, Bal. *EH14*	58	AK27
High Pk Ri, Pen. *EH26*	69	BB39
High Riggs *EH3*	6	BE12
High Sch Yards *EH1*	7	BG12
High St *EH1*	7	BF11
High St, Bonny. *EH19*	55	BR27
High St, Dalk. *EH22*	57	BW24
High St, K'lis. *EH29*	20	AD10
High St, Lass. *EH18*	55	BQ26
High St, Lnhd *EH20*	54	BL27
High St, Muss. *EH21*	31	BY13
High St, Pen. *EH26*	69	BB39
High St, Pres. *EH32*	18	CG10
High St (Cock.), Pres. *EH32*	19	CL7
High St, S Q'fry *EH30*	8	AD2
High St, Tran. *EH33*	35	CM13
Highway, The *EH8*	29	BN11
Hillcoat Ln *EH15* **4**	29	BQ10
Hillcoat Pl *EH15* **5**	29	BQ10
Hill Ct, S Q'fry *EH30* **2**	8	AD2
HILLEND	53	BE25
Hillend *EH10*	53	BE25
Hillend Pl *EH8* **10**	28	BL10
Hillhead, Bonny. *EH19*	55	BR27
Hillhouse Rd *EH4*	24	AV8
Hillpark Av *EH4*	24	AV8
Hillpark Brae *EH4*	24	AV10
Hillpark Ct *EH4*	24	AV8
Hillpark Cres *EH4*	24	AV9
Hillpark Dr *EH4*	24	AV8
Hillpark Gdns *EH4*	24	AV9
Hillpark Grn *EH4*	24	AV9
Hillpark Gro *EH4*	24	AV9
Hillpark Ln *EH4*	25	AW9
Hillpark Rd *EH4*	24	AV9
Hillpark Ter *EH4*	24	AV9
Hillpark Way *EH4*	25	AW9
Hillpark Wd *EH4*	25	AW9
Hill Pl *EH8*	7	BG12
Hill Pl (Mayf.), Dalk. *EH22*	71	CA30
HILLSIDE	27	BH9
Hillside Cres *EH7*	27	BG9
Hillside Cres N, Gore. *EH23*	70	BZ35
Hillside Cres S, Gore. *EH23*	70	BZ35
Hillside Rd (Craig.), S Q'fry *EH30*	22	AM7
Hillside St *EH7*	27	BH9
Hillside Ter (Craig.), S Q'fry *EH30*	10	AM6
Hill Sq *EH8*	7	BG12
Hill St *EH2*	6	BD10
Hill St La N *EH2*	6	BD10
Hill St La S *EH2*	6	BE11
Hilltown Ter (Wool.), Dalk. *EH22*	46	BS18
Hillview *EH4*	25	AX9
Hillview Cotts (Ratho), Newbr. *EH28*	37	AF18
Hillview Cres *EH12*	24	AT12
Hillview Dr *EH12*	24	AS12
Hillview Gdns, Lnhd *EH20*	61	BH28
Hillview Rd *EH12*	24	AS12
Hillview Ter *EH12*	24	AS12
Hillwood Av (Ratho Sta), Newbr. *EH28*	37	AE14
Hillwood Cres (Ratho Sta), Newbr. *EH28*	37	AE14
Hillwood Gdns (Ratho Sta), Newbr. *EH28*	37	AE13
Hillwood Pl, S Q'fry *EH30* **4**	8	AD2
Hillwood Prim Sch *EH28*	37	AE14
Hillwood Ri (Ratho Sta), Newbr. *EH28*	37	AE14
Hillwood Rd (Ratho Sta), Newbr. *EH28*	37	AE14
Hillwood Ter (Ratho Sta), Newbr. *EH28*	37	AE14
Hilton Edinburgh Airport Hotel *EH28*	22	AJ12
Hilton Edinburgh Grosvenor *EH12*	6	BC12
HM Prison Edinburgh *EH11*	41	AW16
Hogarth Av, Gore. *EH23*	65	BX33
Holiday Inn Edinburgh *EH12*	25	AW13
Holiday Inn Edinburgh North *EH4*	25	AY10
Holiday Inn Express Leith Hotel *EH6*	15	BG5

Hollybank (Mayf.), Dalk. *EH22*	71	CA28
Hollybank Ter *EH11*	42	BA15
Holly Ter, Bonny. *EH19*	63	BR29
Holly Wk, Lnhd *EH20*	61	BG28
Holy Cross RC Prim Sch *EH6*	15	BE6
Holyrood Ct *EH8*	7	BH11
Holyrood Hotel, The *EH8*	7	BH11
Holyrood Park *EH8*	7	BH11
Holyrood Pk *EH16*	28	BJ11
Holyrood Pk Rd *EH16*	43	BH14
Holy Rood RC High Sch *EH15*	28	BM13
Holyrood Rd *EH8*	7	BG11
Home St *EH3*	6	BD13
HOPEFIELD	63	BR29
Hopefield Pk, Bonny. *EH19*	63	BQ29
Hopefield Pl, Bonny. *EH19*	63	BQ29
Hopefield Prim Sch *EH19*	63	BQ29
Hopefield Ter *EH6*	15	BG5
Hopefield Ter, Bonny. *EH19*	63	BQ29
Hope La *EH15*	29	BR12
Hope La N *EH15*	29	BR11
Hope Pk Cres *EH8*	7	BG13
Hope Pk Sq *EH8* **1**	7	BG13
Hope Pk Ter *EH8*	7	BG13
Hope Pl, Muss. *EH21*	32	CB13
Hope Pl, Tran. *EH33* **3**	35	CL12
Hope St *EH2*	6	BD11
Hope St, S Q'fry *EH30*	8	AD3
Hope St La *EH2*	6	BD11
Hope Ter *EH9*	43	BE15
Hopetoun Cres *EH7*	27	BG9
Hopetoun Rd, S Q'fry *EH30*	8	AD2
Hopetoun St *EH7*	27	BG9
Horne Ter *EH11*	6	BC13
Horsburgh Bk, Bal. *EH14*	48	AL24
Horsburgh Gdns, Bal. *EH14*	48	AL24
Horsburgh Gro, Bal. *EH14*	48	AL24
Horse Wynd *EH8*	7	BH11
Hoseason Gdns *EH4*	24	AT10
Hosie Rigg *EH15*	29	BR14
House o'Hill Av *EH4*	25	AW8
House o'Hill Brae *EH4*	25	AW8
House o'Hill Cres *EH4*	25	AW8
House o'Hill Gdns *EH4*	25	AX8
House o'Hill Grn *EH4*	25	AW8
House o'Hill Gro *EH4*	25	AW8
House o'Hill Pl *EH4*	25	AW8
House o'Hill Rd *EH4*	25	AW8
House o'Hill Row *EH4*	25	AX8
House o'Hill Ter *EH4*	25	AX9
Howard Pl *EH3*	27	BE8
Howard St *EH3*	27	BE8
Howden Hall Ct *EH16*	53	BH21
Howden Hall Cres *EH16*	53	BH22
Howden Hall Dr *EH16*	53	BH21
Howden Hall Gdns *EH16*	44	BJ21
Howden Hall Ln *EH16*	53	BH21
Howden Hall Pk *EH16*	53	BH21
Howden Hall Rd *EH16*	54	BJ22
Howden Hall Way *EH16*	54	BJ22
Howden St *EH8*	7	BG12
Howe Dean *EH16*	43	BG19
Howe Pk *EH10*	52	BB22
Howe St *EH3*	6	BE10
Hub, The *EH1*	6	BE12
Hughes Cres (Mayf.), Dalk. *EH22*	71	CB29
Hugh Miller Pl *EH3*	26	BD9
Hugh Russell Pl, S Q'fry *EH30*	8	AD3
Huly Hill Rd, Newbr. *EH28*	36	AC14
Humbie Rd, K'lis. *EH29*	20	AC9
Hungerage Sq, Tran. *EH33*	35	CM14
Hunt Cl, Dalk. *EH22*	57	BW23
Hunter Av, Lnhd *EH20*	54	BM27
Hunter Ct, Lnhd *EH20*	54	BM27
Hunterfield Ct, Gore. *EH23*	70	BY35
Hunterfield Pk, Gore. *EH23*	70	BY34
Hunterfield Rd, Gore. *EH23*	70	BY34
Hunterfield Ter, Gore. *EH23*	70	BX34
Hunter's Cl *EH1* **13**	6	BE12
Hunter's Hill, Pen. *EH26*	68	AZ37
Hunter Sq *EH1*	7	BF11
Hunter Sq, Gore. *EH23*	70	BZ35
Hunter's Tryst Prim Sch *EH13*	52	BB20
Hunter Ter, Bonny. *EH19*	63	BR28
Hunter Ter, Lnhd *EH20*	54	BM27
Huntingdon Pl *EH7*	27	BG9
Huntly House Museum (Museum of Edinburgh) *EH8* **14**	7	BG11
Huntly St *EH3*	27	BE8
Hursted Av (Easth.), Dalk. *EH22*	57	BZ28
Hutchison Av *EH14*	41	AY16
Hutchison Cotts *EH14*	41	AY16
Hutchison Crossway *EH14*	41	AY15
Hutchison Gdns *EH14*	41	AY16
Hutchison Gro *EH14*	41	AZ16
Hutchison Ho *EH14*	41	AZ15
Hutchison Ln *EH14*	41	AY16
Hutchison Medway *EH14*	41	AZ15
Hutchison Pk *EH14*	41	AY15
Hutchison Pl *EH14*	41	AY16
Hutchison Rd *EH14*	41	AZ15
Hutchison Ter *EH14*	41	AY16
Hutchison Vw *EH14*	41	AY15
Hutton Cl *EH8*	7	BH11
Hutton Rd *EH8*	7	BH11
Hyvot Av *EH17*	44	BM21
Hyvot Bk Av *EH17*	45	BN21
Hyvot Ct *EH17*	54	BM22
Hyvot Gdns *EH17*	44	BM21
Hyvot Grn *EH17*	54	BM22
Hyvot Gro *EH17*	44	BM21
Hyvot Ln *EH17*	44	BM21
Hyvot Pk *EH17*	44	BM21
HYVOTS BANK	44	BL20
Hyvot Ter *EH17*	44	BM21
Hyvot Vw *EH17*	54	BM22

I

Ibis Edinburgh Hotel *EH1*	7	BF11
Imperial Dock *EH6*	16	BJ4
Imrie Pl, Pen. *EH26*	69	BB38
INCH	44	BJ18
Inchcolm Ct *EH4*	13	AY6
Inchcolm Ter, S Q'fry *EH30*	8	AD3
Inchgarvie Ct *EH4*	13	AZ7
Inchgarvie Pk, S Q'fry *EH30*	8	AC2
Inchkeith Av, S Q'fry *EH30*	9	AE3
Inchkeith Ct *EH7*	27	BG8
Inchmickery Ct *EH4*	13	AW6
Inchview, Pres. *EH32*	18	CG10
Inchview Cres (Wall.), Muss. *EH21*	33	CE14
Inchview N, Pres. *EH32*	18	CG10
Inchview Rd (Wall.), Muss. *EH21*	33	CD14
Inchview Ter *EH7*	29	BP10
India Bldgs *EH1* **3**	7	BF12
India Pl *EH3*	6	BD10
India St *EH3*	6	BD10
Industrial Rd *EH6*	16	BJ7
Industry Home *EH6* **1**	15	BG6
Industry La *EH6*	15	BG6
Infirmary St *EH1*	7	BG12
Inglewood Pl *EH16*	44	BK19
Inglis Av (Port S.), Pres. *EH32*	19	CL7
Inglis Ct *EH1* **2**	6	BE12
Inglis Fm (Cock.), Pres. *EH32*	19	CL7
Inglis Grn Gait *EH14*	41	AX17
Inglis Grn Rigg *EH14*	41	AX17
Inglis Grn Rd *EH14*	41	AX17
INGLISTON	21	AG12
Ingliston Rd (Inglis.), Newbr. *EH28*	37	AH13
Inkerman Ct, Pen. *EH26*	66	BC35
International Language Academy *EH3*	6	BC11
Inveralmond Dr *EH4*	11	AQ6
Inveralmond Gdns *EH4*	11	AQ6
Inveralmond Gro *EH4*	11	AQ6
Inveravon Rd, Lnhd *EH20*	54	BK26
Inveravon Ter, Muss. *EH21*	31	BY14
INVERESK	31	BZ15
Inveresk Brae, Muss. *EH21*	31	BZ14
Inveresk Est, The (Inv.), Muss. *EH21*	31	BZ15
Inveresk Gate (Inv.), Muss. *EH21* **2**	31	BZ14
Inveresk Lodge Gdns (NTS) *EH21*	31	BZ15
Inveresk Mills Ind Pk, Muss. *EH21*	31	BX14
Inveresk Rd, Muss. *EH21*	31	BY14
Inveresk Village Rd, Muss. *EH21*	31	BY14
INVERLEITH	14	BB7
Inverleith Av *EH3*	14	BD7
Inverleith Av S *EH3*	14	BD7
Inverleith Gdns *EH3*	14	BC7
Inverleith Gro *EH3*	26	BB8
Inverleith Pl *EH3*	14	BC7
Inverleith Pl La *EH3*	14	BD7
Inverleith Row *EH3*	14	BD7
Inverleith Ter *EH3*	26	BD8
Inverleith Ter La *EH3*	26	BD8
Iona St *EH6*	27	BH8
Ironmills Rd, Dalk. *EH22*	56	BV24
Ivanhoe Cres *EH16*	44	BK18
Ivy Ter *EH11*	42	BA14

J

Jackson's Entry *EH8* **7**	7	BH11
Jackson St, Pen. *EH26*	68	BA38
Jacobite Way, Pres. *EH32*	19	CL10
Jacobs Way, Gore. *EH23*	70	BY35
Jamaica Ms *EH3*	6	BD10
Jamaica St *EH3*	6	BD10
Jamaica St N La *EH3*	6	BD10
Jamaica St S La *EH3*	6	BD10
Jamaica St W *EH3* **2**	6	BD10
James' Ct *EH1* **4**	7	BF11
James Craig Wk *EH1*	7	BF10
James Gillespie's High Sch *EH9*	43	BE14
James Gillespie's Prim Sch *EH9*	43	BE14
James Lean Av, Dalk. *EH22*	57	BX24
James Leary Way, Bonny. *EH19*	56	BS27
Jameson Pl *EH6*	27	BH8
James St *EH15*	30	BS11
James St, Muss. *EH21*	31	BZ13
James St La *EH15*	30	BS11
Janefield *EH17*	54	BJ23
Jane St *EH6*	15	BH7

Entry	Page	Grid
Jane Ter *EH7* 2	28	BJ10
Jarnac Ct, Dalk. *EH22* 5	57	BW24
Jawbone Wk *EH3*	7	BF13
Jean Armour Av *EH16*	44	BJ18
Jean Armour Dr, Dalk. *EH22*	57	BZ25
Jeffrey Av *EH4*	25	AX10
Jeffrey St *EH1*	7	BF11
Jenks Ln (Newt.), Dalk. *EH22*	64	BV30
Jessfield Ter *EH6*	15	BF5
Jewel, The *EH15*	29	BR14
Jewel & Esk Valley Coll (Eskbank Campus) *EH22*	56	BV26
Jewel & Esk Valley Coll (Milton Rd Campus) *EH15*	30	BT13
JOCK'S LODGE	28	BL10
John Bernard Way, Gore. *EH23* 1	70	BY37
John Cotton Business Cen *EH7*	16	BJ9
John Cres, Tran. *EH33*	35	CL13
John Humble St (Mayf.), Dalk. *EH22*	71	CA30
John Knox House *EH1* 11	7	BG11
John Knox Pl, Pen. *EH26*	69	BB38
John Mason Ct, S Q'fry *EH30*	9	AE3
John Moat Pl, Pres. *EH32*	18	CH10
John Muir Way, Muss. *EH21*	31	BY12
Johnnie Cope's Rd, Pres. *EH32*	34	CJ11
Johnnie Cope's Rd, Tran. *EH33*	34	CJ12
Johnsburn Grn, Bal. *EH14*	58	AK26
Johnsburn Haugh, Bal. *EH14*	58	AK26
Johnsburn Pk, Bal. *EH14*	58	AK27
Johnsburn Rd, Bal. *EH14*	58	AK26
John's La *EH6*	16	BJ6
John's Pl *EH6*	16	BJ7
Johnston Pl, Pen. *EH26*	66	BB35
Johnston Ter *EH1*	6	BE12
Johnston Ter (Port S.), Pres. *EH32*	19	CM7
John St *EH15*	30	BS11
John St, Pen. *EH26*	69	BB38
John St La *EH15*	30	BS11
John St La, Pen. *EH26*	68	BA38
John St La E *EH15*	30	BS11
John St La W *EH15*	30	BS11
JOPPA	30	BT12
Joppa Gdns *EH15*	30	BS12
Joppa Gro *EH15*	30	BS12
Joppa Pans *EH15*	30	BU12
Joppa Pk *EH15*	30	BS12
Joppa Rd *EH15*	30	BS12
Joppa Ter *EH15*	30	BS12
Jordan La *EH10*	42	BD16
Jubilee Cres, Gore. *EH23*	70	BY34
Jubilee Rd *EH12*	21	AH12
Junction Pl *EH6*	15	BH7
Junction Two Ind Est, Newbr. *EH28*	36	AB16
Juner Pl, Gore. *EH23*	70	BY34
Juniper Av, Jun. Grn *EH14*	50	AS21
Juniper Gdns, Jun. Grn *EH14*	50	AS21
JUNIPER GREEN	50	AS21
Juniper Green Prim Sch *EH14*	50	AT21
Juniper Gro, Jun. Grn *EH14*	50	AS21
Juniper La, Jun. Grn *EH14* 1	50	AT21
Juniperlee, Jun. Grn *EH14*	50	AT21
Juniper Pk Rd, Jun. Grn *EH14*	50	AT21
Juniper Pl, Jun. Grn *EH14*	50	AS22
Juniper Ter, Jun. Grn *EH14*	50	AS21
Jurys Inn Edinburgh Hotel *EH1*	7	BG11

K

Entry	Page	Grid
Kaimes Rd *EH12*	24	AU12
Kaimes Sch *EH16*	44	BL21
Kaimes Vw (Dand.), Dalk. *EH22*	45	BR20
Katesmill Rd *EH14*	41	AX19
Kay Gdns (Cock.), Pres. *EH32*	19	CL7
Kedslie Pl *EH16*	53	BH20
Kedslie Rd *EH16*	53	BH20
Keir Hardie Dr (Mayf.), Dalk. *EH22*	71	CA30
Keir St *EH3*	6	BE12
Keith Cres *EH4*	25	AX10
Keith Row *EH4*	25	AY10
Keith Ter *EH4*	25	AY10
Kekewich Av *EH7*	17	BP9
Kemp Pl *EH3*	26	BD9
Kempston Pl, S Q'fry *EH30*	9	AE3
Kenilworth Dr *EH16*	44	BJ19
Kenmure Av *EH8*	28	BL11
Kennedy Cres, Tran. *EH33*	35	CM12
Kennington Av, Lnhd *EH20*	62	BK28
Kennington Ter, Lnhd *EH20*	54	BK27
Kentigern Mall, Pen. *EH26*	69	BB38
Kerr Av, Dalk. *EH22*	56	BU25
Kerr-McNeill Service Rd, Tran. *EH33* 3	35	CL14
Kerr Rd, Tran. *EH33*	35	CL13
Kerr St *EH3*	26	BD9
Kerr's Wynd, Muss. *EH21*	31	BZ13
Kerr Way, Tran. *EH33* 5	35	CL14
Kevock Rd, Lass. *EH18*	55	BP27
Kevock Vale Caravan Pk, Lass. *EH18*	55	BQ27
Kew Ter *EH12*	26	BA12
Kilchurn Ct *EH12* 3	23	AQ12
Kilgraston Ct *EH9*	43	BE15
Kilgraston Rd *EH9*	43	BF15
Kilmaurs Rd *EH16*	28	BJ15
Kilmaurs Ter *EH16*	28	BJ15
Kilncroftside *EH14*	41	AX17
Kilngate Brae *EH17*	54	BM22
Kilwinning Pl, Muss. *EH21*	31	BY13
Kilwinning St, Muss. *EH21*	31	BZ13
Kilwinning Ter, Muss. *EH21*	31	BZ13
Kincaid's Ct *EH1*	7	BF12
King Edwards Way, K'lis. *EH29*	20	AC10
King George V Pk, Bonny. *EH19*	63	BQ28
Kinghorn Pl *EH6*	15	BF6
King Malcolm Cl *EH10*	53	BF22
Kings Acre Golf Course *EH18*	55	BQ24
King's Br *EH1*	6	BE12
King's Bldgs *EH9*	43	BH17
Kingsburgh Rd *EH12*	25	AY12
King's Cramond *EH4*	11	AR6
Kings Haugh *EH16*	28	BL15
Kingsinch Sch *EH16*	44	BJ17
KINGSKNOWE	40	AV18
Kingsknowe Av *EH14*	41	AW18
Kingsknowe Ct *EH14*	40	AV18
Kingsknowe Cres *EH14*	41	AW18
Kingsknowe Dr *EH14*	41	AW18
Kingsknowe Gdns *EH14*	41	AW19
Kingsknowe Golf Course *EH14*	41	AW19
Kingsknowe Gro *EH14*	41	AW19
Kingsknowe Pk *EH14*	41	AW19
Kingsknowe Pl *EH14*	40	AV18
Kingsknowe Rd N *EH14*	41	AW17
Kingsknowe Rd S *EH14*	41	AW18
Kingsknowe Sta *EH14*	41	AW18
Kingsknowe Ter *EH14*	41	AW18
Kingslaw Ct, Tran. *EH33*	35	CM14
Kings Manor Hotel *EH15*	30	BT13
King's Meadow *EH16*	28	BK15
Kings Park Prim Sch *EH22*	57	BW25
King's Pl *EH15*	17	BQ9
King's Rd *EH15*	29	BQ10
King's Rd, Tran. *EH33*	35	CL14
King's Stables La *EH1*	6	BE12
King's Stables Rd *EH1*	6	BE12
King's Ter *EH15*	29	BP10
Kings Theatre *EH3*	6	BD13
Kingston Av *EH16*	44	BL18
King St *EH6*	15	BH6
King St, Muss. *EH21*	31	BZ14
Kinleith Ind Est, Currie *EH14*	49	AR23
Kinnear Rd *EH3*	14	BB7
Kippielaw Dr (Easth.), Dalk. *EH22*	57	BY25
Kippielaw Gdns (Easth.), Dalk. *EH22*	57	BY26
Kippielaw Medway (Easth.), Dalk. *EH22*	57	BY26
Kippielaw Pk (Mayf.), Dalk. *EH22*	57	BZ27
Kippielaw Rd (Easth.), Dalk. *EH22*	57	BY26
Kippielaw Wk (Easth.), Dalk. *EH22*	57	BY25
Kirk Brae *EH16*	44	BJ18
Kirk Cramond *EH4*	12	AS5
Kirkgate *EH6*	16	BJ6
Kirkgate *EH16*	44	BJ20
Kirkgate, Currie *EH14*	49	AQ23
KIRKHILL	69	BC38
Kirkhill Ct, Gore. *EH23*	70	BY36
Kirkhill Dr *EH16*	28	BJ15
Kirkhill Gdns *EH16*	28	BJ14
Kirkhill Gdns, Pen. *EH26*	69	BB38
Kirkhill Rd *EH16*	28	BJ14
Kirkhill Rd, Pen. *EH26*	69	BB38
Kirkhill Ter *EH16*	28	BJ14
Kirkhill Ter, Gore. *EH23*	65	BW34
Kirkhill Way, Pen. *EH26*	69	BB38
Kirklands *EH12*	40	AT15
Kirklands, Pen. *EH26*	68	BA38
Kirklands Pk Cres, K'lis. *EH29*	20	AB9
Kirklands Pk Gdns, K'lis. *EH29*	20	AB9
Kirklands Pk Gro, K'lis. *EH29*	20	AB9
Kirklands Pk Rigg, K'lis. *EH29*	20	AC9
Kirklands Pk St, K'lis. *EH29*	20	AB9
KIRKLISTON	20	AD10
Kirkliston Prim Sch *EH29*	20	AC9
Kirkliston Rd, Newbr. *EH28*	20	AB12
Kirkliston Rd, S Q'fry *EH30*	8	AD3
Kirk Ln *EH12*	24	AU13
Kirk Pk *EH16*	44	BJ19
Kirk St *EH6*	15	BH7
Kirk St, Pres. *EH32*	18	CH10
Kirkstyle Gdns, K'lis. *EH29*	20	AD10
Kirkton Bk, Pen. *EH26*	68	AZ38

Name	Page	Grid
Kirk Vw, Pen. *EH26*	69	BB39
Kirkwood Pl *EH7* **3**	28	BJ10
Kisimul Ct *EH12* **1**	23	AR12
Kittle Yards *EH9*	43	BG14
Klondyke St (Newcr.), Muss. *EH21*	30	BU15
Klondyke Way (Newcr.), Muss. *EH21*	30	BT15
Knightslaw Pl, Pen. *EH26*	68	AZ38
Knowetop Pl, Ros. *EH25*	67	BH32
Komarom Pl, Dalk. *EH22*	57	BZ24
Kyle Pl *EH7*	7	BH10
L		
Laburnum Av (Port S.), Pres. *EH32*	19	CM7
Laburnum Pl (Mayf.), Dalk. *EH22*	71	CA29
Lade, The, Bal. *EH14*	58	AM27
Ladehead *EH6*	15	BF7
Ladiemeadow *EH12*	40	AU14
Lady Brae, Gore. *EH23*	70	BZ36
Lady Brae Pl, Gore. *EH23*	70	CA35
Ladycroft, Bal. *EH14*	58	AL26
Lady Emily Way, Gore. *EH23*	70	BY35
Lady Lawson St *EH3*	6	BE12
Lady Menzies Pl *EH7*	28	BJ10
Lady Nairne Cres *EH8*	28	BM12
Lady Nairne Gro *EH8*	28	BM12
Lady Nairne Ln *EH8*	28	BM12
Lady Nairne Pl *EH8*	28	BM12
Lady Rd *EH16*	44	BJ16
Lady Rd Pl (Newt.), Dalk. *EH22* **1**	65	BX29
Ladysmith Rd *EH9*	43	BF17
Lady Stair's Cl *EH1* **6**	7	BF11
Ladywell, Muss. *EH21*	31	BY13
Ladywell Av *EH12*	24	AT13
Ladywell Ct *EH12*	24	AT13
Ladywell Gdns *EH12*	24	AT13
Ladywell Ho *EH12*	24	AT13
Ladywell Rd *EH12*	24	AS13
Ladywell Way, Muss. *EH21*	31	BY13
LADYWOOD	69	BC37
Ladywood Prim Sch EH26	69	BC36
Lady Wynd *EH1*	6	BE12
Laichfield *EH14*	41	AX16
Laichpark Ln *EH14* **1**	41	AX16
Laichpark Pl *EH14*	41	AX16
Laichpark Rd *EH14*	41	AX16
Laing Ter *EH15*	30	BS11
Laing Ter, Pen. *EH26*	69	BB36
Laird Ter, Bonny. *EH19*	64	BS29
Lamb's Cl *EH8* **2**	7	BG13
Lamb's Ct *EH6* **1**	15	BE4
Lamb's Pend, Pen. *EH26*	69	BB39
Lammermoor Gdns, Tran. *EH33*	34	CK13
Lammermoor Ter *EH16*	44	BL18
Lammermoor Ter, Tran. *EH33*	34	CK13
Lammerview, Tran. *EH33*	35	CL14
Lampacre Rd *EH12*	40	AU14
Lanark Rd *EH13*	50	AV20
Lanark Rd *EH14*	41	AW19
Lanark Rd, Jun. Grn *EH14*	50	AT22
Lanark Rd W, Bal. *EH14*	58	AJ25
Lanark Rd W, Currie *EH14*	49	AQ23
Langlaw Prim Sch EH22	57	BZ27
Langlaw Rd, Dalk. *EH22*	57	BZ27
Lang Linn Path *EH10*	43	BE18
Lang Ln *EH17*	54	BK25
Lang Ln, Lnhd *EH20*	54	BK25
Langton Rd *EH9*	43	BG16
Lansbury Ct, Dalk. *EH22*	57	BW24
Lansdowne Cres *EH12*	26	BB12
Lapicide Pl *EH6*	15	BG6
Larbourfield *EH11*	40	AT18
Larch Cres (Mayf.), Dalk. *EH22*	71	CB29
Larchfield, Bal. *EH14*	58	AL25
Larchfield Neuk, Bal. *EH14*	58	AL25
Largo Pl *EH6*	15	BG6
Larkfield Dr, Dalk. *EH22*	56	BT26
Larkfield Rd, Dalk. *EH22*	56	BU25
Laserquest EH11	26	BB12
Lasswade Bk *EH17*	54	BL22
Lasswade Gro *EH17*	54	BL22
Lasswade High Sch Centre EH19	63	BQ28
Lasswade Prim Sch EH19	56	BS27
Lasswade Rd *EH16*	44	BK20
Lasswade Rd *EH17*	44	BL21
Lasswade Rd, Dalk. *EH22*	56	BT25
Lasswade Rd, Lass. *EH18*	55	BP26
Lasswade Rd, Lnhd *EH20*	54	BM27
Latch Pk *EH13*	51	AZ20
Lauderdale St *EH9*	43	BE14
Lauder Ln *EH9*	43	BG15
Lauder Rd *EH9*	43	BF14
Lauder Rd, Dalk. *EH22*	57	BX25
Laurel Bk, Dalk. *EH22*	57	BY25
Laurelbank Pl (Mayf.), Dalk. *EH22* **1**	71	CA29
Laurelbank Rd (Mayf.), Dalk. *EH22*	71	CA29
Laurel Ter *EH11* **1**	42	BA14
Laurie St *EH6*	16	BJ7
Lauriston Castle EH4	12	AU6
Lauriston Fm Rd *EH4*	12	AU7
Lauriston Gdns *EH3*	6	BE12
Lauriston Pk *EH3*	6	BE12
Lauriston Pl *EH3*	6	BD13
Lauriston St *EH3*	6	BE12
Lauriston Ter *EH3*	6	BE12
Laverockbank Av *EH5*	15	BE5
Laverockbank Cres *EH5*	15	BE5
Laverockbank Gdns *EH5*	15	BE5
Laverockbank Gro *EH5*	15	BE5
Laverockbank Rd *EH5*	15	BE5
Laverockbank Ter *EH5*	15	BE5
Laverockdale Cres *EH13*	51	AX21
Laverockdale Ln *EH13*	51	AX22
Laverockdale Pk *EH13*	51	AX22
Laverock Dr, Pen. *EH26*	68	AZ36
Lawers Sq, Pen. *EH26*	69	BC36
Lawfield Rd (Mayf.), Dalk. *EH22*	57	BZ28
Lawhead Pl, Pen. *EH26*	68	AY38
Lawnmarket *EH1*	7	BF11
Law Pl *EH15* **10**	29	BQ10
Lawrie Dr, Pen. *EH26*	68	BA36
Lawrie Ter, Lnhd *EH20*	62	BK28
Lawson Cres, S Q'fry *EH30*	9	AE3
Leadervale Rd *EH16*	43	BH19
Leadervale Ter *EH16*	43	BH19
Leamington Pl *EH10*	6	BD13
Leamington Rd *EH3*	6	BC13
Leamington Ter *EH10*	6	BD13
Learmonth Av *EH4*	26	BB9
Learmonth Ct *EH4*	26	BB10
Learmonth Cres *EH4*	26	BB10
Learmonth Gdns *EH4*	26	BB10
Learmonth Gdns La *EH4*	26	BB10
Learmonth Gdns Ms *EH4*	26	BC9
Learmonth Gro *EH4*	26	BB9
Learmonth Pk *EH4*	26	BB9
Learmonth Pl *EH4*	26	BB9
Learmonth Ramada Jarvis Hotel EH4	26	BB10
Learmonth Ter *EH4*	26	BB10
Learmonth Ter La *EH4*	26	BB10
Learmonth Vw *EH4* **1**	6	BC10
Ledi Ter, Pen. *EH26*	69	BC36
Lee Cres *EH15*	29	BQ11
Leighton Cres (Easth.), Dalk. *EH22*	57	BY28
LEITH	16	BJ6
Leith Academy EH6	16	BJ8
Leith Docks *EH6*	15	BH4
Leith Links *EH6*	16	BJ7
Leith Prim Sch EH6	16	BJ7
Leith St *EH1*	7	BF10
Leith Wk *EH6*	27	BH8
Leith Wk *EH7*	27	BG9
Leith Walk Prim Sch EH7	27	BG9
Le Meridien Edinburgh Hotel EH7	7	BG10
Lennel Av *EH12*	25	AY11
Lennie Cotts *EH12*	22	AM11
Lennox Row *EH5*	14	BD5
Lennox St *EH4*	6	BC10
Lennox St La *EH4*	6	BC10
Lennymuir *EH12*	22	AK10
Leopold Pl *EH7*	27	BG9
Leslie Pl *EH4*	26	BC9
Leven Cl *EH3* **1**	6	BD13
LEVENHALL	32	CC13
Leven St *EH3*	6	BD13
Leven Ter *EH3*	6	BE13
Lewis Ter *EH11* **12**	6	BC12
Lewisvale Av, Muss. *EH21*	32	CA14
Lewisvale Ct, Muss. *EH21*	32	CA14
Leyden Pk, Bonny. *EH19*	55	BR27
Leyden Pl, Bonny. *EH19* **1**	63	BR28
LIBERTON	44	BJ19
Liberton Brae *EH16*	44	BJ19
Liberton Dr *EH16*	43	BH19
Liberton Gdns *EH16*	44	BJ21
Liberton Golf Course EH16	44	BL18
Liberton High Sch EH17	44	BL19
Liberton Hosp EH16	44	BK20
Liberton Pl *EH16*	44	BJ20
Liberton Prim Sch EH16	44	BK17
Liberton Rd *EH16*	44	BJ18
Liddesdale Pl *EH3*	26	BD9
Lidgate Shot (Ratho), Newbr. *EH28*	37	AF17
Lilac Av (Mayf.), Dalk. *EH22*	71	CB29
Lilyhill Ter *EH8*	28	BL10
Lily Ter *EH11* **1**	42	BA15
Limefield *EH17*	55	BN22
Lime Gro (Mayf.), Dalk. *EH22*	71	CA29
Lime Pl, Bonny. *EH19*	63	BR29
Limes, The *EH10*	42	BC15
Lindean Pl *EH6*	16	BK7
Linden Pl, Lnhd *EH20* **3**	54	BM27
Lindores Dr, Tran. *EH33*	35	CM13
Lindsay Pl *EH6*	15	BG5
Lindsay Rd *EH6*	15	BG5
Lindsay St *EH6*	15	BG5
Lingerwood Cotts (Newt.), Dalk. *EH22* **1**	65	BX31
Lingerwood Rd (Newt.), Dalk. *EH22*	65	BW31
Lingerwood Wk (Newt.), Dalk. *EH22*	65	BX31
Linkfield Ct, Muss. *EH21* **1**	32	CA13
Linkfield Rd, Muss. *EH21*	31	BZ13
Links Av, Muss. *EH21*	31	BX12

Name	No.	Grid
Links Ct (Port S.), Pres. EH32	19	CM7
Links Gdns EH6	16	BK6
Links Gdns La EH6	16	BK6
Links La EH6 **3**	16	BJ6
Links Pl EH6	16	BJ6
Links Pl (Port S.), Pres. EH32	19	CN7
Links Rd (Port S.), Pres. EH32	19	CN7
Links St, Muss. EH21	31	BY13
Links Vw, Muss. EH21	31	BX12
Links Vw (Port S.), Pres. EH32	19	CN7
Linksview Ho EH6	16	BJ6
Links Wk (Port S.), Pres. EH32	19	CN7
Linn Mill, S Q'fry EH30	8	AA2
Linty La, Pen. EH26	68	AZ37
Lismore Av EH8	28	BL10
Lismore Cres EH8	28	BL10
Lismore Prim Sch EH15	29	BP14
Liston Dr, K'lis. EH29	20	AC9
Liston Pl, K'lis. EH29	20	AC9
Liston Rd, K'lis. EH29	20	AC10
Little Acre, Dalk. EH22	57	BZ27
Little France Cres EH16	44	BM18
Little France Dr EH16	45	BN18
Little France Ho EH17	44	BM19
Little France Mills EH16	44	BM18
Littlejohn Rd EH10	42	BA19
Little King St EH1	7	BF10
Little Rd EH16	44	BJ20
Livesey Ter, Pen. EH26	66	BC35
Livingstone Pl EH9	43	BF14
Lixmount Av EH5	15	BE5
Lixmount Gdns EH5	15	BE5
Loan, The, Lnhd EH20	62	BK28
Loan, The, S Q'fry EH30	8	AD2
LOANBURN	68	BA38
Loanburn, Pen. EH26	68	BA38
Loanburn Av, Pen. EH26	69	BB37
LOANHEAD	54	BM26
Loanhead Hosp EH20	54	BM27
Loanhead Prim Sch EH20	54	BL27
Loanhead Rd (Strait.), Lnhd EH20	54	BJ25
Loaning Cres EH7	16	BM9
Loaning Rd EH7	16	BL9
LOANSTONE	69	BD38
Lochend (Ratho Sta.), Newbr. EH28	36	AD13
Lochend Av EH7	16	BK9
Lochend Castle Barns EH7	16	BK9
Lochend Cl EH8	7	BH11
Lochend Cres EH7	16	BL9
Lochend Dr EH7	16	BK9
Lochend Gdns EH7	16	BK9
Lochend Gro EH7	16	BL9
Lochend Ind Est, Newbr. EH28	36	AD14
Lochend Pk EH7	16	BK9
Lochend Quad EH7	16	BL9
Lochend Rd EH6	16	BK8
Lochend Rd EH7	16	BK8
Lochend Rd, K'lis. EH29	20	AC11
Lochend Rd, Newbr. EH28	20	AC12
Lochend Rd N, Muss. EH21	31	BX13
Lochend Rd S EH7	16	BK9
Lochend Rd S, Muss. EH21	31	BX13
Lochend Sq EH7	16	BK9
Loch Pl, S Q'fry EH30	8	AD2
Lochrin Bldgs EH3	6	BD13
Lochrin Pl EH3	6	BD13
Lochrin Ter EH3 **3**	6	BD13
Loch Rd EH4	25	AW9
Loch Rd, S Q'fry EH30	8	AD2
Loch Rd, Tran. EH33	35	CM13
Lochside Av EH12	39	AP14
Lochside Ct EH12	39	AQ15
Lochside Cres EH12	39	AQ15
Lochside Pl EH12	39	AQ15
Lochside Vw EH12	39	AP14
Lochside Way EH12	39	AQ15
Loch Sq, Tran. EH33	35	CM13
Lochview Ct EH8	7	BH11
Lockerby Cotts EH16	44	BL21
Lockerby Cres EH16	44	BL21
Lockerby Gro EH16	44	BL21
Lockharton Av EH14	41	AZ17
Lockharton Cres EH14	41	AZ17
Lockharton Gdns EH14	42	BA16
Lockhart Ter, Ros. EH25	67	BH32
Loganlea Av EH7	16	BM9
Loganlea Dr EH7	28	BL10
Loganlea Gdns EH7	16	BL9
Loganlea Ln EH7	16	BM9
Loganlea Pl EH7	28	BM10
Loganlea Rd EH7	16	BM9
Loganlea Ter EH7	16	BM9
Logan St EH3	27	BE9
Logie Grn Gdns EH7	27	BE8
Logie Grn Ln EH7	27	BE8
Logie Grn Rd EH7	27	BE8
Logie Mill EH7	27	BE8
Lomond Rd EH5	14	BD5
Lomond Vale, Pen. EH26	69	BC36
Lomond Wk, Lnhd EH20	61	BH26
London Rd EH7	7	BG10
London Rd EH8	28	BL10
London Rd, Dalk. EH22	57	BW24
London St EH3	27	BF9
Long Craig Rigg EH5	13	AY4
Long Craig Rd EH5	13	AY4
Long Craigs (Port S.), Pres. EH32	19	CN8
Long Crook, S Q'fry EH30	8	AC3
Long Dalmahoy Rd, Bal. EH14	48	AL22
Longdykes Rd, Pres. EH32	18	CK9
Longformacus Rd EH16	44	BJ20
LONGSTONE	41	AW17
Longstone Av EH14	41	AW17
Longstone Cotts EH14 **1**	41	AW17
Longstone Cres EH14	41	AW17
Longstone Gdns EH14	40	AV16
Longstone Gro EH14	41	AW17
Longstone Pk EH14	41	AW17
Longstone Pl EH14	41	AW17
Longstone Prim Sch EH14	41	AW18
Longstone Rd EH14	41	AW17
Longstone St EH14	41	AW17
Longstone Ter EH14	40	AV16
Longstone Vw EH14	40	AV16
Lonsdale Ter EH3	6	BE13
Lord Russell Pl EH9 **1**	43	BG14
Loretto Ct, Muss. EH21	31	BX15
Loretto Jun Sch EH21	31	BY13
Loretto RC Prim Sch EH21	31	BZ13
Lorimer Vw, Jun. Grn EH14	50	AU21
Lorne Gro (Strait.), Lnhd EH20	54	BJ26
Lorne Pl EH6	27	BH8
Lorne Prim Sch EH6	27	BH8
Lorne Sq EH6	27	BH8
Lorne St EH6	27	BH8
Lothian Bk, Dalk. EH22	56	BV26
LOTHIANBURN	53	BE24
Lothianburn Golf Course EH10	52	BD24
Lothianburn Junct EH10	52	BD23
Lothian Dr (Easth.), Dalk. EH22	57	BY27
Lothian Rd EH1	6	BD11
Lothian Rd EH3	6	BD11
Lothian Rd, Dalk. EH22	57	BW24
Lothian St EH1	7	BF12
Lothian St, Bonny. EH19	63	BR28
Lothian St, Dalk. EH22	57	BW24
Lothian St, Rose. EH24	62	BM33
Lothian Ter (Newt.), Dalk. EH22	65	BX31
Louisa Sq, Rose. EH24	62	BM33
Lovedale Av, Bal. EH14	58	AK26
Lovedale Cres, Bal. EH14	58	AK26
Lovedale Gdns, Bal. EH14	58	AL26
Lovedale Gro, Bal. EH14	58	AK26
Lovedale Rd, Bal. EH14	58	AL26
Lovers La, S Q'fry EH30	9	AE3
Lovers' Ln EH9	43	BF14
Lower Broomieknowe, Lass. EH18	63	BQ28
Lower Gilmore Pl EH3	6	BC13
Lower Granton Rd EH5	14	BD5
Lower Joppa EH15	30	BS11
Lower London Rd EH7	28	BJ10
Lower Valleyfield Vw, Pen. EH26	69	BB39
Lowrie Av, Pen. EH26	68	AY38
Lufra Bk EH5	14	BC5
Lugton Brae, Dalk. EH22	56	BV23
Lumsden Ct (Ratho), Newbr. EH28	37	AF17
Lussielaw Rd EH9	43	BH17
Lutton Pl EH8	7	BG13
Lygon Rd EH16	43	BH17
Lyndene Sq, Lnhd EH20	61	BH26
Lynedoch Pl EH3	6	BC11
Lynedoch Pl La EH3	6	BC11
Lyne St EH7	28	BJ10
Lyne Ter, Pen. EH26	69	BC36

M

Name	No.	Grid
Maby's Way, Newbr. EH28	21	AF12
Macbeth Moir Rd, Muss. EH21	32	CC13
McCathie Dr (Newt.), Dalk. EH22	65	BX29
Mac Cormick Ter, Pen. EH26	66	BB35
McDiarmid Gro (Newt.), Dalk. EH22	65	BX31
McDonald Pl EH7	27	BF8
McDonald Rd EH7	27	BF8
McDonald St EH7	27	BG8
Macdowall Rd EH9	43	BG16
McGahey Ct (Newt.), Dalk. EH22	65	BX31
McKelvie Par EH5	14	BD4
Mackenzie Pl EH3	6	BD10
McKinlay Ter, Lnhd EH20	62	BJ28
McKinnon Dr (Mayf.), Dalk. EH22	71	CA31
McLaren Rd EH9	28	BJ15
McLaren Ter EH11 **11**	6	BC12
Maclean Pl, Gore. EH23	70	BZ34
Maclean Pl, Lass. EH18	63	BN29
McLean Wk (Newt.), Dalk. EH22	65	BX31
McLeod Cres, Pres. EH32	18	CH10
McLeod St EH11	26	BA13

McNeill Av, Lnhd *EH20* 54 BK27
McNeill Path, Tran. *EH33* 35 CL13
McNeill Pl, Lnhd *EH20* 54 BK27
McNeill St *EH11* 6 BC13
McNeill Ter, Lnhd *EH20* 54 BJ27
McNeill Wk, Tran. *EH33* **4** 35 CL14
McNeill Way, Tran. *EH33* 35 CL14
Mcphail Sq, Tran. *EH33* 35 CM13
McQuade St, Bonny. *EH19* 56 BT27
Mactaggart Ln (Newt.),
Dalk. *EH22* 65 BX31
Madeira Pl *EH6* 15 BG6
Madeira St *EH6* 15 BG5
Maesterton Pl (Newt.),
Dalk. *EH22* 65 BX31
Magdala Cres *EH12* 26 BB12
Magdala Ms *EH12* 26 BB12
Magdalene Av *EH15* 29 BR13
Magdalene Ct *EH15* 29 BQ14
Magdalene Dr *EH15* 29 BR13
Magdalene Gdns *EH15* 29 BR13
Magdalene Ln *EH15* 29 BR13
Magdalene Medway *EH15* 29 BR13
Magdalene Pl *EH15* 29 BR13
Maidencraig Ct *EH4* 25 AY9
Maidencraig Cres *EH4* 25 AY9
Maidencraig Gro *EH4* 25 AY9
Maid of the Forth *EH30* 9 AF2
Main Pt *EH3* 6 BE12
Mains Gdns, Tran. *EH33* 35 CM12
Mains of Craigmillar *EH16* 44 BM17
Main St (David.M.) *EH4* 24 AV8
Main St (Newt.),
Dalk. *EH22* 65 BW30
Main St, Gore. *EH23* 70 BY36
Main St, K'lis. *EH29* 20 AB9
Main St, Lnhd *EH20* 61 BH28
Main St (Ratho),
Newbr. *EH28* 37 AF17
Main St, Ros. *EH25* 61 BH31
Main St (Dalm.),
S Q'fry *EH30* 9 AG4
Maitland Av, Muss. *EH21* 31 BW13
Maitland Br, K'lis. *EH29* 20 AC11
Maitland Hog La, K'lis.
EH29 20 AC10
Maitland Pk Rd, Muss.
EH21 31 BW13
Maitland Rd, K'lis. *EH29* 20 AC9
Maitland St, Muss. *EH21* 31 BW13
Maitland Townhouse Hotel, The
EH2 6 BD11
Malbet Pk *EH16* 44 BK20
Malbet Wynd *EH16* 44 BK20
Mall Av, Muss. *EH21* 31 BY13
Malleny Av, Bal. *EH14* 58 AL26
Malleny Garden (NTS)
EH14 58 AM25
Malleny Millgate, Bal.
EH14 58 AM28
Malmaison Edinburgh Hotel
EH6 16 BJ5
Malta Grn *EH4* **2** 26 BD9
Malta Ter *EH4* 26 BD9
Manderston St *EH6* 15 BH7
Mannering Pl *EH16* 44 BK19
Manor Pl *EH3* 6 BC11
Manse La, Muss. *EH21* 31 BZ13
Manse La (Port S.),
Pres. *EH32* 19 CL7
Manse Rd *EH12* 24 AT13
Manse Rd, K'lis. *EH29* 20 AC10
Manse Rd, Ros. *EH25* 62 BJ32
Manse St *EH12* 24 AT13

Mansfield Av (Newt.),
Dalk. *EH22* 65 BX29
Mansfield Av, Muss. *EH21* 31 BY14
Mansfield Ct, Muss. *EH21* 31 BZ14
Mansfield Pl *EH3* 27 BF9
Mansfield Pl (Newt.),
Dalk. *EH22* 65 BX29
Mansfield Pl, Muss. *EH21* 31 BY14
Mansfield Rd, Bal. *EH14* 58 AL27
Mansfield Rd (Newt.),
Dalk. *EH22* 65 BX29
Mansfield Rd, Muss. *EH21* 31 BY13
Mansionhouse Rd *EH9* 43 BF14
Marchbank Dr, Bal. *EH14* 58 AL27
Marchbank Gdns, Bal. *EH14* 58 AL27
Marchbank Gro, Bal. *EH14* 58 AL27
Marchbank Pl, Bal. *EH14* 58 AL27
Marchbank Way, Bal. *EH14* 58 AL26
Marchburn Dr, Pen. *EH26* 68 AY38
Marchfield Gro *EH4* 25 AW8
Marchfield Pk *EH4* 24 AV8
Marchfield Pk La *EH4* 24 AV8
Marchfield Ter *EH4* 25 AW9
March Gait *EH4* 24 AV9
March Gro *EH4* 24 AV9
Marchhall Cres *EH16* 28 BJ14
Marchhall Pl *EH16* 28 BJ14
Marchhall Rd *EH16* 28 BJ14
MARCHMONT 43 BE14
Marchmont Cres *EH9* 43 BE14
Marchmont Rd *EH9* 43 BE14
Marchmont St *EH9* 43 BE14
March Pines *EH4* 24 AV9
March Rd *EH4* 24 AV9
Mardale Cres *EH10* 42 BC15
Margaret Rose Av *EH10* 53 BE22
Margaret Rose Cres *EH10* 53 BE22
Margaret Rose Dr *EH10* 53 BE22
Margaret Rose Ln *EH10* 53 BE22
Margaret Rose Wk *EH10* 53 BE22
Margaret Rose Way *EH10* 53 BE22
Marine Dr *EH4* 13 AW5
Marine Dr *EH5* 12 AT5
Marine Esplanade *EH6* 16 BL6
Marionville Av *EH7* 16 BK9
Marionville Cres *EH7* 16 BL9
Marionville Dr *EH7* 16 BL9
Marionville Gro *EH7* 16 BL9
Marionville Medway *EH7* **1** 16 BL9
Marionville Pk *EH7* 16 BK9
Marionville Rd *EH7* 28 BJ10
Marischal Pl *EH4* **1** 25 AY10
Maritime La *EH6* 16 BJ6
Maritime St *EH6* 16 BJ6
Market Ln, Tran. *EH33* 35 CL12
Market St *EH1* 7 BF11
Market St, Muss. *EH21* 31 BX13
Market Vw, Tran. *EH33* 35 CL13
Market Way, Tran. *EH33* 35 CL12
Marlborough St *EH15* 29 BR11
Marmion Av, Ros. *EH25* 61 BH31
Marmion Cres *EH16* 44 BK18
Marriott Edinburgh Hotel
EH12 39 AQ13
Marshall Rd, K'lis. *EH29* 20 AC10
Marshall's Ct *EH1* **3** 7 BG10
Marshall St *EH8* **2** 7 BG12
Marshall St (Cock.),
Pres. *EH32* 18 CK7
Martello Ct *EH4* 13 AW6
Martin Gro, Bonny. *EH19* 56 BT27
Martin Pl, Dalk. *EH22* 56 BU25
Maryburn Rd (Easth.),
Dalk. *EH22* 57 BY27
Mary Erskine Sch *EH4* 25 AX10

Maryfield *EH7* 7 BH10
Maryfield *EH15* 29 BR10
Maryfield Pl *EH7* 28 BJ10
Maryfield Pl, Bonny. *EH19* 56 BS28
Mary's Pl *EH4* **1** 26 BC9
Marytree Ho *EH17* 44 BM19
Masefield Way *EH12* 22 AK10
Mason Pl, Lass. *EH18* 63 BP29
Matthews Dr (Newt.),
Dalk. *EH22* 64 BV31
Maulsford Av (Dand.),
Dalk. *EH22* 45 BR20
Maurice Pl *EH9* 43 BF17
MAURICEWOOD 68 BA36
Mauricewood Av, Pen.
EH26 69 BB36
Mauricewood Bk, Pen.
EH26 69 BB36
Mauricewood Gro, Pen.
EH26 69 BB36
Mauricewood Pk, Pen.
EH26 69 BB36
Mauricewood Prim Sch
EH26 66 BB35
Mauricewood Ri, Pen.
EH26 69 BB36
Mauricewood Rd, Pen.
EH26 66 BA34
Mavisbank, Lnhd *EH20* 62 BL28
Mavisbank Pl, Lass. *EH18* 63 BN29
Maxton Ct, Dalk. *EH22* **1** 57 BW24
Maxwell St *EH10* 42 BC17
Maybank Vil *EH12* 24 AT12
Mayburn Av, Lnhd *EH20* 54 BK26
Mayburn Bk, Lnhd *EH20* 54 BK27
Mayburn Br, Lnhd *EH20* 54 BK26
Mayburn Ct, Lnhd *EH20* 54 BK27
Mayburn Cres, Lnhd *EH20* 54 BK26
Mayburn Dr, Lnhd *EH20* 54 BK26
Mayburn Gro, Lnhd *EH20* 54 BK26
Mayburn Hill, Lnhd *EH20* 54 BK27
Mayburn Ln, Lnhd *EH20* 54 BK26
Mayburn Ter, Lnhd *EH20* 54 BK26
Mayburn Vale, Lnhd *EH20* 54 BJ27
Mayburn Wk, Lnhd *EH20* 54 BK27
Maybury Dr *EH12* 23 AR10
Maybury Gdns, Lnhd *EH20* 54 BK26
Maybury Rd *EH4* 23 AQ11
Maybury Rd *EH12* 23 AQ12
May Ct *EH4* 13 AW6
MAYFIELD 71 CB28
Mayfield Av, Muss. *EH21* 31 BX15
Mayfield Ct, Lnhd *EH20* **1** 62 BL28
Mayfield Cres, Lnhd *EH20* 54 BL27
Mayfield Cres, Muss. *EH21* 31 BW15
Mayfield Gdns *EH9* 43 BH15
Mayfield Gdns La *EH9* 43 BH15
Mayfield Ind Est, Dalk.
EH22 65 BY30
Mayfield Pk, Muss. *EH21* 31 BX16
Mayfield Pl *EH12* 24 AT13
Mayfield Pl (Mayf.),
Dalk. *EH22* 65 BZ29
Mayfield Pl, Muss. *EH21* 31 BX16
Mayfield Prim Sch *EH22* 65 BZ30
Mayfield Rd *EH9* 43 BH15
Mayfield Rd (Easth.),
Dalk. *EH22* 57 BZ27
Mayfield Ter *EH9* 43 BH15
Mayshade Rd, Lnhd *EH20* 54 BK26
Mayville Bk, Muss. *EH21* 32 CC13
Mayville Gdns *EH5* 15 BE5
Mayville Gdns E *EH5* 15 BE5
MEADOWBANK 28 BK10
Meadowbank *EH8* 28 BK10

Name	Page	Grid
Meadowbank Av EH8	28	BK10
Meadowbank Cres EH8	28	BK10
Meadowbank Ho EH7	28	BL10
Meadowbank Pl EH8 7	28	BL10
Meadowbank Shopping Park EH7	16	BJ9
Meadowbank Ter EH8	28	BK10
Meadowfield Av EH8	28	BM12
Meadowfield Ct EH8	28	BM12
Meadowfield Dr EH8	28	BM12
Meadowfield Gdns EH8	28	BM13
Meadowfield Rd EH12	23	AN11
Meadowfield Ter EH8	28	BM13
Meadowhouse Rd EH12	24	AU13
Meadow La EH8	7	BF13
Meadow Pl EH9	6	BE13
Meadow Pl (Bils.), Ros. EH25	61	BG29
Meadow Pl La EH9	43	BF14
Meadow Pl Rd EH12	24	AS13
Meadow Rd (Ricc.), Currie EH14	49	AP20
Meadowside, Tran. EH33	35	CN14
Meadowspot EH10	42	BA17
Mearenside EH12	23	AQ11
Medwin Ho EH11	40	AS18
Meeting Ho Dr, Tran. EH33	35	CL13
Meggat Pl, Pen. EH26	69	BC36
Meggetland Gate EH14	41	AY16
Meggetland Ter EH14	42	BA16
Melbourne Pl EH1 7	7	BF11
Melgund Ter EH7	27	BF9
Melville Cres EH3	6	BC11
Melville Dr EH9	6	BE13
Melville Dykes Rd, Lass. EH18	55	BR26
Melville Gate Rd, Dalk. EH22	56	BT24
Melville Golf Course EH18	56	BS25
Melville Golf Range EH18	56	BS26
Melville Pl EH3 6	6	BC11
Melville Rd, Dalk. EH22	56	BU25
Melville St EH3	6	BC11
Melville St La EH3	6	BC11
Melville Ter EH9	43	BF14
Melville Ter, Dalk. EH22	56	BU26
Melville Vw, Lass. EH18 1	55	BQ27
Mentone Av EH15	29	BR10
Mentone Gdns EH9	43	BH15
Mentone Ter EH9	43	BH16
Menzies Belford Hotel EH4	26	BB11
Merchants of Edinburgh Golf Course EH10	42	BB18
Merchant St EH1	7	BF12
MERCHISTON	42	BB15
Merchiston Av EH10	42	BC14
Merchiston Bk Av EH10	42	BC15
Merchiston Bk Gdns EH10	42	BC15
Merchiston Castle Sch EH13	51	AX20
Merchiston Cres EH10	42	BC15
Merchiston Gdns EH10	42	BB16
Merchiston Gro EH11	42	BA14
Merchiston Ms EH10	42	BC14
Merchiston Pk EH10	42	BC14
Merchiston Pl EH10	42	BC15
Merlyon Way, Pen. EH26	68	AZ36
Mertoun Pl EH11	42	BB14
Methven Ter, Lass. EH18	63	BP29
Meuse La EH2	7	BF10
Middleby St EH9	43	BH15
Middlefield EH7	27	BG8
Middleknowe EH14	40	AS19
Middle Meadow Wk EH3	7	BF13
Middlepark EH14 2	40	AS19
Middle Pier EH5	14	BB4
Middleshot EH14 3	40	AS19
Middleshot Sq, Pres. EH32	18	CK9
Mid Gillsland Rd EH10	42	BB15
Mid Gogarloch Syke EH12	39	AQ14
Mid Liberton EH16	44	BJ17
Midlothian Ski Centre EH10	52	BC25
Midmar Av EH10	43	BE17
Midmar Dr EH10	43	BE17
Midmar Gdns EH10	42	BD17
Mid New Cultins EH11	39	AQ17
Mid Rd, Pres. EH32	34	CH11
Mid Rd Ind Est, Pres. EH32	34	CH11
Mid Steil EH10	42	BA18
Mid Ter, S Q'fry EH30 2	9	AE2
Millar Cres EH10	42	BC16
Millar Pl EH10	42	BC16
Millar Pl La EH10	42	BC16
Millar Rd, Tran. EH33	35	CL14
Millbank, Bal. EH14	58	AL26
Millbank Gro, Gore. EH23	70	BY36
Millbrae, Currie EH14	50	AU21
Millbrae Wynd EH14	41	AX17
Miller Ct, Tran. EH33	34	CK14
Millerfield Pl EH9	43	BF14
MILLERHILL	46	BU20
Millerhill Rd, Dalk. EH22	45	BR17
Miller Row EH4	6	BC11
Millhill, Muss. EH21	31	BZ13
Millhill La, Muss. EH21	31	BZ13
Millhill Wynd, Muss. EH21	31	BZ13
Mill La EH6	15	BH6
Mill Wynd, Pres. EH32	18	CH9
Milnacre EH6	15	BF7
MILTON BRIDGE	66	BD33
Milton Br, Pen. EH26	67	BE33
Milton Cres EH15	29	BQ13
Milton Dr EH15	30	BT12
Milton Gdns N EH15	29	BQ13
Milton Gdns S EH15	29	BQ13
Milton Gro EH15	30	BU12
Milton Link EH15	30	BS13
Milton Rd EH15	29	BQ13
Milton Rd E EH15	30	BT13
Milton Rd W EH15	29	BN13
Milton St EH8	28	BJ10
Milton Ter EH15	30	BU12
Miner's Ter (Wall.), Muss. EH21	33	CD14
Minstrel Ct, Ros. EH25	62	BJ32
Minto St EH9	43	BH14
Mitchell St EH6	16	BJ6
Mitchell St, Dalk. EH22	56	BV24
Mitchell Way, Tran. EH33	35	CM12
Moat Dr EH14	41	AZ15
Moat Ho EH14	41	AZ15
Moat House Edinburgh Hotel EH12	24	AU10
Moat Pl EH14	41	AZ15
Moat St EH14	41	AZ15
Moat Ter EH14	41	AZ15
Moat Vw, Ros. EH25	67	BH32
Moffat Av, Bonny. EH19	63	BR29
Moira Pk EH7	29	BN10
Moira Ter EH7	29	BN10
Moira Ter La EH7	29	BN10
Moir Av, Muss. EH21	32	CC13
Moir Cres, Muss. EH21	32	CC13
Moir Dr, Muss. EH21	33	CD13
Moir Pl, Muss. EH21	32	CC13
Moir Ter, Muss. EH21	32	CC13
Moncreiffe Ho EH17	44	BM19
Moncrieff Ter EH9	43	BG14
Monkbarns Gdns EH16	44	BK19
Monksrig Rd, Pen. EH26	68	AY38
Monkswood Rd (Newt.), Dalk. EH22	65	BX31
Monktonhall Pl, Muss. EH21	31	BX16
Monktonhall Ter, Muss. EH21	31	BX15
Monkwood Ct EH9	43	BF15
Monmouth Ter EH3	14	BD6
Montague St EH8	7	BG13
Montagu Ter EH3	14	BD7
Montgomery St EH7	27	BG9
Montgomery St La EH7	27	BG9
Montpelier EH10	42	BC14
Montpelier Pk EH10	42	BC14
Montpelier Ter EH10	42	BC14
Montrose Ter EH7	7	BH10
Moorfield Cotts, Dalk. EH22	46	BS19
Moorfoot Ct, Bonny. EH19 4	63	BR28
Moorfoot Pl, Bonny. EH19	63	BR29
Moorfoot Pl, Pen. EH26	68	BA37
Moorfoot Vw, Bonny. EH19	63	BR29
Moorfoot Vw, Gore. EH23	70	BY36
Moorfoot Vw (Bils.), Ros. EH25	61	BG30
Moray Pk EH7	28	BJ10
Moray Pk Ter EH7	28	BJ10
Moray Pl EH3	6	BD10
MOREDUN	45	BN20
Moredun Dykes Rd EH17	44	BM21
Moredun Ho EH17	44	BM19
Moredun Pk Ct EH17	44	BM20
Moredun Pk Dr EH17	44	BM20
Moredun Pk Gdns EH17	44	BM19
Moredun Pk Grn EH17	45	BN20
Moredun Pk Gro EH17	45	BN20
Moredun Pk Ln EH17	44	BM20
Moredun Pk Rd EH17	44	BM20
Moredun Pk St EH17	44	BM20
Moredun Pk Vw EH17	44	BM20
Moredun Pk Wk EH17	45	BN20
Moredun Pk Way EH17	44	BM20
Moredunvale Bk EH17	44	BM19
Moredunvale Grn EH17	44	BM19
Moredunvale Gro EH17	44	BM19
Moredunvale Ln EH17	44	BM19
Moredunvale Pk EH17	44	BM19
Moredunvale Pl EH17	44	BM19
Moredunvale Rd EH17	44	BM19
Moredunvale Vw EH17	44	BM19
Moredunvale Way EH17	44	BM19
Morham Gait EH10 6	42	BA19
Morham Gdns EH10 3	42	BA19
Morham Lea EH10 1	42	BA19
Morham Pk EH10 5	42	BA19
Morison Gdns, S Q'fry EH30	8	AD2
Morison's Haven, Pres. EH32	33	CE11
MORNINGSIDE	42	BD17
Morningside Ct EH10	42	BC17
Morningside Dr EH10	42	BB17
Morningside Gdns EH10	42	BB17
Morningside Gro EH10	42	BB17
Morningside Pk EH10	42	BC16
Morningside Pl EH10	42	BC16
Morningside Rd EH10	42	BC15
Morningside Ter EH10	42	BC16
Morrison Av, Tran. EH33	35	CN14
Morrison Circ EH3	6	BC12
Morrison Cres EH3	6	BC12
Morrison Link EH3	6	BC12
Morrison St EH3	6	BC12
Morris Rd (Newt.), Dalk. EH22	65	BY29
MORTONHALL	53	BH22

Mortonhall Gate EH16	53	BG22
Mortonhall Golf Course		
EH10	52	BC20
Mortonhall Pk Av EH17	53	BH22
Mortonhall Pk Bk EH17	54	BJ22
Mortonhall Pk Cres EH17	54	BJ22
Mortonhall Pk Dr EH17	54	BJ22
Mortonhall Pk Gdns EH17	53	BH22
Mortonhall Pk Grn EH17	53	BH22
Mortonhall Pk Gro EH17	53	BH22
Mortonhall Pk Ln EH17	53	BH22
Mortonhall Pk Pl EH17	54	BJ22
Mortonhall Pk Ter EH17	54	BJ22
Mortonhall Pk Vw EH17	53	BH22
Mortonhall Pk Way EH17	53	BH22
Mortonhall Rd EH9	43	BE16
Morton St EH15	30	BS12
Morvenside EH14	40	AS19
Morvenside Cl EH14	40	AS19
Morven St EH4	24	AS10
Mossgiel Wk EH16	44	BJ18
Moston Ter EH9	43	BH15
Moubray Gro, S Q'fry EH30	9	AE3
Mound, The EH1	6	BE11
Mound, The EH2	6	BE11
Mound Pl EH1	6	BE11
Mount Alvernia EH16	44	BK20
Mountcastle Bk EH8	29	BP11
Mountcastle Cres EH8	29	BN11
Mountcastle Dr N EH8	29	BN11
Mountcastle Dr N EH15	29	BN11
Mountcastle Dr S EH15	29	BP12
Mountcastle Gdns EH8	29	BN11
Mountcastle Grn EH8	28	BM10
Mountcastle Gro EH8	29	BN11
Mountcastle Ln EH8	29	BN11
Mountcastle Pk EH8	29	BN10
Mountcastle Pl EH8	29	BN10
Mountcastle Ter EH8	29	BN11
Mount Gra EH15	43	BE15
Mounthooly Ln EH10	53	BE22
Mountjoy Ter, Muss. EH21	31	BY12
Mount Lo Pl EH15	29	BR11
Mount Royal		
Ramada Jarvis Hotel EH2	7	BF11
Mount Vernon Rd EH16	44	BK19
Mucklets Av, Muss. EH21	31	BW15
Mucklets Ct, Muss. EH21	31	BW15
Mucklets Cres, Muss. EH21	31	BW16
Mucklets Dr, Muss. EH21	31	BW15
Mucklets Pl, Muss. EH21	31	BW15
Mucklets Rd, Muss. EH21	30	BV16
Muirdale Ter EH4 1	25	AX9
Muirend Av, Jun. Grn EH14	50	AU20
Muirfield Gdns, Lnhd EH20	62	BL28
Muirhead Pl, Pen. EH26	66	BB35
MUIRHOUSE	13	AX6
Muirhouse Av EH4	13	AX7
Muirhouse Av N EH4	13	AX6
Muirhouse Bk EH4	13	AX7
Muirhouse Cl EH4	13	AW7
Muirhouse Ct EH4	13	AX6
Muirhouse Cres EH4	13	AX6
Muirhouse Dr EH4	13	AW6
Muirhouse Gdns EH4	13	AW6
Muirhouse Grn EH4	13	AX7
Muirhouse Gro EH4	13	AW6
Muirhouse Ln EH4	13	AX6
Muirhouse Medway EH4	13	AW6
Muirhouse Pk EH4	13	AW7
Muirhouse Parkway EH4	13	AX6
Muirhouse Pl E EH4	13	AX7
Muirhouse Pl W EH4	13	AX7
Muirhouse Ter EH4	13	AW7
Muirhouse Vw EH4	13	AW6

Muirhouse Way EH4	13	AX7
Muirpark, Dalk. EH22	56	BU26
Muirpark Ct, Tran. EH33	35	CN14
Muirpark Dr, Tran. EH33	35	CN14
Muirpark Gdns, Tran. EH33	35	CN14
Muirpark Gro, Tran. EH33	35	CN14
Muirpark Pl, Tran. EH33	35	CN14
Muirpark Rd, Tran. EH33	35	CN14
Muirpark Ter, Tran. EH33	35	CN14
Muirpark Wynd, Tran. EH33	35	CN14
Muirside EH13	52	BA22
Muirside Dr, Tran. EH33	35	CL14
Muir Wd Cres, Currie EH14	49	AR22
Muir Wd Dr, Currie EH14	49	AR22
Muir Wd Gro, Currie EH14	49	AR22
Muir Wd Pl, Currie EH14	49	AR21
Muir Wd Rd, Currie EH14	49	AR21
Mulberry Pl EH6 1	15	BF6
Multrees Wk EH1	7	BF10
Munro Dr EH13	51	AW22
Munro Pl EH3 1	27	BE8
Murano Pl EH7	27	BH9
Murderean Rd (Newt.),		
Dalk. EH22	65	BW30
Murdoch Ter EH11	6	BC13
Murieston Cres EH11	26	BA13
Murieston Cres La EH11 2	26	BB13
Murieston La EH11	26	BA13
Murieston Pl EH11	26	BA13
Murieston Rd EH11	26	BA13
Murieston Ter EH11	26	BA13
Murrayburn App EH14	40	AT18
Murrayburn Dr EH14	40	AT18
Murrayburn Gdns EH14	40	AU18
Murrayburn Gate EH14	40	AT19
Murrayburn Grn EH14	40	AU18
Murrayburn Gro EH14	40	AU18
Murrayburn Pk EH14	40	AT18
Murrayburn Pl EH14	40	AT18
Murrayburn Prim Sch EH11	40	AT17
Murrayburn Rd EH14	40	AU17
Murray Cotts EH12	24	AS13
MURRAYFIELD	25	AY12
Murrayfield Av EH12	25	AZ12
Murrayfield Dr EH12	25	AY12
Murrayfield Gdns EH12	25	AZ11
Murrayfield Golf Course		
EH4	25	AX11
Murrayfield Pl EH12 1	25	AZ12
Murrayfield Rd EH12	25	AY11
Murrayfield Stadium EH12	25	AZ13
Murrays, The EH17	54	BL23
Murrays Brae, The EH17	54	BL23
Museum of Childhood		
EH1 10	7	BG11
Museum of Fire EH3	6	BE12
Museum of Scotland EH1	7	BF12
MUSSELBURGH	31	BX15
Musselburgh Burgh Prim Sch		
EH21	31	BY13
Musselburgh Dolls Museum		
EH21	31	BY13
Musselburgh Golf Course		
EH21	31	BX16
Musselburgh Gram Sch		
EH21	31	BY14
Musselburgh Links Golf Course		
(The Old Course) EH21	31	BZ12
Musselburgh Racecourse		
EH21	31	BZ12
Musselburgh Rd EH15	30	BT12
Musselburgh Rd, Dalk.		
EH22	57	BX23
Musselburgh Sta EH21	31	BW15
Myre Dale, Bonny. EH19	64	BS29

Myreside Ct EH10	42	BB17
Myreside Rd EH10	42	BB16
Myrtle Cres (Bils.),		
Ros. EH25	61	BG29
Myrtle Gro (Mayf.),		
Dalk. EH22	57	BZ28
Myrtle Ter EH11	42	BA14

N

Namur Rd, Pen. EH26	66	BB35
Nantwich Dr EH7	17	BN8
Napier Ln EH10	42	BB15
Napier Rd EH10	42	BB15
Napier Uni (Canaan La Campus)		
EH9	43	BE16
Napier Uni (Comely Bank Campus)		
EH4	26	BA9
Napier Uni (Craighouse Campus)		
EH10	42	BA17
Napier Uni (Craiglockhart Campus)		
EH14	41	AZ18
Napier Uni (Marchmount Campus)		
EH9	43	BE14
Napier Uni (Merchiston Campus)		
EH10	42	BC15
Napier Uni (Morningside Campus)		
EH10	42	BD15
Napier Uni (Redwood Campus)		
EH10	42	BB15
Napier Uni (Sighthill Campus)		
EH11	40	AT17
National Gallery of Scotland		
EH2	6	BE11
National Lib of Scotland		
EH1	7	BF12
National War Mus of Scotland		
(Edinburgh Castle) EH1	6	BE11
Neidpath Ct EH12 4	23	AQ12
Nellfield EH16	44	BK19
Nelson Monument EH7	7	BG10
Nelson Pl EH3 1	6	BE10
Nelson St EH3	6	BE10
Nether Bakehouse EH8 9	7	BH11
Netherbank EH16	53	BH21
Netherbank Vw EH16	53	BH21
Netherby Rd EH5	14	BC6
Nether Craigour EH17	44	BM18
Nether Craigwell EH8	7	BH10
Nether Currie Cres, Currie		
EH14	49	AR22
Nether Currie Pl, Currie		
EH14	49	AR22
Nether Currie Prim Sch		
EH14	49	AR22
Nether Currie Rd, Currie		
EH14	49	AR22
Nether Lennie EH12	22	AL8
Nether Liberton Ct EH16 1	44	BJ17
Nethershot Rd, Pres. EH32	18	CJ9
Nevis Gdns, Pen. EH26	69	BC36
New Arthur Pl EH8	7	BG12
New Arthur St EH8 5	7	BG12
NEWBATTLE	57	BW27
Newbattle Abbey Coll		
EH22	57	BW26
Newbattle Abbey Cres,		
Dalk. EH22	56	BV27
Newbattle Gdns, Dalk.		
EH22	57	BW26
Newbattle Golf Course		
EH22	57	BW25
Newbattle High Sch EH22	57	BY28
Newbattle Ind Est, Dalk.		
EH22	65	BY29

Name	Page	Ref
Newbattle Rd, Dalk. *EH22*	56	BV25
Newbattle Ter *EH10*	42	BD15
New Belfield *EH8*	29	BN12
New Bells Ct *EH6* 4	16	BJ6
Newbigging, Muss. *EH21*	31	BZ14
NEWBRIDGE	36	AC13
New Br, Newbr. *EH28*	36	AB13
Newbridge Ind Est, Newbr. *EH28*	36	AC14
Newbridge Rd, Newbr. *EH28*	36	AC14
New Broompark *EH5*	14	BA4
New Broughton *EH3*	27	BF9
Newbyres Av, Gore. *EH23*	70	BY34
Newbyres Cres, Gore. *EH23*	70	BY35
Newbyres Gdns, Gore. *EH23*	70	BY35
NEWCRAIGHALL	30	BT14
Newcraighall Dr (Newcr.), Muss. *EH21*	30	BT15
Newcraighall Prim Sch *EH21*	30	BU15
Newcraighall Rd *EH15*	29	BR15
Newcraighall Rd, Muss. *EH21*	30	BT15
Newcraighall Sta *EH21*	30	BT15
New Cut Rigg *EH6*	15	BF6
NEWHAILES	30	BV13
Newhailes Av, Muss. *EH21*	31	BW13
Newhailes Cres, Muss. *EH21*	30	BV13
Newhailes Ind Est, Muss. *EH21*	30	BV14
Newhailes (NTS) *EH21*	30	BV13
Newhailes Rd, Muss. *EH21*	30	BV14
New Halls Rd, S Q'fry *EH30*	9	AF2
NEWHAVEN	15	BF5
Newhaven Heritage Museum *EH6*	15	BF4
Newhaven Main St *EH6*	15	BE4
Newhaven Pl *EH6*	15	BF4
Newhaven Rd *EH6*	15	BG7
New Hunterfield, Gore. *EH23*	65	BX33
NEWINGTON	43	BH14
Newington Rd *EH9*	43	BG14
New John's Pl *EH8*	7	BG13
Newkirkgate *EH6* 2	15	BH7
New Lairdship Pl *EH11*	40	AT16
New Lairdship Yards *EH11*	40	AT16
Newlands Pk *EH9*	43	BH15
New La *EH6*	15	BF5
New Liston Rd, K'lis. *EH29*	20	AC11
Newmains Fm La, K'lis. *EH29*	20	AC9
Newmains Rd, K'lis. *EH29*	20	AC9
New Mkt Rd *EH14*	41	AY16
New Mart Rd *EH14*	41	AX16
New Meadowspott, Dalk. *EH22* 1	56	BV25
Newmills Av, Bal. *EH14*	48	AM23
Newmills Cres, Bal. *EH14*	48	AM23
Newmills Gro, Bal. *EH14*	48	AM24
Newmills Rd, Bal. *EH14*	48	AM24
Newmills Rd, Dalk. *EH22*	57	BW24
Newmills Ter, Dalk. *EH22* 1	57	BX24
New Orchardfield *EH6*	15	BH7
NEW PENTLAND	61	BH27
New Poltonhall, Bonny. *EH19*	63	BP31
New Row, Tran. *EH33*	35	CL13
New Skinner's Cl *EH1*	7	BG11
News Steps *EH1*	7	BF11
New Star Bk (Newt.), Dalk. *EH22*	65	BW30
New St *EH8*	7	BG11
New St *EH17*	54	BM22
New St, Muss. *EH21*	31	BW13
New St, Pres. *EH32*	18	CH10
New St (Cock.), Pres. *EH32*	19	CL7
New St, Tran. *EH33*	35	CL12
New Swanston *EH10*	52	BB22
Newtoft St *EH17*	55	BN22
Newton Ch Rd (Dand.), Dalk. *EH22*	45	BR20
NEWTONGRANGE	64	BV29
Newtongrange Pl (Newt.), Dalk. *EH22*	65	BW30
Newtongrange Prim Sch *EH22*	65	BX30
NEWTONLOAN	65	BW32
Newtonloan Ct, Gore. *EH23*	65	BX33
Newton St *EH11*	42	BA14
Newton St (Easth.), Dalk. *EH22*	57	BY27
NEWTON VILLAGE	46	BT19
Newton Village, Dalk. *EH22*	46	BT19
New Twr Pl *EH15* 1	29	BR10
Nichollfield *EH6*	15	BF5
Nicolson Sq *EH8*	7	BF12
Nicolson St *EH8*	7	BG12
NIDDRIE	29	BQ15
Niddrie Cotts *EH15* 1	30	BS15
Niddrie Fm Gro *EH16*	29	BN15
Niddrie Ho Av *EH16*	45	BP16
Niddrie Ho Dr *EH16*	45	BQ16
Niddrie Ho Gdns *EH16*	45	BP16
Niddrie Ho Gro *EH16* 2	45	BQ16
Niddrie Ho Pk *EH16*	45	BP16
Niddrie Ho Sq *EH16*	45	BP16
Niddrie Mains Dr *EH16*	29	BN15
Niddrie Mains Rd *EH16*	29	BN15
Niddrie Mains Rd *EH16*	29	BN15
Niddrie Mains Ter *EH16*	29	BN15
Niddrie Marischal Cres *EH16*	29	BP15
Niddrie Marischal Dr *EH16*	45	BP16
Niddrie Marischal Gdns *EH16*	29	BP15
Niddrie Marischal Grn *EH16*	45	BP16
Niddrie Marischal Gro *EH16*	29	BQ15
Niddrie Marischal Ln *EH16*	29	BP15
Niddrie Marischal Pl *EH16*	45	BP16
Niddrie Marischal Rd *EH16*	29	BQ15
Niddrie Marischal St *EH16*	29	BP15
Niddrie Mill Av *EH15*	29	BQ14
Niddrie Mill Cres *EH15*	29	BQ14
Niddrie Mill Dr *EH15*	29	BQ15
Niddrie Mill Gro *EH15*	29	BQ15
Niddrie Mill Pl *EH15*	29	BQ15
Niddrie Mill Prim Sch *EH15*	29	BQ15
Niddrie Mill Ter *EH15*	29	BQ15
Niddry St *EH1*	7	BF11
Niddry St S *EH1* 3	7	BG12
Nigel Ln *EH16*	44	BK19
Nile Gro *EH10*	42	BD16
Nimmo Av, Pres. *EH32*	18	CJ10
Ninth St (Newt.), Dalk. *EH22*	65	BX29
Nisbet Ct *EH7*	16	BK8
Nivensknowe Caravan Pk, Lnhd *EH20*	61	BG28
Niven's Knowe Rd, Lnhd *EH20*	61	BH28
No. 28 Charlotte Square (NTS) *EH2*	6	BD11
Nobel Pl, Ros. *EH25*	67	BH32
Noble Pl *EH6*	16	BK7
North Bk Rd, Pres. *EH32*	18	CG10
North Bk St *EH1*	7	BF11
North Br *EH1*	7	BF11
North Br Arc *EH1* 10	7	BF11
North Bughtlin Bk *EH12*	23	AR10
North Bughtlin Brae *EH12*	23	AR10
North Bughtlinfield *EH12*	23	AQ10
North Bughtlin Gate *EH12*	23	AR10
North Bughtlin Neuk *EH12* 3	23	AR10
North Bughtlin Pl *EH12* 2	23	AR10
North Bughtlinrig *EH12*	23	AQ10
North Bughtlin Rd *EH12*	23	AQ10
North Bughtlinside *EH12*	23	AQ10
North Cairntow *EH16*	28	BM14
North Castle St *EH2*	6	BD10
North Charlotte St *EH2*	6	BD10
North Clyde St La *EH1* 1	7	BF10
Northcote St *EH11*	26	BB13
North Cres, Pres. *EH32*	18	CJ10
North E Circ Pl *EH3*	6	BD10
North Edinburgh Arts Centre *EH4*	13	AX6
NORTHFIELD	29	BN12
Northfield, Pres. *EH32*	34	CH11
Northfield, Tran. *EH33*	35	CN13
Northfield Av *EH8*	28	BM11
Northfield Bdy *EH8*	28	BM10
Northfield Circ *EH8*	28	BM11
Northfield Ct, Pres. *EH32*	34	CH11
Northfield Cres *EH8*	28	BM11
Northfield Dr *EH8*	29	BN12
Northfield E, Tran. *EH33*	35	CN13
Northfield Fm Av *EH8*	29	BN12
Northfield Fm Rd *EH8*	29	BN11
Northfield Gdns *EH8*	29	BN11
Northfield Gdns, Pres. *EH32*	34	CH11
Northfield Gro *EH8*	29	BN12
Northfield Pk *EH8*	29	BN11
Northfield Pk Gro *EH8*	29	BN11
Northfield Rd *EH8*	28	BM11
Northfield Sq *EH8*	29	BN11
Northfield Ter *EH8*	28	BM11
North Fort St *EH6*	15	BG5
North Gra Av, Pres. *EH32*	34	CG11
North Gra Gro, Pres. *EH32*	18	CH10
North Gra Rd, Pres. *EH32*	18	CH10
North Grns *EH15*	29	BR14
North Gyle Av *EH12*	39	AQ13
North Gyle Dr *EH12*	23	AQ12
North Gyle Fm Ct *EH12*	39	AQ13
North Gyle Fm La *EH12*	39	AQ13
North Gyle Gro *EH12*	39	AQ13
North Gyle Ln *EH12*	23	AQ12
North Gyle Pk *EH12*	23	AQ12
North Gyle Rd *EH12*	23	AR12
North Gyle Ter *EH12*	39	AQ13
North High St, Muss. *EH21*	31	BX13
North Hillhousefield *EH6*	15	BG5
North Junct St *EH6*	15	BG5
Northlawn Ct *EH4* 6	12	AU7
Northlawn Ter *EH4*	12	AU7
NORTH LEITH	15	BG6
North Leith Mill *EH6* 4	15	BG5
North Leith Sands *EH6*	15	BG5
North Lorimer Pl (Cock.), Pres. *EH32*	18	CK7
North Meadow Wk *EH3*	6	BE13
North Meadow Wk *EH8*	6	BE13
North Meggetland *EH14*	41	AZ16
North Pk Ter *EH4*	26	BC9
North Peffer Pl *EH16*	28	BM15
North Richmond St *EH8* 1	7	BG12
North St. Andrew La *EH2*	7	BF10
North St. Andrew St *EH2*	7	BF10
North St. David St *EH2*	7	BF10

Name	Page	Grid
North Seton Pk (Port S.), Pres. *EH32*	19	CL7
North St (Ratho), Newbr. *EH28*	37	AF17
Northumberland Pl *EH3* **2**	6	BE10
Northumberland Pl La *EH3*	6	BE10
Northumberland St *EH3*	6	BE10
Northumberland St N E La *EH3*	6	BE10
Northumberland St N W La *EH3*	6	BE10
Northumberland St S E La *EH3*	6	BE10
Northumberland St S W La *EH3*	6	BE10
Northview Ct *EH4*	13	AX6
North Wk, The *EH10*	42	BC17
North Way, The *EH8*	28	BM11
North Werber Pk *EH4*	26	BA8
North Werber Pl *EH4*	14	BA7
North Werber Rd *EH4*	26	BA8
North W Circ Pl *EH3*	6	BD10
North Wynd, Dalk. *EH22*	57	BW24
Norton House Hotel *EH28*	37	AF15
Norton Pk *EH7*	16	BJ9
Nottingham Pl *EH7*	7	BG10

O

Name	Page	Grid
Oak Av, Lnhd *EH20*	61	BH28
Oak Cres (Mayf.), Dalk. *EH22*	71	CA29
Oakfield Pl *EH8*	7	BG12
Oaklands Sch *EH11*	40	AU16
Oak La *EH12*	24	AU10
Oak Pl (Mayf.), Dalk. *EH22*	71	CA29
Oakville Ter *EH6*	16	BK7
Observatory Grn *EH9*	43	BG17
Observatory Rd *EH9*	43	BG17
Ocean Dr *EH6*	15	BG5
Ocean Terminal Shopping Centre *EH6*	15	BG4
Ochil Ct, S Q'fry *EH30*	9	AE3
Ochiltree Gdns *EH16*	44	BL18
Odeon Cinema (Lothian Road) *EH3*	6	BD12
Odeon Cinema (Wester Hailes) *EH14*	40	AT19
Ogilvie Ter *EH11*	42	BA15
Old Assembly Cl *EH1* **9**	7	BF11
Old Broughton *EH3* **2**	27	BF9
Old Burdiehouse Rd *EH17*	54	BJ24
Old Ch La *EH15*	28	BL13
OLD CRAIGHALL	47	BW17
Old Craighall Rd, Dalk. *EH22*	46	BU20
Old Dalkeith Rd *EH16*	44	BK16
Old Dalkeith Rd *EH17*	45	BP20
Old Dalkeith Rd (Dand.), Dalk. *EH22*	46	BS21
Old Edinburgh Rd, Dalk. *EH22*	56	BV24
Old Fm Av *EH13*	51	AY20
Old Fm Pl *EH13*	51	AX20
Old Fishmarket Cl *EH1*	7	BF11
Old Kirk Rd *EH12*	24	AU12
Old Liston Rd, Newbr. *EH28*	36	AC13
Old Mill La *EH16*	44	BJ17
Old Newmills Rd, Bal. *EH14*	48	AM24
OLD PENTLAND	61	BG26
Old Pentland Rd *EH10*	53	BE25
Old Pentland Rd, Lnhd *EH20*	61	BG26
Old Star Rd (Newt.), Dalk. *EH22*	65	BW30
Old Tolbooth Wynd *EH8*	7	BG11
Old Waverley Hotel *EH2*	7	BF11
Oliphant Gdns (Wall.), Muss. *EH21*	33	CD14
Olivebank Retail Pk, Muss. *EH21*	31	BW13
Olive Bk Rd, Muss. *EH21*	31	BW13
Omni *EH1*	7	BG10
Orchard, The, Tran. *EH33*	35	CL12
Orchard Bk *EH4*	26	BA10
ORCHARD BRAE	26	BA10
Orchard Brae *EH4*	26	BB9
Orchard Brae Av *EH4*	26	BA10
Orchard Brae Gdns *EH4*	26	BA10
Orchard Brae Gdns W *EH4*	26	BA10
Orchard Brae W *EH4*	26	BB9
Orchard Cres *EH4*	25	AZ10
Orchard Cres, Pres. *EH32*	18	CH10
Orchard Dr *EH4*	25	AZ10
Orchardfield Av *EH12*	24	AT13
Orchardfield La *EH6*	27	BH8
Orchard Gro *EH4*	26	BB9
Orchardhead Ln *EH16*	44	BJ19
Orchardhead Rd *EH16*	44	BJ18
Orchard Pk, Tran. *EH33*	35	CL12
Orchard Pl *EH4*	26	BA9
Orchard Rd *EH4*	26	BA10
Orchard Rd S *EH4*	25	AZ10
Orchard Ter *EH4*	26	BA10
Orchard Toll *EH4*	26	BA10
Orchard Vw, Dalk. *EH22*	56	BU25
Ormelie Ter *EH15*	30	BS11
Ormidale Ter *EH12*	25	AY12
Ormiston Av, Tran. *EH33*	35	CN13
Ormiston Cres E, Tran. *EH33*	35	CN13
Ormiston Cres W, Tran. *EH33*	35	CN13
Ormiston Pl, Pres. *EH32*	18	CG10
Ormiston Rd, Tran. *EH33*	35	CM13
Ormiston Ter *EH12*	24	AT13
Orrok Pk *EH16*	44	BJ17
Orwell Pl *EH11*	26	BB13
Orwell Prim Sch *EH11*	26	BB13
Orwell Ter *EH11*	26	BB13
Osborne Ct (Cock.), Pres. *EH32*	19	CL7
Osborne Ter *EH12*	26	BB12
Osborne Ter (Cock.), Pres. *EH32*	19	CL7
Oswald Ct *EH9*	43	BF16
Oswald Rd *EH9*	43	BF16
Oswald Ter *EH12* **1**	24	AT13
Oswald Ter, Pres. *EH32*	18	CJ10
Otterburn Pk *EH14*	41	AX18
Oxcars Ct *EH4*	13	AW6
Oxcraig St *EH5*	14	BB4
Oxford St *EH8*	7	BH13
Oxford Ter *EH4*	6	BC10
OXGANGS	52	BA21
Oxgangs Av *EH13*	52	BA21
Oxgangs Bk *EH13*	52	BB21
Oxgangs Brae *EH13*	52	BB21
Oxgangs Bdy *EH13* **2**	52	BB21
Oxgangs Cres *EH13*	52	BB20
Oxgangs Dr *EH13*	52	BB20
Oxgangs Fm Av *EH13*	52	BA21
Oxgangs Fm Dr *EH13*	52	BA21
Oxgangs Fm Gdns *EH13*	52	BA21
Oxgangs Fm Gro *EH13*	52	BA21
Oxgangs Fm Ln *EH13*	52	BA21
Oxgangs Fm Ter *EH13*	52	BA21
Oxgangs Gdns *EH13*	52	BA20
Oxgangs Grn *EH13*	52	BB20
Oxgangs Gro *EH13*	52	BB20
Oxgangs Hill *EH13*	52	BB20
Oxgangs Ln *EH13*	52	BB20
Oxgangs Medway *EH13*	52	BB21
Oxgangs Pk *EH13*	52	BB21
Oxgangs Path *EH13*	52	BB21
Oxgangs Path E *EH13* **1**	52	BB21
Oxgangs Pl *EH13*	52	BA20
Oxgangs Prim Sch *EH13*	51	AZ20
Oxgangs Ri *EH13*	52	BB20
Oxgangs Rd *EH10*	52	BB22
Oxgangs Rd *EH13*	52	BB21
Oxgangs Rd N *EH13*	41	AZ19
Oxgangs Rd N *EH14*	41	AZ19
Oxgangs Row *EH13*	52	BB21
Oxgangs St *EH13*	52	BB21
Oxgangs Ter *EH13*	52	BA21
Oxgangs Vw *EH13*	52	BB21

P

Name	Page	Grid
Paddock, The, Muss. *EH21* **1**	31	BZ12
Paddockholm, The *EH12*	24	AU13
Paisley Av *EH8*	28	BM11
Paisley Cres *EH8*	28	BL11
Paisley Dr *EH8*	28	BM12
Paisley Gdns *EH8*	28	BL11
Paisley Gro *EH8*	28	BM12
Paisley Ter *EH8*	28	BL11
Palace of Holyrood House *EH8*	7	BH11
Palmer Pl, Currie *EH14*	49	AP23
Palmer Rd, Currie *EH14*	49	AP22
Palmerston Pl *EH12*	6	BC11
Palmerston Pl La *EH12*	6	BC12
Palmerston Rd *EH9*	43	BF14
Pankhurst Ln, Dalk. *EH22*	57	BZ24
Panmure Pl *EH3*	6	BE13
Pape's Cotts *EH12*	25	AZ12
Paradykes Av, Lnhd *EH20*	54	BJ27
Paradykes Prim Sch *EH20*	54	BK27
Park Av *EH15*	29	BQ12
Park Av, Gore. *EH23*	70	BY34
Park Av, Lnhd *EH20*	62	BJ28
Park Av, Muss. *EH21*	32	CA14
Park Av (Bils.), Ros. *EH25*	61	BF29
Park Ct, Muss. *EH21*	32	CA14
Park Cres *EH16*	44	BK19
Park Cres, Bonny. *EH19*	63	BR28
Park Cres (Easth.), Dalk. *EH22*	57	BY27
Park Cres, Lnhd *EH20*	62	BK28
Parker Av *EH7*	29	BN10
Parker Rd *EH7*	29	BN10
Parker Ter *EH7*	29	BP10
Park Gdns *EH16*	44	BK19
Park Gdns, Muss. *EH21*	32	CA14
Park Gro *EH16*	44	BK20
Parkgrove Av *EH4*	24	AS9
Parkgrove Bk *EH4*	24	AS9
Parkgrove Cres *EH4*	24	AS9
Parkgrove Dr *EH4*	23	AR9
Parkgrove Gdns *EH4*	24	AS9
Parkgrove Grn *EH4*	24	AS9
Parkgrove Ln *EH4*	24	AS9
Parkgrove Neuk *EH4*	24	AS9
Parkgrove Path *EH4*	24	AT9
Parkgrove Pl *EH4*	24	AS9
Park Gro Pl, Muss. *EH21*	32	CA14
Parkgrove Rd *EH4*	24	AS9
Parkgrove Row *EH4*	24	AS9
Parkgrove St *EH4*	24	AT9

Name	Page	Grid
Parkgrove Ter *EH4*	24	AS9
Park Gro Ter, Muss. *EH21*	32	CA14
Parkgrove Vw *EH4*	24	AS9
PARKHEAD	40	AV17
Parkhead Av *EH11*	40	AU17
Parkhead Cres *EH11*	40	AU17
Parkhead Dr *EH11*	40	AV17
Parkhead Gdns *EH11*	40	AU17
Parkhead Gro *EH11*	40	AU17
Parkhead Ln *EH11*	40	AV17
Parkhead Pk (Easth.), Dalk. *EH22* 1	57	BY27
Parkhead Pl *EH11*	40	AU17
Parkhead Pl (Easth.), Dalk. *EH22*	57	BY27
Parkhead St *EH11*	40	AU17
Parkhead Ter *EH11*	40	AV16
Parkhead Vw *EH11*	40	AU17
Park Hill, Gore. *EH23*	70	BX34
Park La *EH15*	29	BQ12
Park La, Dalk. *EH22*	56	BV25
Park La, Muss. *EH21*	32	CA14
Park Pl *EH6*	15	BE5
Park Rd *EH6*	15	BE5
Park Rd, Bonny. *EH19*	63	BR28
Park Rd, Dalk. *EH22*	56	BV25
Park Rd (Newt.), Dalk. *EH22*	65	BX29
Park Rd, Gore. *EH23*	70	BY34
Park Rd (Port S.), Pres. *EH32*	19	CM7
Parkside, Newbr. *EH28*	36	AC13
Parkside Ct, Dalk. *EH22* 6	57	BW24
Parkside Pl, Dalk. *EH22*	57	BW24
Parkside St *EH8*	7	BH13
Parkside Ter *EH16*	7	BH13
Park Ter (Newcr.), Muss. *EH21*	30	BU15
Parkvale Pl *EH6*	16	BK7
Park Vw, Lnhd *EH20*	62	BK28
Park Vw, Muss. *EH21*	32	CA14
Park Vw (Newcr.), Muss. *EH21*	30	BT15
Park Vw, Pres. *EH32*	18	CJ10
Park Vw E (Port S.), Pres. *EH32*	19	CM7
Park Vw W (Port S.), Pres. *EH32*	19	CM7
Parliament Building Visitor Centre *EH8*	7	BH11
Parliament House Hotel *EH1*	7	BG10
Parliament Sq *EH1*	7	BF11
Parliament St *EH6*	15	BH6
Parrot La, Gore. *EH23*	70	BY35
Parrotshot *EH15*	29	BQ14
Parsonage, Muss. *EH21*	31	BZ13
Parson's Green Prim Sch *EH8*	28	BM12
Parsonspool, Bonny. *EH19*	64	BS30
Path Brae, K'lis. *EH29*	20	AC10
Patie's Rd *EH14*	41	AY19
Patrick Geddes Steps *EH1* 14	6	BE12
Patriothall *EH3* 3	26	BD9
Pattison St *EH6*	16	BJ6
Peacock Av, Bonny. *EH19*	64	BU29
Peacock Ct *EH6*	15	BF4
Peacock Parkway, Bonny. *EH19*	64	BU29
Peacock Pl, Bonny. *EH19*	64	BT29
Peacocktail Cl *EH15*	29	BR15
Pearce Av *EH12*	24	AS12
Pearce Gro *EH12*	24	AS12
Pearce Rd *EH12*	24	AS12
Peatville Gdns *EH14*	41	AW18
Peatville Ter *EH14*	41	AW18
Peebles Rd, Pen. *EH26*	69	BB39
Peel Ter *EH9*	43	BH15
Peffer Bk *EH16*	28	BM15
Peffermill Ct *EH16* 1	44	BM16
Peffermill Ind Est *EH16*	28	BM15
Peffermill Rd *EH16*	44	BK16
Peffer Pl *EH16*	28	BM15
Peffer St *EH16*	28	BM15
Peggy's Mill Rd *EH4*	23	AQ7
Pembroke Pl *EH12*	26	BA12
Pendreich Av, Bonny. *EH19*	56	BS27
Pendreich Dr, Bonny. *EH19*	56	BS27
Pendreich Gro, Bonny. *EH19*	56	BS27
Pendreich Ter, Bonny. *EH19*	56	BS27
Pendreich Vw, Bonny. *EH19*	56	BS27
PENICUIK	69	BB39
Penicuik High Sch *EH26*	68	BA38
Penicuik Rd, Ros. *EH25*	67	BF32
Pennywell Cotts *EH4*	13	AX5
Pennywell Ct *EH4*	13	AX6
Pennywell Gdns *EH4*	13	AW6
Pennywell Gro *EH4*	13	AX6
Pennywell Medway *EH4*	13	AW6
Pennywell Pl *EH4*	13	AX6
Pennywell Rd *EH4*	13	AX6
Pennywell Vil *EH4*	13	AX5
Pentland Av *EH13*	50	AV21
Pentland Av, Currie *EH14*	49	AP23
Pentland Av (Gowks.), Gore. *EH23*	65	BX32
Pentland Av, Pen. *EH26*	68	BA37
Pentland Br *EH10*	61	BG26
Pentland Caravan Pk, Lnhd *EH20*	61	BG27
Pentland Ct (Bils.), Ros. *EH25*	61	BG29
Pentland Cres *EH10*	52	BC20
Pentland Cres, Rose. *EH24*	62	BM32
Pentland Dr *EH10*	52	BB21
Pentland Gait *EH11*	39	AR18
Pentland Gdns *EH10*	52	BC20
Pentland Gro *EH10*	52	BC20
Pentland Ind Est, Lnhd *EH20*	54	BJ27
Pentland Pl, Currie *EH14*	49	AP23
Pentland Rd *EH13*	51	AW20
Pentland Rd, Bonny. *EH19*	63	BP29
Pentland Ter *EH10*	42	BC19
Pentland Ter, Pen. *EH26*	68	BA37
Pentland Vw *EH10*	52	BC21
Pentland Vw, Currie *EH14*	49	AP23
Pentland Vw, Dalk. *EH22*	57	BY25
Pentland Vw Ct, Currie *EH14* 1	49	AQ23
Pentland Vw Cres, Ros. *EH25*	67	BH32
Pentland Vw Pl, Ros. *EH25*	67	BH32
Pentland Vw Rd, K'lis. *EH29*	20	AC10
Pentland Vw Rd, Ros. *EH25*	67	BH32
Pentland Vw Ter, Ros. *EH25*	67	BH32
Pentland Vil, Jun. Grn *EH14* 1	50	AT22
People's Story Museum, The *EH8* 13	7	BG11
Perdrixknowe *EH14*	41	AZ16
Persevere Ct *EH6*	15	BH5
Perth St *EH3*	26	BD9
Pettigrew's Cl, Dalk. *EH22* 3	57	BW24
Peveril Ter *EH16*	44	BJ19
Philip Pl, Pen. *EH26*	68	BA36
Picardy Pl *EH1*	7	BG10
Pier Pl *EH6*	15	BE4
Piersfield Gro *EH8*	28	BM10
Piersfield Pl *EH8*	28	BM10
Piersfield Ter *EH8*	28	BM10
PIERSHILL	28	BM11
Piershill La *EH8* 3	28	BL10
Piershill Pl *EH8* 4	28	BL10
Piershill Sq E *EH8*	28	BM10
Piershill Sq W *EH8*	28	BL10
Piershill Ter *EH8*	28	BM11
Pillars, The *EH17*	44	BM20
PILRIG	15	BG7
Pilrig Cotts *EH6*	27	BH8
Pilrig Gdns *EH6*	15	BG7
Pilrig Glebe *EH6*	27	BH8
Pilrig Ho Cl *EH6*	15	BG7
Pilrig Ind Est *EH6*	15	BG7
Pilrig Park Sch *EH6*	15	BG7
Pilrig Pl *EH6*	27	BH8
Pilrig St *EH6*	15	BG7
PILTON	13	AZ6
Pilton Av *EH5*	13	AZ6
Pilton Cres *EH5*	14	BB6
Pilton Dr *EH5*	14	BA6
Pilton Dr N *EH5*	14	BA5
Pilton Gdns *EH5*	14	BB6
Pilton Ln *EH5*	14	BA6
Pilton Pk *EH5*	14	BA6
Pilton Pl *EH5*	14	BA6
Pine Gro Gdns *EH4*	23	AR9
Pinewood Pl (Mayf.), Dalk. *EH22*	71	CA29
Pinewood Rd (Mayf.), Dalk. *EH22*	71	CA29
Pinewood Vw (Mayf.), Dalk. *EH22*	71	CA29
Pinkhill *EH12*	24	AV13
PINKIE	32	CB14
Pinkie Av, Muss. *EH21*	32	CA14
Pinkie Dr, Muss. *EH21*	32	CA14
Pinkie Hill Cres, Muss. *EH21*	32	CA14
Pinkie Pl, Muss. *EH21*	32	CA14
Pinkie Rd, Muss. *EH21*	32	CA14
Pinkie St. Peter's Prim Sch *EH21*	32	CA13
Pinkie Ter, Muss. *EH21*	32	CA14
Pinkie Wk, Tran. *EH33* 7	35	CL14
Pipe La *EH15*	29	BQ10
Pipe St *EH15*	29	BQ10
Pirniefield Bk *EH6*	16	BL7
Pirniefield Gdns *EH6*	16	BL7
Pirniefield Gro *EH6*	16	BL7
Pirniefield Pl *EH6*	16	BL7
Pirniefield Ter *EH6*	16	BL7
Pirniehall Prim Sch *EH4*	13	AY6
Pirrie St *EH6*	15	BH7
Pitlochry Pl *EH7*	16	BJ9
Pitsligo Rd *EH10*	42	BD15
Pittencrieff Ct, Muss. *EH21* 1	32	CB13
Pitt St *EH6*	15	BF6
Pittville St *EH15*	29	BR11
Pittville St La *EH15*	29	BR11
Place Charente, Dalk. *EH22*	57	BY24
Platinum Pt *EH6*	15	BF3
Playfair Steps *EH2* 1	6	BE11
Playhouse Theatre *EH1*	7	BG10
Pleasance *EH8*	7	BG12
Pleasance Theatre *EH8*	7	BG12
Plewlandcroft, S Q'fry *EH30*	8	AD2
Plewlands Av *EH10*	42	BB17
Plewlands Gdns *EH10*	42	BB17
Plewlands Pl, S Q'fry *EH30*	8	AD3
Plewlands Ter *EH10*	42	BB17

Name	Page	Grid
Pleydell Pl *EH16*	44	BK19
Plough La, Tran. *EH33* 2	35	CM13
Plummer Ct; Dalk. *EH22* 2	57	BW24
Poetry Lib *EH8*	7	BH11
Point Hotel *EH3*	6	BD12
Pollard Glebe *EH11*	41	AW15
Polson Gdns, Tran. *EH33*	34	CK13
POLTON	62	BM29
Polton Av Rd, Bonny. *EH19*	63	BP29
Polton Bk, Lass. *EH18*	63	BN29
Polton Bk Ter, Lass. *EH18*	63	BN29
Polton Cotts, Lass. *EH18*	62	BM29
Polton Ct, Bonny. *EH19*	63	BP29
Polton Dr, Lass. *EH18*	63	BP29
Polton Gdns, Lass. *EH18*	63	BQ28
POLTONHALL	63	BP29
Poltonhall, Bonny. *EH19* 2	63	BQ30
Polton Pl, Bonny. *EH19*	63	BR28
Polton Rd, Lass. *EH18*	63	BQ28
Polton Rd (Polt.), Lass. *EH18*	62	BM29
Polton Rd, Lnhd *EH20*	62	BL28
Polton Rd W, Lass. *EH18*	63	BN29
Polton St, Bonny. *EH19*	63	BR29
Polton Ter, Lass. *EH18* 1	63	BQ28
Polton Vale, Lnhd *EH20*	62	BL28
POLWARTH	42	BA14
Polwarth Cres *EH11*	42	BC14
Polwarth Cres, Pres. *EH32*	18	CJ10
Polwarth Gdns *EH11*	42	BB14
Polwarth Gro *EH11*	42	BB15
Polwarth Pk *EH11*	42	BB14
Polwarth Pl *EH11*	42	BB14
Polwarth Ter *EH11*	42	BB15
Polwarth Ter, Pres. *EH32*	18	CJ10
Pomathorn Bk, Pen. *EH26*	69	BB39
Pomathorn Rd, Pen. *EH26*	69	BB39
Ponton St *EH3*	6	BD13
Poplar La *EH6*	16	BJ6
Poplar Pk (Port S.), Pres. *EH32*	19	CM8
Poplar Path, Lnhd *EH20*	61	BH28
Poplar St (Mayf.), Dalk. *EH22*	71	CA29
Poplar Ter, Bonny. *EH19*	63	BR29
PORT EDGAR	8	AB1
Port Edgar Marina & Sailing Sch *EH30*	8	AC1
Porterfield Rd *EH4*	26	BA8
Portgower Pl *EH4*	26	BC9
Port Hamilton *EH3*	6	BD12
Portland Gdns *EH6*	15	BG6
Portland Pl *EH6*	15	BG5
Portland Row *EH6*	15	BG5
Portland St *EH6*	15	BG5
Portland Ter *EH6* 3	15	BG5
PORTOBELLO	29	BR10
Portobello High Sch *EH15*	29	BP12
Portobello High St *EH15*	29	BQ10
Portobello Pubic Golf Course *EH15*	29	BQ12
Portobello Rd *EH8*	28	BM10
Port Royal Golf Range *EH28*	21	AH12
Portsburgh Sq *EH1* 5	6	BE12
Port Seton Harbour (Port S.), Pres. *EH32*	19	CL7
Post Rd, Tran. *EH33*	34	CJ13
POST SETON	19	CL6
Potterrow *EH8*	7	BF12
Potter's Path, Tran. *EH33* 4	35	CL13
Pottery, The *EH15* 14	29	BQ10
Pottery, The, Pres. *EH32*	18	CG10
Povert Rd, Bonny. *EH19*	64	BV33
Povert Rd, Gore. *EH23*	64	BV34
Powderhall Brae *EH7*	15	BF7
Powderhall Rigg *EH7*	15	BF7
Powderhall Rd *EH7*	27	BF8
Powdermill Brae, Gore. *EH23*	70	BY37
Premier Lodge (Edinburgh East) *EH21*	30	BT15
PRESTON	34	CJ11
Preston Av, Pres. *EH32*	18	CK10
Preston Ct, Pres. *EH32*	34	CH11
Preston Cres, Pres. *EH32*	18	CK9
Preston Cross Cotts, Pres. *EH32* 3	18	CJ10
PRESTONFIELD	28	BK15
Prestonfield Av *EH16*	28	BJ15
Prestonfield Bk *EH16*	28	BJ15
Prestonfield Cres *EH16*	28	BJ15
Prestonfield Gdns *EH16*	28	BJ15
Prestonfield Golf Course *EH16*	28	BJ14
Prestonfield House Hotel *EH16*	28	BK14
Prestonfield Prim Sch *EH16*	44	BK16
Prestonfield Rd *EH16*	28	BJ15
Prestonfield Ter *EH16*	28	BJ15
Prestongrange, Pres. *EH32*	33	CF11
Prestongrange Museum *EH32*	33	CE11
Prestongrange Ter, Pres. *EH32*	34	CG11
Prestonhall Cres, Rose. *EH24*	62	BM32
Prestonhall Rd, Rose. *EH24*	62	BM33
Preston Lodge High Sch *EH32*	18	CJ10
PRESTONPANS	18	CG9
Prestonpans Ind Est, Pres. *EH32*	34	CJ11
Prestonpans Inf Sch *EH32*	18	CH10
Prestonpans Prim Sch *EH32*	34	CJ11
Prestonpans Sta *EH32*	34	CJ11
Preston Rd, Pres. *EH32*	34	CH11
Preston St, Rose. *EH24*	62	BM33
Preston Street Prim Sch *EH16*	43	BH14
Preston Ter, Pres. *EH32*	18	CK10
Priestfield Av *EH16*	28	BK15
Priestfield Cres *EH16*	28	BK15
Priestfield Gdns *EH16*	28	BK15
Priestfield Gro *EH16*	28	BJ14
Priestfield Rd *EH16*	28	BJ15
Priestfield Rd N *EH16*	28	BJ14
Primrose Bk Rd *EH5*	14	BD5
Primrose Cres, Dalk. *EH22*	57	BY25
Primrose Dr (Craig.), S Q'fry *EH30*	22	AM8
Primrose Gdns, S Q'fry *EH30*	9	AE3
Primrose St *EH6*	16	BJ7
Primrose Ter *EH11*	42	BA14
Primrose Ter, Dalk. *EH22* 1	57	BY25
Prince of Wales Dock *EH6*	15	BH4
Prince Regent St *EH6*	15	BG5
Princes Mall *EH2*	7	BF11
Princes Mall *EH1*	7	BF11
Princess Alexandra Eye Pavilion *EH3*	6	BE13
Princes St *EH1*	6	BE11
Princes St *EH2*	6	BE11
Priory Gro, S Q'fry *EH30*	8	AD3
Private Rd, Gore. *EH23*	70	BZ36
Promenade *EH15*	17	BP8
Promenade, Muss. *EH21*	31	BX12
Promenade, The (Port S.), Pres. *EH32*	19	CM7
Promenade Ter *EH15*	29	BQ10
Prospect Bk Cres *EH6*	16	BK7
Prospect Bk Gdns *EH6*	16	BK8
Prospect Bk Gro *EH6*	16	BL7
Prospect Bk Pl *EH6*	16	BL7
Prospect Bk Rd *EH6*	16	BK7
Prospect Bank Sch *EH6*	16	BK7
Prospect Bk Ter *EH6*	16	BL7
Provost Haugh, Currie *EH14*	49	AR22
Provost Milne Gro, S Q'fry *EH30*	9	AF4
Pryde Av, Bonny. *EH19*	63	BQ28
Pryde Ter, Bonny. *EH19*	63	BQ28
Pypers Wynd, Pres. *EH32*	18	CH9

Q

Name	Page	Grid
Quadrant, The, Pen. *EH26*	69	BB37
Quality Hotel Edinburgh Airport, The *EH28*	21	AG12
Quality St *EH4*	24	AV8
Quality St La *EH4*	24	AV8
Quarrybank *EH14*	40	AS19
Quarrybank Cl *EH14*	40	AS19
Quarrybank Ct *EH14*	40	AS19
Quarrybank End *EH14*	40	AS19
Quarry Cl *EH8*	7	BG13
Quarry Cotts *EH15*	29	BR15
Quarryfoot Gdns, Bonny. *EH19*	63	BR28
Quarryfoot Grn, Bonny. *EH19*	56	BS28
Quarryfoot Pl, Bonny. *EH19*	63	BR28
QUARRYHEAD		
Quarry Howe, Bal. *EH14* 1	58	AL26
Quarryview *EH14* 1	40	AS19
Quayside Mills *EH6* 3	15	BH6
Quayside St *EH6*	15	BH6
Queen Anne Dr, Newbr. *EH28*	36	AD13
Queen Charlotte La *EH6*	16	BJ6
Queen Charlotte St *EH6*	16	BJ6
Queen Margaret Cl *EH10*	53	BE22
Queen Margaret Dr, S Q'fry *EH30*	9	AE2
Queen Margaret Uni Coll (Corstorphine Campus) *EH12*	24	AT11
Queen Margaret Uni Coll (Leith Campus) *EH6*	16	BJ7
Queen's Av *EH4*	25	AX9
Queen's Av S *EH4*	25	AY9
Queen's Bay Cres *EH15*	30	BT12
Queen's Cres *EH9*	43	BH15
Queen's Dr *EH8*	7	BH12
Queensferry High Sch *EH30*	9	AF3
Queensferry Mus *EH30*	9	AE2
Queensferry Prim Sch *EH30*	9	AE2
Queensferry Rd *EH4*	26	BB10
Queensferry Rd (Cram.) *EH4*	24	AS9
Queensferry Rd, K'lis. *EH29*	20	AC9
Queensferry St *EH2*	6	BC11
Queensferry St La *EH2*	6	BC11
Queensferry Ter *EH4*	26	BA10
Queen's Gall (Palace of Holyroodhouse) *EH8*	7	BH11
Queen's Gdns *EH4*	25	AY9
Queen's Pk Av *EH8*	28	BK10
Queen's Pk Ct *EH8*	28	BL11
Queen's Rd *EH4*	25	AY9

Queens's Hall Thea EH8   7   BG13
Queen St EH2   6   BD10
Queen St Gdns E EH3   6   BE10
Queen St Gdns W EH3   6   BE10
Queen's Wk EH16   29   BN15
Queensway, Pen. EH26   68   BA36
Quilts, The EH6   15   BG6
Quilts Wynd EH6   15   BG6

R

Raeburn Ms EH4   26   BC9
Raeburn Pl EH4   26   BC9
Raeburn St EH4   26   BC9
Rae's Ct EH16   54   BJ22
Raes Gdns, Bonny. EH19   63   BR28
Ramada Jarvis Edinburgh Murrayfield EH12   25   AY12
Ramillies Ct, Pen. EH26   66   BC35
Ramsay Cres (Mayf.), Dalk. EH22   71   CA30
Ramsay Gdn EH1   6   BE11
Ramsay La EH1   6   BE11
Ramsay Pl EH15 9   29   BQ10
Ramsay Pl, Pen. EH26   68   AY37
Ramsay Ter, Lass. EH18   63   BP29
Ramsay Wk (Mayf.), Dalk. EH22 4   71   CA30
Randolph Cliff EH3   6   BC11
Randolph Cres EH3   6   BC11
Randolph La EH3   6   BD11
Randolph Pl EH3   6   BD11
Rankeillor St EH8   7   BG13
Rankin Av EH9   43   BH17
Rankin Dr EH9   43   BG17
Rankin Rd EH9   43   BH16
Rannoch Gro EH4   24   AT10
Rannoch Pl EH4   24   AT10
Rannoch Rd EH4   24   AU10
Rannoch Ter EH4   24   AT10
Ransome Gdns EH4   24   AT10
Ratcliffe Ter EH9   43   BG14
RATHO   37   AG17
Ratho Pk (Ratho Sta), Newbr. EH28   37   AE13
Ratho Park Golf Course EH28   38   AJ17
Ratho Pk Rd (Ratho), Newbr. EH28   37   AG17
Ratho Prim Sch EH28   37   AF17
RATHO STATION   37   AF14
Ravelrig Gait, Bal. EH14   58   AK25
Ravelrig Hill, Bal. EH14   58   AK25
Ravelrig Pk, Bal. EH14   58   AK25
Ravelrig Rd, Bal. EH14   48   AK22
RAVELSTON   25   AY10
Ravelston Ct EH12   25   AZ11
Ravelston Dykes EH4   25   AZ11
Ravelston Dykes EH12   25   AY11
Ravelston Dykes La EH4   25   AW11
Ravelston Dykes Rd EH4   25   AX10
Ravelston Gdn EH4   25   AY11
Ravelston Golf Course EH4   25   AX10
Ravelston Hts EH4   25   AY10
Ravelston Ho Gro EH4   25   AY10
Ravelston Ho Ln EH4   25   AY10
Ravelston Ho Pk EH4   25   AY10
Ravelston Ho Rd EH4   25   AY10
Ravelston Pk EH4   26   BA11
Ravelston Pl EH4 4   25   BB11
Ravelston Ri EH4   25   AY11
Ravelston Ter EH4   26   BB10
Ravelsykes Rd, Pen. EH26   68   AY38

Ravendean Gdns, Pen. EH26   68   AY38
Ravenscroft Gdns EH17   55   BN22
Ravenscroft Pl EH17   55   BN22
Ravenscroft St EH17   55   BN22
Ravensheugh Cres, Muss. EH21   32   CC13
Ravensheugh Rd, Muss. EH21   32   CC13
Ravenswood Av EH16   44   BK18
Real Mary King's Cl EH1 7   7   BF11
Redbraes Gro EH7   15   BF7
Redbraes Pl EH7   15   BF7
Redburn Rd, Pres. EH32   18   CG10
Redburn Rd N, Pres. EH32   18   CG10
Redcroft St, Dalk. EH22   45   BQ19
Redford Av EH13   51   AX21
Redford Bk EH13   51   AY21
Redford Barracks EH13   51   AY20
Redford Cres EH13   51   AY21
Redford Dr EH13   51   AX21
Redford Gdns EH13   51   AY21
Redford Gro EH13   51   AZ20
Redford Ln EH13   51   AX21
Redford Neuk EH13   51   AZ21
Redford Rd EH13   52   BA21
Redford Ter EH13   51   AY21
Red Fox Cres, Pen. EH26   66   BC34
Redgauntlet Ter EH16   44   BK18
Redhall Av EH14   41   AW17
Redhall Bk Rd EH14   41   AX18
Redhall Cres EH14   41   AW17
Redhall Dr EH14   41   AW17
Redhall Gdns EH14   41   AW17
Redhall Gro EH14   41   AW17
Redhall Ho Dr EH14   41   AY18
Redhall Pl EH14   41   AW17
Redhall Rd EH14   41   AW17
Redhall Vw EH14   41   AX18
Redheugh Ln, Gore. EH23 2   70   BY34
Redheughs Av EH12   39   AQ15
Redheughs Rigg EH12   39   AQ14
Redwood Gro (Newt.), Dalk. EH22   64   BV30
Redwood Wk (Newt.), Dalk. EH22   65   BW30
Reed Dr (Newt.), Dalk. EH22   65   BX29
Reekie's Ct EH8   7   BG12
Regent Br EH1 2   7   BF10
Regent Pl EH7   28   BJ10
Regent Rd EH1   7   BG10
Regent Rd EH7   7   BG10
Regent's Ct EH11 1   26   BB13
Regent St EH15   29   BR11
Regent St La EH15   29   BR11
Regent Ter EH7   7   BG10
Regent Ter Ms EH7   7   BH10
Regis Ct EH4   23   AR7
Register Pl EH2   7   BF10
Reid's Cl EH8   7   BH11
Reid's Ct EH8 1   7   BH11
Reid Ter EH3   26   BC9
Relugas Gdns EH9   43   BG16
Relugas Pl EH9   43   BG16
Relugas Rd EH9   43   BG16
Rennie's Isle EH6   15   BH5
Research Av N (Ricc.), Currie EH14   49   AN19
Research Av S (Ricc.), Currie EH14   49   AP20
RESTALRIG   16   BL9

Restalrig Av EH7   28   BL10
Restalrig Circ EH7   16   BL8
Restalrig Cres EH7   16   BL8
Restalrig Dr EH7   16   BL9
Restalrig Gdns EH7   16   BL9
Restalrig Pk EH7   16   BK8
Restalrig Rd EH6   16   BK7
Restalrig Rd EH7   16   BK8
Restalrig Rd S EH7   28   BL10
Restalrig Sq EH7   16   BL8
Restalrig Ter EH6   16   BJ7
RICCARTON   49   AN20
Riccarton Av, Currie EH14   49   AP22
Riccarton Cres, Currie EH14   49   AQ22
Riccarton Dr, Currie EH14   49   AQ22
Riccarton Gro, Currie EH14   49   AQ22
Riccarton Mains Rd, Currie EH14   39   AP18
Riccarton Prim Sch EH14   49   AQ23
Richard Corsie Leisure EH15   30   BT13
Richmond La EH8   7   BG12
Richmond Pl EH8   7   BG12
Richmond Ter EH11   6   BC12
Riding Pk EH4   23   AR7
Riego St EH3   6   BD12
Rigley Ter, Pres. EH32   34   CG11
Rillbank Cres EH9   43   BF14
Rillbank Ter EH9   43   BF14
Ringwood Pl EH16   44   BK19
Rintoul Pl EH3   26   BD9
Riselaw Cres EH10   52   BC20
Riselaw Pl EH10   42   BC19
Riselaw Rd EH10   42   BC19
Riselaw Ter EH10   42   BC19
Ritchie Pl EH11   42   BB14
River Gore Gro, Gore. EH23   70   BY35
River Gore Rd, Gore. EH23   70   BY35
River Gore Vw, Gore. EH23   70   BY35
Riversdale Cres EH12   25   AY13
Riversdale Gro EH12   25   AY12
Riversdale Rd EH12   25   AX12
Riverside EH4 1   11   AR4
Riverside, Newbr. EH28   36   AB13
Riverside Gdns, Muss. EH21   31   BX14
Riverside Rd (Craig.), S Q'fry EH30   23   AN8
Roanshead Rd (Easth.), Dalk. EH22   57   BY27
Robb's Ln EH14   41   AY15
Robb's Ln Gro EH14   41   AY15
Robert Burns Dr EH16   44   BJ18
Robert Burns Ms, Dalk. EH22 1   57   BZ24
Robert William Av (Mayf.), Dalk. EH22   71   CA30
Robertson Av EH11   41   AZ14
Robertson Av, Pres. EH32   18   CJ9
Robertson Av, Tran. EH33   35   CM13
Robertson Bk, Gore. EH23   70   BZ36
Robertson Dr, Tran. EH33   35   CM12
Robertson's Cl EH1   7   BG12
Robertson's Cl, Dalk. EH22   57   BW24
Robertson's Ct EH8 2   7   BH11
Rocheid Pk EH4   14   BB7
Rocheid Path EH3   26   BD8
Rochester Ter EH10   42   BC15
Rockville Ter, Bonny. EH19   55   BR27
Roddinglaw Rd EH12   38   AK15
Rodney Pl EH7   27   BE9
Rodney St EH7   27   BE8
Romero Pl EH16   43   BH14
Ronaldson's Wf EH6   15   BH6
Rope Wk, Pres. EH32   18   CG10

Name		
Rosabelle Rd, Ros. *EH25*	67	BH32
Rose Av, Bonny. *EH19*	64	BT29
Rosebank Cotts *EH3*	6	BC12
Rosebank Gdns *EH5*	14	BC6
Rosebank Gro *EH5*	14	BC6
Rosebank Rd *EH5*	14	BC6
Rosebery Av, S Q'fry *EH30*	9	AE3
Rosebery Ct, S Q'fry *EH30*	9	AE3
Rosebery Cres *EH12*	26	BB12
Rosebery Cres, Gore. *EH23*	70	BY37
Rosebery Cres La *EH12*	26	BB12
ROSEBURN	25	AZ12
Roseburn Av *EH12*	25	AZ12
Roseburn Cliff *EH12*	25	AZ12
Roseburn Cres *EH12*	25	AZ13
Roseburn Dr *EH12*	25	AZ12
Roseburn Gdns *EH12* **2**	25	AZ12
Roseburn Maltings *EH12*	26	BA12
Roseburn Pl *EH12*	25	AZ12
Roseburn Prim Sch *EH12*	25	AZ13
Roseburn St *EH12*	25	AZ13
Roseburn Ter *EH12*	25	AZ12
Rose Cotts, Bonny. *EH19*	64	BT29
Rose Ct *EH4* **7**	12	AU7
Rosefield Av *EH15*	29	BQ11
Rosefield Av La *EH15*	29	BQ11
Rosefield La *EH15*	29	BQ11
Rosefield Pl *EH15*	29	BQ11
Rosefield St *EH15*	29	BQ11
Rose Gdns, Bonny. *EH19*	64	BT29
Rose Gro, Bonny. *EH19*	64	BT29
Rose La, S Q'fry *EH30*	8	AD2
Rosemount Bldgs *EH3*	6	BC12
Rosemount Ms, Pres. *EH32* **4**	18	CH9
Roseneath Pl *EH9*	43	BE14
Roseneath St *EH9*	43	BF14
Roseneath Ter *EH9*	43	BF14
Rose Neuk, Bonny. *EH19*	64	BT29
Rose Pk *EH5*	14	BD6
Rose Pk, Bonny. *EH19*	64	BT29
Rose Path, Bonny. *EH19*	64	BT29
Rose Pl, Bonny. *EH19*	64	BT29
Rose St *EH2*	6	BD11
Rose St N La *EH2*	6	BD11
Rose St S La *EH2*	6	BD11
Rose Ter, Bonny. *EH19*	64	BT29
Rosevale Pl *EH6* **1**	16	BK7
Rosevale Ter *EH6*	16	BJ7
Roseville Gdns *EH5*	15	BE5
Rose Way, Bonny. *EH19*	64	BT29
ROSEWELL	62	BL33
Rosewell Prim Sch *EH24*	63	BN33
Rosewell Rd, Bonny. *EH19*	63	BP31
ROSLIN	67	BH32
Roslin Prim Sch *EH25*	67	BH32
Ross Cres, Tran. *EH33*	35	CM14
Ross Gdns *EH9*	43	BG16
Rossglen Ct, Ros. *EH25*	62	BJ32
Ross High Sch *EH33*	35	CL13
Rosshill Ter (Dalm.), S Q'fry *EH30*	9	AF3
Rossie Pl *EH7*	27	BH9
Rosslyn Chapel *EH25*	62	BJ32
Rosslyn Cres *EH6*	27	BG8
Rosslyn Ter *EH6*	27	BG8
Ross Open Air Theatre *EH2*	6	BE11
Ross Pl *EH9*	43	BH16
Ross Pl (Newt.), Dalk. *EH22*	65	BX29
Ross Rd *EH16*	43	BH16
Rothesay Ms *EH3*	26	BB11
Rothesay Pl *EH3*	26	BB11
Rothesay Pl, Muss. *EH21*	31	BZ14
Rothesay Ter *EH3*	26	BB11
Roull Gro *EH12*	40	AT14
Roull Pl *EH12*	40	AU14
Roull Rd *EH12*	40	AT14
Rowallan Ct *EH12* **2**	23	AQ12
Rowanfield Sch *EH4*	25	AY8
Rowan Gdns, Bonny. *EH19*	63	BR29
Rowanhill Cl (Port S.), Pres. *EH32*	19	CM8
Rowanhill Dr (Port S.), Pres. *EH32*	19	CM8
Rowanhill Pk (Port S.), Pres. *EH32*	19	CL8
Rowanhill Way (Port S.), Pres. *EH32*	19	CM8
Rowan Tree Av, Currie *EH14*	49	AN23
Rowan Tree Gro, Currie *EH14*	49	AN24
Rowantree Rd (Mayf.), Dalk. *EH22*	71	CA28
Roxburghe Hotel *EH2*	6	BD11
Roxburgh Pl *EH8*	7	BG12
Roxburgh St *EH8*	7	BG12
Royal Blind Sch (Canaan Lane) *EH10*	42	BD16
Royal Blind Sch (Craigmillar Park) *EH16*	43	BH16
Royal Botanic Gardens Edinburgh *EH3*	26	BD8
Royal British Hotel *EH2*	7	BF10
Royal Burgess Golf Course *EH4*	23	AR8
Royal Circ *EH3*	6	BD10
Royal Coll of Nursing *EH9*	43	BE16
Royal Commonwealth Pool *EH16*	43	BH14
Royal Ct, Pen. *EH26*	68	AZ36
Royal Cres *EH3*	27	BE9
Royal (Dick) Sch of Veterinary Studies (Easter Bush) *EH25*	61	BE30
Royal (Dick) Sch of Veterinary Studies (Summerhall) *EH9*	7	BG13
Royal Edinburgh Hosp *EH10*	42	BC16
Royal Elizabeth Yd, K'lis. *EH29*	9	AG6
Royal High Prim Sch *EH8*	28	BM11
Royal High Sch, The *EH4*	24	AT8
Royal Hosp for Sick Children *EH9*	43	BF14
Royal Infirmary of Edinburgh (Little France) *EH16*	45	BN17
Royal Lyceum Theatre *EH1*	6	BD12
Royal Mile *EH1*	6	BE11
Royal Mile Prim Sch *EH8*	7	BH11
Royal Mus *EH1*	7	BF12
Royal Pk Pl *EH8*	28	BK10
Royal Pk Ter *EH8*	28	BK10
Royal Scots Dragoon Guards Museum (Edinburgh Castle) *EH1*	6	BE12
Royal Scots Mus (Edinburgh Castle) *EH1*	6	BE12
Royal Scottish Academy *EH2*	6	BE11
Royal Ter *EH7*	7	BG10
Royal Ter Ms *EH7*	7	BH10
Royal Victoria Hosp *EH4*	26	BA9
Royal Yacht Britannia *EH6*	15	BH4
Royston Mains Av *EH5*	13	AZ5
Royston Mains Cl *EH5*	14	BA5
Royston Mains Cres *EH5*	13	AZ5
Royston Mains Gdns *EH5*	14	BA5
Royston Mains Grn *EH5*	14	BA5
Royston Mains Pl *EH5*	13	AZ5
Royston Mains Rd *EH5*	14	BA5
Royston Mains St *EH5*	13	AZ5
Royston Prim Sch *EH5*	14	BA5
Royston Ter *EH3*	14	BD7
Rudolf Steiner Sch *EH10*	42	BB15
Rullion Grn Av, Pen. *EH26*	68	AZ36
Rullion Grn Cres, Pen. *EH26*	68	AZ36
Rullion Grn Gro, Pen. *EH26*	68	AZ36
Rullion Rd, Pen. *EH26*	68	AZ36
Ruskin Pl (Mayf.), Dalk. *EH22* **1**	71	CA30
Russell Gdns *EH12*	26	BA12
Russell Pl *EH5*	14	BD5
Russell Rd *EH11*	26	BA13
Russell Rd *EH12*	26	BA12
Rustic Cotts *EH13* **1**	51	AX20
Rutherford Dr *EH16*	44	BK18
Ruthven Pl *EH16*	44	BK18
Rutland Ct *EH3* **2**	6	BD12
Rutland Ct La *EH3*	6	BD12
Rutland Pl *EH1* **1**	6	BD11
Rutland Sq *EH1*	6	BD11
Rutland St *EH1*	6	BD11
Ryehill Av *EH6*	16	BK7
Ryehill Gdns *EH6*	16	BK7
Ryehill Gro *EH6*	16	BK8
Ryehill Pl *EH6*	16	BK7
Ryehill Ter *EH6*	16	BK7

S

Name		
Sacred Heart RC Prim Sch *EH26*	68	AZ38
Saddletree Ln *EH16* **1**	44	BL17
St. Alban's Rd *EH9*	43	BG16
St. Andrew Pl *EH6*	16	BJ7
St. Andrew Sq *EH1*	7	BF10
St. Andrew Sq *EH2*	7	BF10
St. Andrew's RC Prim Sch *EH23*	65	BW32
St. Andrew St, Dalk. *EH22*	57	BW24
St. Annes Ct, Dalk. *EH22*	65	BW30
St. Annes Path, Lass. *EH18*	63	BN29
St. Ann's Av, Lass. *EH18*	63	BN29
St. Anthony La *EH6*	15	BH6
St. Anthony Pl *EH6* **5**	15	BH6
St. Anthony St *EH6* **6**	15	BH6
St. Augustine's RC High Sch *EH12*	40	AS15
St. Bernard's Cres *EH4*	6	BC10
St. Bernard's Row *EH4*	26	BD9
St. Catherine's Gdns *EH12*	25	AW13
St. Catherine's Pl *EH9*	43	BG14
St. Catherine's Prim Sch *EH16*	54	BK22
St. Clair Av *EH6*	16	BJ8
St. Clair Cres, Ros. *EH25*	62	BJ32
St. Clair Pl *EH6*	16	BJ8
St. Clair Rd *EH6*	16	BJ8
St. Clair St *EH6*	16	BJ8
St. Clair Ter *EH10*	42	BB17
St. Clements Cres (Wall.), Muss. *EH21* **1**	33	CD15
St. Clements Gdns N (Wall.), Muss. *EH21*	33	CD15
St. Clements Gdns S (Wall.), Muss. *EH21*	33	CD15
St. Clements Ter (Wall.), Muss. *EH21*	33	CD15
St. Colme St *EH3*	6	BD11
St. Crispin's Sch *EH9*	43	BG16
St. Cuthbert's RC Prim Sch *EH14*	41	AZ15

Name	Page	Grid
St. Davids (Newt.), Dalk. *EH22*	65	BW30
St. David's Pl *EH3* 9	6	BC12
St. David's RC High Sch *EH22*	47	BZ22
St. David's RC Prim Sch *EH4*	13	AY6
St. David's RC Prim Sch *EH22*	57	BY25
St. David's Ter *EH3* 10	6	BC12
St. Fillan's Ter *EH10*	42	BC17
St. Francis' RC Prim Sch *EH16*	29	BN15
St. Gabriel's RC Prim Sch *EH32*	18	CH10
St. George's Sch *EH12*	26	BA11
St. Giles Cath *EH1*	7	BF11
St. Giles' St *EH1*	7	BF11
St. James Cen *EH1*	7	BF10
St. James' St *EH1*	7	BF10
St. James's Gdns, Pen. *EH26*	68	BA39
St. James Shopping Centre *EH1*	7	BF10
St. James Sq *EH1*	7	BF10
St. James's Vw, Pen. *EH26*	68	BA39
St. John's Av *EH12*	24	AU13
St. John's Cres *EH12*	24	AV13
St. John's Gdns *EH12*	24	AU13
St. John's Hill *EH8* 9	7	BG12
St. John's RC Prim Sch *EH15*	29	BQ12
St. John's Rd *EH12*	24	AT13
St. John's Ter *EH12*	24	AU13
St. John St *EH8*	7	BG11
St. John Vianney RC Prim Sch *EH16*	44	BK18
St. Jospeh's RC Prim Sch *EH11*	40	AV16
St. Katharine's Brae *EH16*	44	BJ21
St. Katharine's Cres *EH16*	44	BJ21
St. Katharine's Ln *EH16*	54	BK22
St. Kentigern Rd, Pen. *EH26*	68	AZ37
St. Leonard's Bk *EH8*	7	BH13
St. Leonard's Crag *EH8* 1	7	BH13
St. Leonard's Hill *EH8*	7	BG13
St. Leonard's La *EH8*	7	BH13
St. Leonard's St *EH8*	7	BG13
St. Luke's RC Prim Sch *EH22*	65	BZ30
St. Margaret's Pl *EH9*	43	BE15
St. Margaret's RC Prim Sch *EH20*	54	BL27
St. Margaret's RC Prim Sch *EH30*	9	AE2
St. Margaret's Rd *EH9*	42	BD15
St. Margaret's Sch *EH16*	44	BJ16
St. Mark's La *EH15*	29	BR11
St. Mark's Pl *EH15*	29	BR11
St. Mark's RC Prim Sch *EH7*	52	BA20
St. Martins La, Tran. *EH33*	35	CN13
St. Martin's RC Prim Sch *EH33*	35	CM13
St. Mary's Episcopal Cath *EH12*	6	BC12
St. Mary's Music Sch *EH12*	26	BB12
St. Mary's Pl *EH15*	30	BS12
St. Mary's Pl La *EH15*	30	BS12
St. Mary's RC Prim Sch *EH6*	16	BK6
St. Mary's RC Prim Sch *EH7*	27	BF9
St. Mary's RC Prim Sch *EH19*	63	BR29
St. Mary's St *EH1*	7	BG11
St. Matthew's RC Prim Sch *EH24*	63	BN33
St. Michael's Av, Muss. *EH21*	31	BY14
St. Mungo's Vw, Pen. *EH26*	69	BB39
St. Nicholas Sch *EH11*	41	AZ14
St. Ninian's Dr *EH12*	24	AT12
St. Ninian's RC Prim Sch *EH7*	16	BL9
St. Ninian's Rd *EH12*	24	AT12
St. Ninian's Row *EH8* 3	7	BF10
St. Ninian's Ter *EH10*	42	BB17
St. Ninians Way, Muss. *EH21*	32	CC13
St. Patrick Sq *EH8*	7	BG13
St. Patrick St *EH8* 3	7	BG13
St. Peter's Bldgs *EH3*	6	BC13
St. Peter's Pl *EH3*	6	BC13
St. Peter's RC Prim Sch *EH10*	42	BD16
St. Ronan's Ter *EH10*	42	BC17
St. Serf's Sch *EH12*	26	BA12
St. Stephen Pl *EH3*	26	BD9
St. Stephen St *EH3*	26	BD9
St. Teresa Pl *EH10*	42	BB15
St. Thomas of Acquin's RC High Sch *EH3*	6	BE13
St. Thomas Rd *EH9*	43	BF15
St. Vincent St *EH3*	27	BE9
Salamanca Cres, Pen. *EH26*	66	BC35
Salamander Pl *EH6*	16	BK6
Salamander St *EH6*	16	BJ6
Salamander Yards *EH6*	16	BL7
Salisbury Crags *EH8*	7	BH12
Salisbury Ms *EH9*	43	BH14
Salisbury Pl *EH9*	43	BG14
Salisbury Rd *EH16*	43	BH14
Salisbury Vw (Mayf.), Dalk. *EH22*	65	BZ29
Salmond Pl *EH7*	16	BJ9
Saltersgate Spec Sch *EH22*	47	BZ22
Salter's Gro, Dalk. *EH22*	57	BY23
Salter's Rd, Dalk. *EH22*	47	BZ20
Salter's Rd (Wall.), Muss. *EH21*	32	CC16
Salter's Ter, Dalk. *EH22*	57	BY24
Salt Preston Pl, Pres. *EH32* 1	18	CH10
Salvesen Cres *EH4*	13	AW5
Salvesen Gdns *EH4*	13	AX5
Salvesen Gro *EH4*	13	AX5
Salvesen Ter *EH4*	13	AX5
Samoa Ter, Pen. *EH26*	66	BC35
Sanderson's Gro, Tran. *EH33*	35	CM12
Sanderson's Wynd, Tran. *EH33*	35	CM12
Sandford Gdns *EH15*	29	BQ11
Sand Port *EH6*	16	BJ5
Sandport Pl *EH6*	15	BH5
Sandport St *EH6*	15	BH5
Sandport Way *EH6*	15	BH6
Sauchiebank *EH11*	26	BA13
Saugh Cotts (Newt.), Dalk. *EH22*	65	BW31
SAUGHTON	41	AX14
Saughton Av *EH11*	41	AY15
Saughton Cres *EH12*	25	AX13
Saughton Gdns *EH12*	25	AX13
Saughton Gro *EH12*	25	AX13
SAUGHTONHALL	25	AX13
Saughtonhall Av *EH12*	25	AX13
Saughtonhall Av W *EH12*	25	AX13
Saughtonhall Circ *EH12*	25	AY13
Saughtonhall Cres *EH12*	25	AX13
Saughtonhall Dr *EH12*	25	AX12
Saughtonhall Gdns *EH12*	25	AY13
Saughtonhall Gro *EH12*	25	AY13
Saughtonhall Pl *EH12*	25	AX13
Saughtonhall Ter *EH12*	25	AY13
Saughton Ln *EH12*	25	AX13
Saughton Mains Av *EH11*	40	AV15
Saughton Mains Bk *EH11*	40	AV15
Saughton Mains Dr *EH11*	40	AV16
Saughton Mains Gdns *EH11*	40	AV16
Saughton Mains Gro *EH11*	41	AW16
Saughton Mains Ln *EH11*	40	AV16
Saughton Mains Pk *EH11*	40	AV15
Saughton Mains Pl *EH11*	40	AV16
Saughton Mains St *EH11*	40	AV15
Saughton Mains Ter *EH11*	40	AV15
Saughton Pk *EH12*	25	AX13
Saughton Rd *EH11*	40	AV15
Saughton Rd N *EH12*	40	AU14
Saunders St *EH3*	6	BD10
Savile Pl *EH9*	43	BH16
Savile Ter *EH9*	43	BH16
Saxe-Coburg Pl *EH3*	26	BD9
Saxe-Coburg St *EH3*	26	BD9
Saxe-Coburg Ter *EH3* 4	26	BD9
Scarlett Pk (Wall.), Muss. *EH21*	32	CC14
Schaw Rd, Pres. *EH32*	18	CK10
School Brae *EH4*	11	AR5
School Brae, Lass. *EH18*	55	BQ26
School Grn, Lass. *EH18*	55	BQ26
School La (Cock.), Pres. *EH32*	19	CL7
School Wynd (Ratho), Newbr. *EH28*	37	AF17
Schoolyard Ct, Ros. *EH25*	62	BJ32
Sciennes *EH9*	43	BG14
Sciennes Gdns *EH9*	43	BG14
Sciennes Hill Pl *EH9*	43	BG14
Sciennes Ho Pl *EH9*	43	BG14
Sciennes Pl *EH9* 2	43	BG14
Sciennes Prim Sch *EH9*	43	BF14
Sciennes Rd *EH9*	43	BF14
Scollon Av, Bonny. *EH19*	56	BS27
Scone Gdns *EH8*	28	BL10
Scotch Whisky Heritage Centre *EH1* 2	6	BE12
Scotland St *EH3*	27	BE9
Scotsman Hotel, The *EH1*	7	BF11
Scotstoun Av, S Q'fry *EH30*	9	AE3
Scotstoun Grn, S Q'fry *EH30*	8	AD3
Scotstoun Gro, S Q'fry *EH30* 2	9	AE3
Scotstoun Pk, S Q'fry *EH30*	9	AE4
Scottish Agricultural Coll (Bush Estate) *EH26*	60	BD31
Scottish Agricultural Coll (King's) *EH9*	43	BH18
Scottish Mining Museum *EH22*	65	BW31
Scottish National Gallery of Modern Art *EH4*	26	BA11
Scottish National Portrait Gallery *EH2*	7	BF10
Scottish Parliament Visitor Centre *EH1* 6	7	BF11
Scottish Storytelling Centre (Netherbow Arts Centre) *EH1* 12	7	BG11
Scott Monument *EH2*	7	BF11
Scott Rd, Pen. *EH26*	68	BA36
Scotway Cen, The, Dalk. *EH22*	46	BU19
Seacot *EH6* 1	16	BL7
SEAFIELD, Leith	16	BM7
SEAFIELD, Roslin	61	BF29

Seafield Av *EH6* 16 BL7
Seafield Cres (Bils.),
  Ros. *EH25* 61 BG29
Seafield Ind Est *EH15* 17 BP9
Seafield Moor Rd *EH10* 61 BE26
Seafield Pl *EH6* 16 BL7
Seafield Rd *EH6* 16 BL7
Seafield Rd (Bils.),
  Ros. *EH25* 61 BF29
Seafield Rd E *EH15* 17 BN8
Seafield St *EH6* 16 BM7
Seafield Way *EH15* 17 BN8
Seaforth Dr *EH4* 25 AY9
Seaforth Ter *EH4* 25 AY9
Seaforth Ter, Bonny. *EH19* 63 BP29
Sealcarr St *EH5* 14 BA4
Seaport St *EH6* **5** 16 BJ6
Seaview Cres *EH15* 30 BT12
Seaview Ter *EH15* 30 BT12
Second Gait (Ricc.),
  Currie *EH14* 49 AN19
Second St (Newt.),
  Dalk. *EH22* 65 BX30
Semple St *EH3* 6 BD12
SETON 19 CN9
Seton Collegiate Ch *EH32* 19 CP8
Seton Ct (Port S.), Pres. *EH32* 19 CN7
Seton Ct, Tran. *EH33* **8** 35 CL14
Seton Pl *EH9* 43 BG14
Seton Pl (Port S.), Pres. *EH32* 19 CM7
Seton Vw (Port S.),
  Pres. *EH32* 19 CN8
Seton Wynd (Port S.),
  Pres. *EH32* 19 CN7
Seventh St (Newt.),
  Dalk. *EH22* 65 BX30
Shadepark Cres, Dalk. *EH22* 57 BX23
Shadepark Dr, Dalk. *EH22* 57 BX23
Shadepark Gdns, Dalk. *EH22* 57 BX23
Shaftesbury Pk *EH11* 42 BA15
Shandon Cres *EH11* 42 BA15
Shandon Pl *EH11* 42 BA15
Shandon Rd *EH11* 42 BA15
Shandon St *EH11* 42 BA15
Shandon Ter *EH11* 42 BA15
Shandwick Pl *EH2* 6 BC12
Shanter Way *EH16* 44 BK18
Shaping a Nation &
  TurboVenture *EH11* 6 BC13
Sharpdale Ln *EH16* 44 BJ17
Shaw Pl (Mayf.), Dalk. *EH22* 57 BZ27
Shaws Ct (Milt.Br),
  Pen. *EH26* 66 BC34
Shaw's Cres (Milt.Br),
  Pen. *EH26* 66 BC34
Shaw's Pl *EH7* 27 BG8
Shaw's Sq *EH1* **2** 27 BG9
Shaw's St *EH7* 27 BG8
Shaw'sTer *EH7* 27 BG8
Sheraton Grand Hotel *EH3* 6 BD12
Sheriff Bk *EH6* 15 BH6
Sheriff Brae *EH6* 15 BH6
Sheriff Pk *EH6* 15 BH6
Sherwood Av, Bonny. *EH19* 64 BS29
Sherwood Ct, Bonny. *EH19* 64 BS29
Sherwood Cres, Bonny.
  EH19 64 BS29
Sherwood Dr, Bonny. *EH19* 64 BS29
Sherwood Gro, Bonny. *EH19* 64 BS29
Sherwood Ind Est, Bonny.
  EH19 56 BS28
Sherwood Ln, Bonny. *EH19* 64 BS29
Sherwood Pk, Bonny. *EH19* 64 BS29
Sherwood Pl, Bonny. *EH19* 64 BS29
Sherwood Ter, Bonny. *EH19* 64 BS29

Sherwood Vw, Bonny. *EH19* 64 BS29
Sherwood Wk, Bonny.
  EH19 **1** 64 BT29
Sherwood Way, Bonny. *EH19* 64 BS29
Shore *EH6* 16 BJ6
Shore Pl *EH6* 16 BJ6
Shore Rd, S Q'fry *EH30* 8 AD1
Shorthope St, Muss. *EH21* 31 BY13
Shrub Mt *EH15* 29 BQ10
Shrub Pl *EH7* 27 BG8
Shrub Pl La *EH7* 27 BG8
Sienna Gdns *EH9* 43 BG14
SIGHTHILL 40 AS17
Sighthill Av *EH11* 40 AU17
Sighthill Bk *EH11* 40 AT17
Sighthill Ct *EH11* 40 AT17
Sighthill Cres *EH11* 40 AT18
Sighthill Dr *EH11* 40 AT18
Sighthill Gdns *EH11* 40 AT17
Sighthill Grn *EH11* 40 AT17
Sighthill Gro *EH11* 40 AU17
Sighthill Ind Est *EH11* 40 AS17
Sighthill Ln *EH11* 40 AT17
Sighthill Neuk *EH11* 40 AT18
Sighthill Pk *EH11* 40 AT17
Sighthill Pl *EH11* 40 AT17
Sighthill Prim Sch *EH11* 40 AS18
Sighthill Ri *EH11* 40 AT18
Sighthill Rd *EH11* 40 AT18
Sighthill Shop Cen *EH11* 40 AT17
Sighthill St *EH11* 40 AT18
SighthillTer *EH11* 40 AT17
Sighthill Vw *EH11* 40 AT17
Sighthill Wynd *EH11* 40 AT17
Silverburn Dr, Pen. *EH26* 68 AY37
SILVERKNOWES 12 AV7
Silverknowes Av *EH4* 12 AU7
Silverknowes Bk *EH4* 12 AV7
Silverknowes Brae *EH4* 12 AV7
Silverknowes Ct *EH4* 12 AV7
Silverknowes Cres *EH4* 12 AV6
Silverknowes Dell *EH4* 13 AW7
Silverknowes Dr *EH4* 12 AV7
Silverknowes Eastway *EH4* 12 AV7
Silverknowes Gdns *EH4* 12 AV6
Silverknowes Golf Course
  EH4 12 AV6
Silverknowes Grn *EH4* 13 AW7
Silverknowes Gro *EH4* 12 AV6
Silverknowes Hill *EH4* 12 AV7
Silverknowes Ln *EH4* 12 AU7
Silverknowes Midway *EH4* 13 AW7
Silverknowes Neuk *EH4* 25 AW8
Silverknowes Parkway *EH4* 12 AV6
Silverknowes Pl *EH4* 12 AV6
Silverknowes Rd *EH4* 12 AV6
Silverknowes Rd E *EH4* 12 AV7
Silverknowes Rd S *EH4* 24 AV8
Silverknowes Southway *EH4* 13 AW7
SilverknowesTer *EH4* 12 AU7
Silverknowes Vw *EH4* 13 AW7
Silvermills *EH3* 26 BD9
Simon Sq *EH8* **4** 7 BG12
Simpsons Hotel *EH3* 6 BE12
Sinclair Cl *EH11* **2** 42 BA15
Sinclair Gdns *EH11* 42 BA14
Sinclair Pl *EH11* 41 AZ14
Sir Harry Lauder Rd *EH15* 29 BP10
Sir Walter Scott Pend, Pres.
  EH32 **1** 18 CH9
Sir William Fraser Homes
  EH13 51 AW20
Sixth St (Newt.), Dalk. *EH22* 65 BW30
Skeltiemuir Av, Bonny. *EH19* 63 BQ30
Skeltiemuir Ct, Bonny. *EH19* 63 BQ30

Skeltiemuir Gro, Bonny.
  EH19 63 BR30
Slaeside, Bal. *EH14* 58 AL26
SLATEFORD 41 AX17
Slateford Grn *EH14* 41 AZ16
Slateford Rd *EH11* 41 AZ15
Slateford Rd *EH14* 41 AY17
Slateford Rd Br *EH11* 42 BA15
Slateford Sta *EH14* 41 AY16
Slater's Steps *EH8* **6** 7 BH11
Sleigh Dr *EH7* 16 BK9
Sleigh Gdns *EH7* 16 BL9
Sloan St *EH6* 27 BH8
Smeaton Gro (Inv.),
  Muss. *EH21* 31 BZ15
Smithfield St *EH11* 41 AZ14
Smith's Land, S Q'fry
  EH30 **5** 9 AE2
Smith's Pl *EH6* 15 BH7
Smithy Grn Av (Dand.),
  Dalk. *EH22* 45 BQ20
Society Rd, S Q'fry *EH30* 8 AB1
Solicitor's Bldgs *EH1* **4** 7 BF12
Somerset Pl *EH6* 16 BJ7
Somers Pk, Tran. *EH33* 35 CL14
Sommerville Gdns, S Q'fry
  EH30 9 AF4
Sour Howe *EH13* 52 BB22
Southbank *EH4* **1** 12 AU7
Southbank Ct *EH4* **2** 12 AU7
South Barnton Av *EH4* 24 AU8
South Beechwood *EH12* 25 AW13
South Br *EH1* 7 BF11
South Br *EH8* 7 BF11
South Charlotte St *EH2* 6 BD11
South Clerk St *EH8* 7 BG13
South Coll St *EH8* 7 BF12
South Cres, Pres. *EH32* 18 CJ10
South Doors (Cock.),
  Pres. *EH32* 19 CL7
South E Circ Pl *EH3* **1** 6 BD10
South Elixa Pl *EH8* 28 BM11
South Ettrick Rd *EH10* 42 BB15
Southfield Bk *EH15* 29 BP13
Southfield Fm Gro *EH15* 29 BN12
Southfield Gdns E *EH15* 29 BP12
Southfield Gdns W *EH15* 29 BP13
Southfield Hosp *EH17* 44 BL20
Southfield Ln *EH15* 29 BP13
Southfield Pl *EH15* 29 BQ11
Southfield Rd E *EH15* 29 BP13
Southfield Rd W *EH15* 29 BN13
Southfield Sq *EH15* 29 BP13
SouthfieldTer *EH15* 29 BP13
Southfield Vil *EH15* **1** 29 BQ12
South Fort St *EH6* 15 BG6
South Gayfield La *EH1* 27 BG9
South Gillsland Rd *EH10* 42 BB15
South Gra Av, Pres. *EH32* 34 CG11
South Gray's Cl *EH1* 7 BG11
South Gray St *EH9* 43 BH15
South Groathill Av *EH4* 25 AY9
SOUTH GYLE 39 AR15
South Gyle Access *EH12* 40 AS15
South Gyle Bdy *EH12* 39 AR14
South Gyle Cres *EH12* 40 AS16
South Gyle Cres La *EH12* 39 AR15
South Gyle Gdns *EH12* 39 AR14
South Gyle Ind Est *EH12* 39 AR15
South Gyle Ln *EH12* 39 AR14
South Gyle Mains *EH12* 40 AS14
South Gyle Pk *EH12* 39 AR14
South Gyle Pk Business Est
  EH12 39 AR15
South Gyle Rd *EH12* 39 AR14

Entry	Map	Grid
South Gyle Wynd *EH12*	40	AS14
SOUTHHOUSE	54	BK23
Southhouse Av *EH17*	54	BK22
Southhouse Boundary *EH17*	54	BK22
Southhouse Bdy *EH17*	54	BK22
Southhouse Cres *EH17*	54	BK23
Southhouse Gdns *EH17*	54	BK23
Southhouse Gro *EH17*	54	BK23
Southhouse Ln *EH17*	54	BK22
Southhouse Medway *EH17*	54	BK22
Southhouse Path *EH17*	54	BK22
Southhouse Rd *EH17*	54	BJ22
Southhouse Sq *EH17* **1**	54	BK23
Southhouse Ter *EH17*	54	BK22
South Lauder Rd *EH9*	43	BG15
South Laverockbank Av *EH5*	15	BE5
Southlawn Ct *EH4* **3**	12	AU7
South Learmonth Av *EH4*	26	BB10
South Learmonth Gdns *EH4*	26	BB10
SOUTH LEITH	16	BJ8
South Lorimer Pl (Cock.), Pres. *EH32*	19	CL8
South Lorne Pl *EH6*	27	BH8
South Maybury *EH12*	39	AQ13
South Meadow Wk *EH9*	6	BE13
South Mellis Pk *EH8*	29	BN11
South Morningside Prim Sch *EH10*	42	BC18
South Morton St *EH15*	30	BS12
South Oswald Rd *EH9*	43	BE16
South Oxford St *EH8*	43	BH14
South Pk *EH6*	15	BF5
South Parrotshot *EH15*	29	BQ14
SOUTH QUEENSFERRY	9	AE1
South St. Andrew St *EH2*	7	BF10
South St. David St *EH2*	7	BF10
South Scotstoun, S Q'fry *EH30*	9	AE4
South Seton Pk (Port S.), Pres. *EH32*	19	CL8
South Sloan St *EH6*	27	BH8
South Steil *EH10*	42	BA19
South St, Dalk. *EH22*	57	BW24
South St, Muss. *EH21*	31	BX13
South Trinity Rd *EH5*	14	BD6
South Vw, Pres. *EH32* **1**	18	CJ10
Soutra Ct *EH16*	44	BK21
Spalding Cres, Dalk. *EH22*	57	BX24
Spa Pl *EH15* **7**	29	BQ10
Speedwell Av, Dalk. *EH22*	45	BQ19
Spencer Pl *EH5*	14	BD5
Spence St *EH16*	43	BH14
Spey St *EH7*	27	BG8
Spey St La *EH7*	27	BG8
Spey Ter *EH7*	27	BG8
Spier's Pl *EH6* **7**	15	BH6
Spinney, The *EH17*	44	BM21
Spittalfield Cres *EH8*	7	BG13
Spittal St *EH3*	6	BD12
Spittal St La *EH3* **3**	6	BE12
Spottiswoode Rd *EH9*	43	BE14
Spottiswoode St *EH9*	43	BE14
Springfield *EH6*	15	BG7
Springfield Bldgs *EH6* **3**	15	BH7
Springfield Cres, S Q'fry *EH30*	8	AB2
Springfield La *EH6*	15	BH7
Springfield Lea, S Q'fry *EH30*	8	AB2
Springfield Pl, Gore. *EH23*	70	BZ36
Springfield Pl, Ros. *EH25*	62	BJ31
Springfield Pl, S Q'fry *EH30*	8	AB2
Springfield Rd, S Q'fry *EH30*	8	AB2
Springfield St *EH6*	15	BH7
Springfield Ter, S Q'fry *EH30*	8	AB2
Springfield Vw, S Q'fry *EH30*	8	AB2
Spring Gdns *EH8*	28	BJ10
Springvalley Gdns *EH10*	42	BC16
Springvalley Ter *EH10*	42	BC16
Springwell Pl *EH11*	26	BB13
Springwell Ter, S Q'fry *EH30*	8	AD2
Springwood Pk *EH16*	44	BK19
Spruce Wk, Lnhd *EH20*	61	BG28
Spylaw Av *EH13*	50	AV20
Spylaw Bk Rd *EH13*	50	AV20
Spylaw Ho *EH13*	51	AW21
Spylaw Pk *EH13*	50	AV20
Spylaw Rd *EH10*	42	BB15
Spylaw St *EH13*	51	AW21
Square, The (Dand.), Dalk. *EH22*	45	BR19
Square, The (Newt.), Dalk. *EH22*	65	BX30
Square, The, K'lis. *EH29* **1**	20	AD10
Square, The, Pen. *EH26*	69	BB39
Stable Cor, Pres. *EH32*	18	CH9
Stable La *EH10*	42	BC16
Stafford St *EH3*	6	BC11
Stair Pk *EH12*	25	AY12
Stair Pk, Tran. *EH33*	34	CK12
Standingstane Rd (Dalm.), S Q'fry *EH30*	9	AG4
Stanedykehead *EH16*	53	BH21
Stanhope Pl *EH12*	26	BA12
Stanhope St *EH12*	26	BA12
Stanley Av (Bils.), Ros. *EH25*	61	BG29
Stanley Pl *EH7*	28	BJ10
Stanley Rd *EH6*	15	BE5
Stanley St *EH15*	29	BQ12
Stanwell St *EH6*	15	BH7
Stapeley Av *EH7*	17	BN9
Starbank Rd *EH5*	15	BE5
Stark's Cotts *EH13* **1**	52	BA20
Station Brae *EH15*	29	BQ11
Station Ln, Bal. *EH14*	48	AL24
Station Rd *EH12*	24	AU13
Station Rd, Dalk. *EH22*	56	BU25
Station Rd (Newt.), Dalk. *EH22*	65	BW29
Station Rd, Gore. *EH23*	70	BY36
Station Rd, K'lis. *EH29*	20	AD9
Station Rd, Lnhd *EH20*	54	BL27
Station Rd, Muss. *EH21*	31	BX14
Station Rd (Ratho Sta), Newbr. *EH28*	37	AE13
Station Rd, Pres. *EH32*	34	CJ11
Station Rd, Ros. *EH25*	62	BJ31
Station Rd, S Q'fry *EH30*	9	AF3
Station Rd, K'lis. *EH29*	20	AD10
Station Vw, S Q'fry *EH30*	9	AF3
Stead's Pl *EH6*	15	BH7
Steele Av (Mayf.), Dalk. *EH22*	71	CB29
Steel's Pl *EH10*	42	BD16
Steil Gro, Tran. *EH33*	35	CM14
Steils, The *EH10*	42	BA18
STENHOUSE	41	AX15
Stenhouse Av *EH11*	41	AW14
Stenhouse Av W *EH11*	41	AW15
Stenhouse Cotts *EH11*	41	AW16
Stenhouse Cres *EH11*	41	AW15
Stenhouse Cross *EH11*	41	AW15
Stenhouse Dr *EH11*	41	AW15
Stenhouse Gdns *EH11*	41	AW15
Stenhouse Gdns N *EH11*	41	AW15
Stenhouse Gro *EH11*	41	AW15
Stenhouse Mill Cres *EH11*	41	AX16
Stenhouse Mill La *EH11*	41	AX16
Stenhouse Mill Wynd *EH11*	41	AX16
Stenhouse Pl E *EH11*	41	AW15
Stenhouse Pl W *EH11*	41	AW15
Stenhouse Prim Sch *EH11*	41	AW15
Stenhouse Rd *EH11*	41	AW16
Stenhouse St E *EH11*	41	AW15
Stenhouse St W *EH11*	40	AV15
Stenhouse Ter *EH11*	41	AX15
Stennis Gdns *EH17* **1**	44	BL20
Ster Century Cinemas (Ocean Terminal) *EH6*	15	BH4
Stevenlaw's Cl *EH1*	7	BF11
Stevenson Av *EH11*	41	AY14
Stevenson Coll (Duncan Pl) *EH6*	16	BJ7
Stevenson Dr *EH11*	41	AW15
Stevenson Gro *EH11*	41	AY14
Stevenson La (Newt.), Dalk. *EH22*	65	BX31
Stevenson Pl, Lass. *EH18*	62	BM29
Stevenson Rd *EH11*	41	AY14
Stevenson Rd, Pen. *EH26*	66	BC35
Stevenson Ter *EH11*	41	AY14
Stewart Av, Currie *EH14*	49	AN24
Stewart Clark Av, S Q'fry *EH30*	9	AE3
Stewart Cres, Currie *EH14*	49	AN23
Stewartfield *EH6*	15	BF7
Stewart Gdns, Currie *EH14*	49	AN23
Stewart Gro, Dalk. *EH22*	45	BQ19
Stewart Pl, Currie *EH14*	49	AN24
Stewart Pl, K'lis. *EH29*	20	AD9
Stewart Rd, Currie *EH14*	49	AN24
Stewart's Melville Coll *EH4*	26	BA10
Stewart Ter *EH11*	41	AZ14
Stewart Ter, S Q'fry *EH30*	8	AD2
Stills Gall *EH1*	7	BF11
Stirling Pl *EH5*	14	BD5
Stirling Rd, K'lis. *EH29*	20	AB9
Stobhill Prim Sch *EH23*	70	BZ35
Stobhill Rd (Newt.), Dalk. *EH22*	65	BX31
Stobhill Rd (Gowks.), Gore. *EH23*	65	BX32
STOCKBRIDGE	26	BD9
Stockbridge Prim Sch *EH3*	26	BD9
Stone Av (Mayf.), Dalk. *EH22*	65	BZ29
Stone Cres (Mayf.), Dalk. *EH22*	65	BZ29
Stone Pl (Mayf.), Dalk. *EH22*	65	BZ30
STONEYBANK	31	BW15
Stoneybank Av, Muss. *EH21*	31	BW15
Stoneybank Ct, Muss. *EH21*	31	BW14
Stoneybank Cres, Muss. *EH21*	31	BX15
Stoneybank Dr, Muss. *EH21*	31	BW14
Stoneybank Gdns, Muss. *EH21*	31	BW14
Stoneybank Gdns N, Muss. *EH21*	31	BW14
Stoneybank Gdns S, Muss. *EH21*	31	BX15
Stoneybank Gro, Muss. *EH21*	31	BX15
Stoneybank Pl, Muss. *EH21*	31	BX15
Stoneybank Rd, Muss. *EH21*	31	BX15
Stoneybank Ter, Muss. *EH21*	31	BX15
Stoneycroft Rd, S Q'fry *EH30*	9	AE2
Stoneyflatts, S Q'fry *EH30*	8	AC2
Stoneyflatts Cres, S Q'fry *EH30*	8	AC2
Stoneyflatts Pk, S Q'fry *EH30*	8	AC3
STONEYHILL	31	BW15

Stoneyhill Av, Muss. *EH21*	31	BW14
Stoneyhill Ct, Muss. *EH21*	31	BW14
Stoneyhill Cres, Muss. *EH21*	31	BW14
Stoneyhill Dr, Muss. *EH21*	31	BW14
Stoneyhill Fm Rd, Muss. *EH21*	31	BW14
Stoneyhill Gdns, Muss. *EH21* **1**	31	BW14
Stoneyhill Gro, Muss. *EH21*	31	BW14
Stoneyhill Pl, Muss. *EH21*	31	BW14
Stoneyhill Prim Sch *EH21*	31	BW14
Stoneyhill Ri, Muss. *EH21*	31	BW14
Stoneyhill Rd, Muss. *EH21*	31	BW14
Stoneyhill Steading, Muss. *EH21*	31	BW14
Stoneyhill Ter, Muss. *EH21*	31	BW14
Stoneyhill Wynd, Muss. *EH21*	31	BW14
Strachan Gdns *EH4*	25	AW9
Strachan Rd *EH4*	25	AX10
STRAITON	54	BJ25
Straiton Mains (Strait.), Lnhd *EH20*	54	BJ26
Straiton Pk (Strait.), Lnhd *EH20*	54	BJ26
Straiton Pk Caravan Site (Strait.), Lnhd *EH20*	61	BH26
Straiton Pl *EH15*	29	BR10
Straiton Rd (Strait.), Lnhd *EH20*	54	BJ25
Strathalmond Ct *EH4*	23	AP8
Strathalmond Grn *EH4*	23	AP8
Strathalmond Pk *EH4*	23	AP9
Strathalmond Rd *EH4*	23	AP8
Strathearn Pl *EH9*	42	BD15
Strathearn Rd *EH9*	43	BE15
Strathesk Gro, Pen. *EH26*	69	BC37
Strathesk Pl, Pen. *EH26*	69	BC37
Strathesk Rd, Pen. *EH26*	69	BC37
Strawberry Bk, Dalk. *EH22*	56	BU26
Stuart Cres *EH12*	23	AR11
Stuart Grn *EH12*	23	AR11
Stuart Pk *EH12*	23	AR11
Stuart Sq *EH12*	23	AR11
Stuart Wynd *EH12*	23	AR11
Succoth Av *EH12*	25	AZ11
Succoth Ct *EH12*	25	AZ11
Succoth Gdns *EH12*	25	AZ11
Succoth Pk *EH12*	25	AY11
Succoth Pl *EH12*	25	AZ11
Suffolk Rd *EH16*	43	BH16
Suffolk Rd La *EH16*	43	BH16
Summerbank *EH3*	27	BE9
Summerfield Gdns *EH6*	16	BK7
Summerfield Pl *EH6*	16	BK7
Summerhall *EH9* **4**	43	BG14
Summerhall Cres *EH9* **4**	7	BG13
Summerhall Pl *EH9* **5**	43	BG14
Summerhall Sq *EH9*	43	BG14
Summerlee, Pres. *EH32*	18	CG10
Summer Pl *EH3*	27	BE8
Summerside Pl *EH6*	15	BF6
Summerside St *EH6*	15	BF6
Summertrees Ct *EH16*	44	BK18
Sunbury Ms *EH4*	26	BB11
Sunbury Pl *EH4*	26	BB11
Sunbury St *EH4*	26	BB11
Sunnybank *EH7*	28	BK10
Sunnybank Pl *EH7*	28	BK10
Sunnybank Ter *EH7* **4**	28	BJ10
Sunnyside *EH7*	16	BJ9
Surrey Pl *EH12* **2**	26	BA12
Sutherland St *EH12*	26	BA12
Suttieslea Cres (Newt.), Dalk. *EH22*	65	BY29
Suttieslea Dr (Newt.), Dalk. *EH22*	65	BY29
Suttieslea Pl (Newt.), Dalk. *EH22*	65	BY29
Suttieslea Rd (Newt.), Dalk. *EH22*	65	BY29
Suttieslea Wk (Newt.), Dalk. *EH22*	65	BY29
Swan Cres, Gore. *EH23*	70	BY34
Swanfield *EH6*	15	BH6
Swan Rd, Tran. *EH33*	35	CL14
Swan Spring Av *EH10*	52	BC20
Swanston Av *EH10*	52	BC22
Swanston Cres *EH10*	52	BC22
Swanston Dr *EH10*	52	BD23
Swanston Gdns *EH10*	52	BC22
Swanston Golf Course *EH10*	52	BB24
Swanston Grn *EH10*	52	BC22
Swanston Gro *EH10*	52	BD22
Swanston Ln *EH10*	52	BC22
Swanston Muir *EH10*	52	BA22
Swanston Pk *EH10*	52	BC22
Swanston Pl *EH10*	52	BC22
Swanston Rd *EH10*	52	BB22
Swanston Row *EH10*	52	BC22
Swanston Ter *EH10*	52	BD22
Swanston Vw *EH10*	52	BC22
SWANSTON VILLAGE	52	BC24
Swanston Way *EH10*	52	BC22
Sycamore Av (Port S.), Pres. *EH32*	19	CM8
Sycamore Gdns *EH12*	24	AT13
Sycamore Path, Lnhd *EH20* **1**	61	BG28
Sycamore Rd (Mayf.), Dalk. *EH22*	71	CA29
Sycamore Ter *EH12*	24	AU13
Sydney Pk *EH7*	17	BN9
Sydney Pl *EH7*	17	BN9
Sydney Ter *EH7*	17	BN9
Sylvan Pl *EH9*	43	BF14
Syme Cres *EH10*	42	BA19
Syme Pl *EH10* **2**	42	BA19
Syme Rigg *EH10* **4**	42	BA19

T

Tait Dr, Pen. *EH26*	69	BB38
Tait St, Dalk. *EH22*	57	BW24
Talbot Rice Gall *EH1*	7	BF12
Talisman Pl *EH16*	44	BK18
Tanfield *EH3*	27	BE8
Tantallon Pl *EH9*	43	BG14
Tarvit St *EH3*	6	BD13
Tattoo Office *EH1*	7	BF11
Taylor Gdns *EH6*	15	BH6
Taylor Pl *EH7*	28	BJ10
Taylor Pl, Dalk. *EH22*	57	BY25
Tay St *EH11*	42	BB14
Telfer Sub *EH11*	26	BB13
Telferton *EH7*	29	BP10
Telford Coll (North Campus) *EH5*	13	AZ6
Telford Coll (South Campus) *EH3*	14	BA7
Telford Coll (West Campus) *EH4*	25	AZ8
Telford Cotts, Pen. *EH26*	69	BB39
Telford Dr *EH4*	25	AZ8
Telford Gdns *EH4*	25	AZ8
Telford Pl *EH4*	25	AZ8
Telford Rd *EH4*	25	AZ9
Templar's Cramond *EH4*	23	AQ7
Templeland Gro *EH12*	24	AT12
Templeland Rd *EH12*	24	AS12
Temple Pk Cres *EH11*	42	BB14
Tennant St *EH6*	15	BH7
Tenth St (Newt.), Dalk. *EH22*	65	BX29
Terrars Cft *EH8*	7	BH13
Terregles, Pen. *EH26*	68	AZ37
Teviotdale Pl *EH3*	26	BD9
Teviot Gro, Pen. *EH26*	69	BB36
Teviot Pl *EH1*	7	BF12
Teviot Pl *EH8*	7	BF12
Theatre DuPif *EH5*	13	AZ6
Third Gait (Ricc.), Currie *EH14*	49	AN19
Third St (Newt.), Dalk. *EH22*	65	BW31
Thirlestane La *EH9*	43	BE15
Thirlestane Rd *EH9*	43	BE14
Thistle Ct *EH2* **3**	6	BE10
Thistle Pl *EH11*	6	BC13
Thistle St *EH2*	6	BE10
Thistle St N E La *EH2*	6	BE10
Thistle St N W La *EH2*	6	BE10
Thistle St S E La *EH2*	6	BE10
Thistle St S W La *EH2*	6	BE10
Thistle Hotel, The *EH1*	7	BF10
Thomson Cres, Currie *EH14*	49	AR22
Thomson Cres (Port S.), Pres. *EH32*	19	CM7
Thomson Dr, Currie *EH14*	49	AR22
Thomson Gro, Currie *EH14*	49	AR22
Thomson Rd, Currie *EH14*	49	AR22
Thomson's Ct *EH1* **8**	6	BE12
Thorburn Gro *EH13*	51	AY21
Thorburn Rd *EH13*	51	AX20
Thorburn Ter, Pen. *EH26*	68	BA39
Thorntree Cres, Pres. *EH32*	18	CK10
Thorntreeside *EH6*	16	BJ7
Thorntree St *EH6*	15	BH7
Thornville Ter *EH6*	16	BJ8
Thornybank, Dalk. *EH22*	57	BY23
Thornybank Ind Est, Dalk. *EH22*	57	BY23
Thornybauk *EH3*	6	BD12
Thornyhall, Dalk. *EH22*	57	BY23
Threipmuir Av, Bal. *EH14*	58	AL27
Threipmuir Gdns, Bal. *EH14*	58	AL27
Threipmuir Pl, Bal. *EH14*	58	AL27
Timber Bush *EH6*	16	BJ5
Timmins Ct (Ratho), Newbr. *EH28*	37	AF17
Tinto Pl *EH6*	15	BG7
Tipperlinn Rd *EH10*	42	BC15
Toddshill Rd, K'lis. *EH29*	20	AC10
Tolbooth Wynd *EH6*	15	BH6
Tollcross Prim Sch *EH3*	6	BD13
Torduff Rd *EH13*	51	AW23
Torphichen Pl *EH3*	6	BC12
Torphichen St *EH3*	6	BC12
Torphin Bk *EH13*	50	AV22
Torphin Hill Golf Course *EH13*	50	AV22
Torphin Rd *EH13*	50	AV22
Torrance Pk *EH4*	24	AS10
Torsonce Rd, Dalk. *EH22*	56	BV25
Toscana Ct, Dalk. *EH22*	45	BQ19
Toward Ct *EH12* **1**	23	AQ12
Towerbank Prim Sch *EH15*	29	BR10
Tower Pl *EH6*	16	BJ5
Tower St *EH6*	16	BJ5
Tower St La *EH6*	16	BJ5
Townswomen's Guild Wk *EH3*	7	BF13
Trafalgar La *EH6*	15	BF6

Trafalgar St *EH6* 15 BG6
TRANENT 35 CL14
Tranent Inf Sch *EH33* 35 CM12
Tranent Prim Sch *EH33* 35 CM12
Traprain Ter, Lnhd *EH20* 62 BL28
Traquair Pk E *EH12* 24 AV13
Traquair Pk W *EH12* 24 AU13
Travel Inn Edinburgh City *EH3* 6 BC12
Travel Inn Leith *EH6* 15 BF4
Travel Inn South Queensferry *EH30* 8 AC3
Travelodge Edinburgh Central *EH1* 7 BG11
Travelodge Edinburgh East *EH21* 47 BX17
Travelodge Edinburgh South *EH13* 51 AZ22
Traverse Theatre *EH1* 6 BD12
Trelawney Ter, Pen. *EH26* 66 BC35
Trench Knowe *EH10* 52 BC22
Tressilian Gdns *EH16* 44 BK18
TRINITY 14 BD5
Trinity Academy *EH6* 15 BE5
Trinity Ct *EH6* 14 BD6
Trinity Cres *EH5* 14 BD4
Trinity Gro *EH5* 14 BD5
Trinity Mains *EH5* 14 BD6
Trinity Prim Sch *EH6* 15 BF5
Trinity Rd *EH5* 14 BD5
Trinity Way *EH5* 14 BD6
Tron Old Town Information Centre The *EH1* 8 7 BF11
Tron Sq *EH1* 12 7 BF11
Trotter Haugh *EH9* 43 BF16
Tryst Pk *EH10* 52 BB22
Turner Av, Bal. *EH14* 48 AK24
Turner Pk, Bal. *EH14* 48 AL24
TURNHOUSE 22 AL10
Turnhouse Fm Rd *EH12* 22 AL10
Turnhouse Golf Course *EH12* 22 AM11
Turnhouse Rd *EH12* 22 AM11
Turret Gdns, Pres. *EH32* 34 CH11
Tyler's Acre Av *EH12* 40 AU14
Tyler's Acre Gdns *EH12* 40 AU14
Tyler's Acre Rd *EH12* 40 AU14
Tynecastle High Sch *EH11* 26 BA13
Tynecastle La *EH11* 42 BA14
Tynecastle Park (Hearts FC) *EH11* 42 BA14
Tynecastle Ter *EH11* 42 BA14
Tytler Ct *EH8* 28 BJ10
Tytler Gdns *EH8* 7 BH10

U

UCI Cinema (Fort Kinnaird) *EH15* 30 BS15
UGC Cinema (Fountain Park) *EH11* 6 BC13
Ulster Cres *EH8* 28 BL11
Ulster Dr *EH8* 28 BL11
Ulster Gdns *EH8* 28 BM11
Ulster Gro *EH8* 28 BM12
Ulster Ter *EH8* 28 BM12
Union Pk, Bonny. *EH19* 63 BR29
Union Pl *EH1* 2 7 BG10
Union St *EH1* 27 BF9
University of Edinburgh (Central Campus) *EH8* 7 BF13
University of Edinburgh (King's Buildings) *EH9* 43 BH17
University of Edinburgh Medical Sch *EH16* 45 BN18

Upper Bow *EH1* 8 7 BF11
Upper Broomieknowe, Lass. *EH18* 55 BQ27
Upper Coltbridge Ter *EH12* 25 AZ11
Upper Craigour *EH17* 45 BN18
Upper Craigour Way *EH17* 44 BM18
Upper Cramond Ct *EH4* 23 AR7
UPPER DALHOUSIE 64 BS32
Upper Damside *EH4* 26 BB11
Upper Dean Ter *EH4* 6 BC10
Upper Gilmore Pl *EH3* 6 BD13
Upper Gilmore Ter *EH3* 6 BD13
Upper Gray St *EH9* 43 BG14
Upper Greenside La *EH1* 7 7 BG10
Upper Gro Pl *EH3* 6 BC13
Upper Hermitage *EH6* 16 BJ7
Usher Hall *EH1* 6 BD12

V

VALLEYFIELD 69 BB39
Valleyfield Rd, Pen. *EH26* 69 BB39
Valleyfield St *EH3* 6 BD13
Valleyfield Vw, Pen. *EH26* 69 BB39
Vanburgh Pl *EH6* 16 BJ7
Vandeleur Av *EH7* 29 BN10
Vandeleur Gro *EH7* 29 BP10
Vandeleur Pl *EH7* 17 BN9
Vaucluse Pl, Pen. *EH26* 68 BA39
Veitch's Sq *EH4* 26 BD9
Vennel *EH1* 6 BE12
Vennel, S Q'fry *EH30* 3 9 AE2
Ventnor Pl *EH9* 28 BJ15
Ventnor Ter *EH9* 43 BH15
Vernon Cotts *EH15* 1 29 BR11
Vexhim Pk *EH15* 29 BR14
Victoria Dock *EH6* 15 BH5
Victoria Gdns (Newt.), Dalk. *EH22* 64 BV29
Victoria Prim Sch *EH6* 15 BF4
Victoria Rd (Newt.), Dalk. *EH22* 64 BV29
Victoria St *EH1* 7 BF12
Victoria St, Rose. *EH24* 62 BM33
Victoria Ter *EH1* 9 6 BE12
Victoria Ter, Muss. *EH21* 32 CA13
Victor Pk Ter *EH12* 24 AT12
Viewbank Av, Bonny. *EH19* 56 BT27
Viewbank Cres, Bonny. *EH19* 1 56 BS27
Viewbank Dr, Bonny. *EH19* 56 BS27
Viewbank Rd, Bonny. *EH19* 55 BR27
Viewbank Vw, Bonny. *EH19* 56 BS27
Viewcraig Gdns *EH8* 7 BG11
Viewcraig St *EH8* 7 BG11
Viewfield, Bonny. *EH19* 56 BT27
Viewfield Rd, Jun. Grn *EH14* 50 AU20
Viewforth *EH10* 42 BC14
Viewforth *EH11* 6 BC13
Viewforth (Port S.), Pres. *EH32* 19 CM7
Viewforth Bk, S Q'fry *EH30* 8 AD2
Viewforth Gdns *EH10* 42 BD14
Viewforth Gdns, Tran. *EH33* 6 35 CL13
Viewforth Pl, S Q'fry *EH30* 8 AD3
Viewforth Rd, S Q'fry *EH30* 8 AD2
Viewforth Sq *EH10* 42 BC14
Viewforth Ter *EH10* 42 BC14
Viewforth Ter, Tran. *EH33* 5 35 CL13
Viewpark Gdns, Bonny. *EH19* 55 BR27
Villa Rd, S Q'fry *EH30* 8 AD2
Violet Ter *EH11* 42 BA14

Vivian Ter *EH4* 24 AV8
Vogrie Cres S, Gore. *EH23* 70 BZ36
Vogrie Pl, Gore. *EH23* 70 BZ35
Vogrie Rd, Gore. *EH23* 70 BZ35
Vorlich Cres, Pen. *EH26* 69 BC36

W

Wadingburn La, Lass. *EH18* 55 BP26
Wadingburn Rd, Lass. *EH18* 55 BN27
Wakefield Av *EH7* 17 BP9
Walker Cres, Dalk. *EH22* 56 BT26
Walker Dr, S Q'fry *EH30* 8 AC2
Walker Pl, Lass. *EH18* 63 BN29
Walkers Ct *EH14* 1 40 AU18
Walkers Rigg *EH14* 40 AU18
Walker St *EH3* 6 BC11
Walkers Wynd *EH14* 40 AU18
Walker Ter *EH11* 6 6 BC12
Wallace Cres, Ros. *EH25* 62 BJ31
Wallace Pl, Tran. *EH33* 1 35 CL12
WALLYFORD 33 CE15
Wallyford Ind Est (Wall.), Muss. *EH21* 33 CD15
Wallyford Ln Rd (Wall.), Muss. *EH21* 33 CD13
Wallyford Prim Sch *EH21* 33 CD14
Wallyford Sta *EH21* 33 CD14
Wallyford Toll (Wall.), Muss. *EH21* 33 CE13
Walter Scott Av *EH16* 44 BK18
Wanless Ct, Muss. *EH21* 31 BZ13
Warden's Cl *EH1* 7 BF12
WARDIE 14 BC5
Wardie Av *EH5* 14 BC6
Wardieburn Dr *EH5* 14 BB5
Wardieburn Pl E *EH5* 14 BB5
Wardieburn Pl N *EH5* 14 BB5
Wardieburn Pl S *EH5* 14 BB5
Wardieburn Pl W *EH5* 14 BA5
Wardieburn Rd *EH5* 14 BA5
Wardieburn St E *EH5* 14 BB5
Wardieburn St W *EH5* 14 BA5
Wardieburn Ter *EH5* 14 BA5
Wardie Cres *EH5* 14 BB5
Wardie Dell *EH5* 14 BC5
Wardiefield *EH5* 14 BB5
Wardie Gro *EH5* 14 BB5
Wardie Ho La *EH5* 14 BC4
Wardie Pk *EH5* 14 BC6
Wardie Prim Sch *EH5* 14 BC6
Wardie Rd *EH5* 14 BC5
Wardie Sq *EH5* 14 BC5
Wardie Steps *EH5* 14 BC5
Wardlaw Pl *EH11* 42 BA14
Wardlaw St *EH11* 42 BA14
Wardlaw Ter *EH11* 42 BA14
Warner Village Cinema *EH1* 7 BG10
Warrender Pk Cres *EH9* 42 BD14
Warrender Pk Rd *EH9* 43 BE14
Warrender Pk Ter *EH9* 43 BE14
WARRISTON 15 BE7
Warriston Av *EH3* 15 BE7
Warriston Cres *EH3* 27 BE8
Warriston Dr *EH3* 14 BD7
Warriston Fm Rd, Currie *EH14* 48 AL21
Warriston Gdns *EH3* 14 BD7
Warriston Gro *EH3* 14 BD7
Warriston Pl *EH3* 27 BE8
Warriston Rd *EH3* 27 BE8
Warriston Rd *EH7* 15 BE6
Warriston Ter *EH3* 14 BD7
Washington La *EH11* 26 BB13
Washington St *EH11* 26 BB13

Name		Page	Grid
Waterfall Wk, Dalk. *EH22*		57	BX25
Waterloo Bk, Pen. *EH26*		69	BB39
Waterloo Pl *EH1*		7	BF10
Water of Leith Visitor Centre *EH14*		41	AY17
Water of Leith Walkway *EH13*		41	AW19
Water of Leith Walkway *EH14*		41	AW19
Water's Cl *EH6* **6**		16	BJ6
Water St *EH6*		16	BJ6
Watertoun Rd *EH9*		43	BG16
Watson Cres *EH11*		42	BB14
Watson St, Pen. *EH26*		68	BA38
Watt Gro (Mayf.), Dalk. *EH22*		71	CA30
Watt Pk (Newt.), Dalk. *EH22*		65	BX31
Watt's Cl, Muss. *EH21*		31	BX13
Wauchope Av *EH16*		29	BN15
Wauchope Cres *EH16*		29	BN15
Wauchope Ho *EH16*		45	BP16
Wauchope Pl *EH16*		29	BN15
Wauchope Rd *EH16*		29	BP15
Wauchope Sq *EH16*		29	BP15
Wauchope Ter *EH16*		29	BP15
Waugh Path, Bonny. *EH19*		56	BT27
Waulkmill Dr, Pen. *EH26*		69	BB39
Waulkmill Ln, Currie *EH14*		49	AN24
Waulkmill Rd, Pen. *EH26*		69	BC38
Waulkmill Vw, Pen. *EH26*		69	BB38
Waverley Br *EH1*		7	BF11
Waverley Ct, Bonny. *EH19*		56	BS28
Waverley Cres, Bonny. *EH19*		56	BS28
Waverley Dr, Bonny. *EH19*		56	BS28
Waverley Pk *EH8*		28	BJ10
Waverley Pk, Bonny. *EH19*		56	BS28
Waverley Pk (Mayf.), Dalk. *EH22*		65	BZ29
Waverley Pk Ter *EH8*		28	BJ10
Waverley Pl *EH7*		28	BJ10
Waverley Rd, Bonny. *EH19*		56	BS28
Waverley Rd, Dalk. *EH22*		56	BV25
Waverley Sta *EH1*		7	BF11
Waverley St *EH2*		7	BF11
Waverley St (Mayf.), Dalk. *EH22*		65	BZ30
Waverley Ter, Bonny. *EH19*		56	BS28
Waverley Ter (Mayf.), Dalk. *EH22*		65	BZ29
Weaver's Knowe Cres, Currie *EH14*		49	AP22
Websters Land *EH1* **10**		6	BE12
Wedderburn Ter (Inv.), Muss. *EH21*		31	BZ16
Wee Brae, Lass. *EH18*		55	BQ26
Weir Ct *EH11*		40	AT17
Weir Ct, Dalk. *EH22* **1**		56	BU25
Weir Cres, Dalk. *EH22*		56	BU25
Well Ct *EH4* **4**		6	BC11
Wellflats Rd, K'lis. *EH29*		20	AD10
Wellhead Cl, S Q'fry *EH30*		9	AF3
Wellington Pl *EH6*		16	BJ6
Wellington St *EH7*		27	BH9
Well Wynd, Tran. *EH33*		35	CM13
Wemyss Gdns (Wall.), Muss. *EH21*		33	CE14
Wemyss Pl *EH3*		6	BD10
Wemyss Pl (Port S.), Pres. *EH32*		19	CL7
Wemyss Pl Ms *EH3*		6	BD10
Werberside Ms *EH4*		14	BA7
Wesley Cres, Bonny. *EH19*		56	BT28
West Adam St *EH8*		7	BG12
West Annandale St *EH7*		27	BF8
West App Rd *EH3*		6	BD12
West App Rd *EH11*		26	BB13
Westbank *EH4* **4**		12	AU7
Westbank Ln *EH15* **1**		29	BQ10
Westbank Pl *EH15*		29	BQ10
Westbank St *EH15*		29	BQ10
West Bow *EH1*		7	BF12
West Bowl Grn St *EH6*		15	BG6
West Brighton Cres *EH15*		29	BQ11
West Bryson Rd *EH11*		42	BB14
Westburn Av *EH14*		40	AS19
Westburn Gro *EH14*		40	AS19
Westburn Middlefield *EH14*		40	AS19
Westburn Pk *EH14*		40	AT19
Westburn Prim Sch *EH11*		40	AT18
West Cairn Cres, Pen. *EH26*		68	BA37
West Caiystane Rd *EH10*		52	BC22
West Camus Rd *EH10*		52	BC21
West Carnethy Av *EH13*		51	AW22
West Castle Rd *EH10*		42	BC14
West Catherine Pl *EH12*		26	BA12
West Cherrybank *EH6*		15	BE5
West Coates *EH12*		26	BA12
West Coll St *EH8*		7	BF12
West Ct *EH4*		25	AY10
West Ct *EH16*		45	BN16
WEST CRAIGS		23	AP12
West Craigs Av *EH12*		39	AP13
West Craigs Cres *EH12*		39	AP13
West Craigs Ind Est *EH12*		23	AP12
West Cft (Ratho), Newbr. *EH28*		37	AG17
West Cromwell St *EH6* **1**		15	BH5
West Crosscauseway *EH8*		7	BG13
WEST END		6	BC11
West End *EH2*		6	BD11
West End Pl *EH11*		26	BB13
Wester Auchendinny Br, Pen. *EH26*		67	BE35
Wester Broom Av *EH12*		40	AS14
Wester Broom Dr *EH12*		40	AS14
Wester Broom Gdns *EH12*		40	AS14
Wester Broom Gro *EH12*		40	AS14
Wester Broom Pl *EH12*		40	AS14
Wester Broom Ter *EH12*		40	AS14
Wester Cl *EH6* **3**		15	BF4
Wester Coates Av *EH12*		26	BA12
Wester Coates Gdns *EH12*		26	BA12
Wester Coates Pl *EH12*		26	BA11
Wester Coates Rd *EH12*		26	BA12
Wester Coates Ter *EH12*		26	BA12
Wester Drylaw Av *EH4*		25	AX8
Wester Drylaw Dr *EH4*		25	AX8
Wester Drylaw Pk *EH4*		25	AY8
Wester Drylaw Pl *EH4*		25	AX8
Wester Drylaw Row *EH4*		25	AY9
WESTER HAILES		40	AT19
Wester Hailes Education Centre *EH14*		40	AS18
Wester Hailes Pk *EH14*		40	AU19
Wester Hailes Rd *EH11*		40	AS17
Wester Hailes Rd *EH14*		40	AS17
Wester Hailes Rd, Jun. Grn *EH14*		50	AU20
Wester Hailes Sta *EH14*		40	AT19
Wester Hill *EH10*		42	BA19
Westerlea Sch *EH12*		25	AY12
Wester Millerhill, Dalk. *EH22*		46	BU20
Western Cor *EH12* **1**		25	AX12
Western Gdns *EH12*		25	AY12
Western General Hosp *EH4*		25	AZ8
Western Harbour *EH6*		15	BG4
Western Pl *EH12*		25	AY12
Western Ter *EH12*		25	AY12
Wester Row, Currie *EH14*		39	AN18
Wester Steil *EH10*		42	BA18
West Ferryfield *EH5*		14	BB6
Westfield Av *EH11*		41	AY14
Westfield Bk, Dalk. *EH22*		56	BU26
Westfield Ct *EH11*		41	AY14
Westfield Ct, Dalk. *EH22* **2**		56	BU26
Westfield Dr, Dalk. *EH22* **3**		56	BU26
Westfield Gro, Dalk. *EH22*		56	BU26
Westfield Pk, Dalk. *EH22*		56	BU26
Westfield Rd *EH11*		41	AZ14
Westfield St *EH11*		41	AZ14
West Fountain Pl *EH11*		26	BB13
Westgarth Av *EH13*		51	AX21
West Gorgie Pk *EH14*		41	AY15
West Gorgie Pl *EH14*		41	AY16
West Gra Gdns *EH9*		43	BF15
West Granton Access *EH5*		13	AZ5
West Granton Rd *EH5*		14	BA5
Westgrove *EH11*		40	AU17
Westhall Gdns *EH10*		42	BD14
West Harbour (Cock.), Pres. *EH32*		18	CK7
West Harbour Rd *EH5*		14	BA4
West Harbour Rd (Cock.), Pres. *EH32*		18	CK7
West Holmes Gdns, Muss. *EH21*		31	BX13
Westhouses Av (Mayf.), Dalk. *EH22*		71	CA30
Westhouses Dr (Mayf.), Dalk. *EH22* **3**		71	CA30
Westhouses Rd (Mayf.), Dalk. *EH22*		71	CA30
Westhouses St (Mayf.), Dalk. *EH22* **2**		71	CA30
Westland Cotts *EH17*		55	BN22
West Ln, Pres. *EH32*		18	CH10
West Ln Ct, Pres. *EH32* **1**		34	CH11
West Lorimer Pl (Cock.), Pres. *EH32*		18	CK7
WEST MAINS		43	BH18
West Mains Rd *EH9*		43	BG17
West Maitland St *EH12*		6	BC12
West Mayfield *EH9*		43	BH15
West Mill Bk *EH13*		51	AW21
West Mill Ct, Lass. *EH18* **1**		55	BQ26
West Mill La *EH4*		6	BC11
West Mill Rd *EH13*		50	AV21
Westmill Rd, Lass. *EH18*		55	BQ27
Westmill Wynd, Lass. *EH18*		55	BQ27
West Montgomery Pl *EH7*		27	BG9
West Newington Pl *EH9*		43	BG14
West Nicolson St *EH8*		7	BG12
West Norton Pl *EH7*		7	BH10
West One Business Pk *EH11*		39	AR17
WESTPANS		32	CC12
West Pk Pl *EH11*		26	BB13
West Pier *EH5*		14	BA4
WEST PILTON		13	AZ6
West Pilton Av *EH4*		13	AY7
West Pilton Bk *EH4*		13	AX6
West Pilton Cres *EH4*		13	AX6
West Pilton Crossway *EH4*		13	AY6
West Pilton Dr *EH4*		13	AY6
West Pilton Gdns *EH4*		13	AY6
West Pilton Grn *EH4*		13	AY6
West Pilton Gro *EH4*		13	AY7
West Pilton Lea *EH4*		13	AY6
West Pilton Ln *EH4*		13	AY6
West Pilton March *EH4*		13	AZ5
West Pilton Pk *EH4*		13	AY6
West Pilton Pl *EH4*		13	AZ6
West Pilton Ri *EH4*		13	AY6
West Pilton Rd *EH4*		13	AZ6

West Pilton St EH4 13 AY6
West Pilton Ter EH4 13 AY6
West Pilton Vw EH4 13 AY7
West Port EH1 6 BE12
West Port EH3 6 BE12
West Powburn EH9 43 BG16
West Preston St EH8 43 BG14
West Register St EH2 7 BF10
West Register St La EH2 4 7 BF10
West Relugas Rd EH9 43 BF16
West Richmond St EH8 7 BG12
West Savile Gdns EH9 43 BG16
West Savile Rd EH16 43 BH16
West Savile Ter EH9 43 BG16
West Scotland St La EH3 27 BE9
West Seaside, Pres. EH32 18 CG10
West Shore Rd EH5 13 AX5
West Shore Rd Trd Est EH5 13 AY4
Westside Gdns EH11 40 AU16
Westside Plaza Shop Cen
  EH14 40 AT19
West Silvermills La EH3 26 BD9
West Stanhope Pl EH12 1 26 BA12
West St, Pen. EH26 68 BA39
West Telferton EH7 29 BP10
West Ter, S Q'fry EH30 3 8 AD2
West Tollcross EH3 6 BD13
West Werberside EH4 14 BA7
West Windygoul Gdns, Tran.
  EH33 34 CK15
West Winnelstrae EH5 14 BB7
West Wds EH4 26 BA8
Wheatfield Gro, Lnhd EH20 54 BJ27
Wheatfield Ln, Lnhd EH20 54 BK26
Wheatfield Pl EH11 41 AZ14
Wheatfield Rd EH11 41 AZ14
Wheatfield St EH11 42 BA14
Wheatfield Ter EH11 1 41 AZ14
Wheatfield Wk, Lnhd EH20 54 BJ27
Wheatsheaf La, Dalk. EH22 57 BW23
Whin Pk (Cock.), Pres. 18 CK8
Whin Pk Ind Est, Pres. EH32 18 CK8
Whins Pl EH15 2 29 BQ11
White Dales EH10 53 BE22
Whitehall Ct EH4 25 AX9
White Hart St, Dalk. EH22 7 57 BW24
Whitehead Gro, S Q'fry EH30 9 AE3
WHITEHILL 31 BW15
Whitehill Av, Muss. EH21 31 BW14
Whitehill Dr, Dalk. EH22 57 BZ25
Whitehill Fm Rd, Muss. EH21 31 BW15
Whitehill Gdns, Muss. EH21 31 BW15
Whitehill Gro, Dalk. EH22 57 BZ26
Whitehill Rd EH15 30 BS15
Whitehill Rd, Dalk. EH22 30 BS16
Whitehill Rd (Newcr.),
  Muss. EH21 30 BT16
Whitehill St (Newcr.),
  Muss. EH21 30 BT15
White Horse Cl EH8 7 BH11
Whitehouse Ln EH9 42 BD14
Whitehouse Rd EH4 23 AQ8
Whitehouse Ter EH9 43 BE15
Whitelea Cres, Bal. EH14 58 AL27
Whitelea Rd, Bal. EH14 58 AL27
White Pk EH11 42 BA14
White's Cl, Dalk. EH22 57 BW24
Whitingford EH6 15 BF6
Whitson Cres EH11 41 AX14
Whitson Gro EH11 41 AX14
Whitson Pl E EH11 41 AX14
Whitson Pl W EH11 41 AX14
Whitson Rd EH11 41 AX14
Whitson Ter EH11 41 AX14
Whitson Wk EH11 41 AW14

Whitson Way EH11 41 AX14
Whyte Pl EH7 28 BJ10
Wilfrid Ter EH8 5 28 BL10
Wilkieston Rd (Ratho),
  Newbr. EH28 37 AE17
William Black Pl, S Q'fry
  EH30 9 AE3
Williamfield Sq EH15 1 29 BQ11
William Jameson Pl EH15 8 29 BQ10
William St EH3 6 BC11
William St La N E EH3 6 BC11
William St La N W EH3 6 BC11
William St La S E EH3 6 BC11
William St La S W EH3 6 BC12
Willow Av, Bonny. EH19 63 BR29
Willowbank Row EH6 15 BF5
WILLOWBRAE 28 BL12
Willowbrae Av EH8 28 BL11
Willowbrae Gdns EH8 28 BM11
Willowbrae Rd EH8 28 BL11
Willowpark Sch EH11 41 AZ14
Willow Path, Lnhd EH20 2 61 BH28
Willow Rd (Mayf.),
  Dalk. EH22 71 CA29
Willow Tree Pl, Bal. EH14 48 AM24
Wilson Av, Dalk. EH22 57 BY24
Wilson Av, Pres. EH32 18 CH10
Wilson Rd, Gore. EH23 70 BZ34
Wilson's Ct EH8 3 7 BG11
Wilson's Pk EH15 29 BR10
Wilson St, Pen. EH26 68 BA38
Wilson Wk, Tran. EH33 2 35 CL14
Wilton Rd EH16 43 BH17
Windmill La EH8 7 BF13
Windmill Pl EH8 6 7 BG13
Windmill St EH8 7 BF13
Windsor Cres, Pen. EH26 69 BC37
Windsor Dr, Pen. EH26 69 BC38
Windsor Gdns, Muss. EH21 32 CA13
Windsor Pk, Muss. EH21 32 CB13
Windsor Pk Dr, Muss. EH21 32 CB13
Windsor Pk Pl, Muss. EH21 32 CB13
Windsor Pk Ter, Muss. EH21 32 CA13
Windsor Pl EH15 29 BR11
Windsor Rd, Pen. EH26 69 BC37
Windsor Sq, Pen. EH26 69 BC37
Windsor St EH7 27 BG9
Windsor St La EH7 27 BG9
Windsor Ter, Pen. EH26 69 BC37
Windygoul Cres, Tran. EH33 35 CM14
Windy Wynd, Muss. EH21 31 BZ15
Winton Cl, Tran. EH33 35 CM15
Winton Ct (Cock.), Pres.
  EH32 1 19 CL7
Winton Ct, Tran. EH33 35 CN15
Winton Dr EH10 52 BD23
Winton Gdns EH10 53 BE23
Winton Gro EH10 52 BD22
Winton Gro, Tran. EH33 35 CN15
Winton Ln EH10 53 BE23
Winton Pk EH10 52 BD23
Winton Pk (Cock.),
  Pres. EH32 19 CL8
Winton Pl, Tran. EH33 35 CM13
Winton Ter EH10 52 BD23
Winton Way, Tran. EH33 35 CM15
Wishart Av, Bonny. EH19 56 BT27
Wishart Pl, Dalk. EH22 56 BU25
Wishaw Ter EH7 28 BK10
Wisp, The EH16 45 BR16
Wisp Grn EH15 29 BR15
Witholm (Whitehill),
  Dalk. EH22 71 CA26
Wolrige Rd EH16 44 BJ19
Wolseley Cres EH8 28 BL10

Wolseley Gdns EH8 8 28 BL10
Wolseley Pl EH8 9 28 BL10
Wolseley Ter EH8 6 28 BL10
Wolsey Av, Bonny. EH19 64 BS29
Woodbine Gdns, Pres.
  EH32 2 18 CH10
Woodbine Ter EH6 16 BJ8
WOODBURN 57 BY24
Woodburn Av, Dalk. EH22 57 BY24
Woodburn Bk, Dalk. EH22 57 BY24
Woodburn Dr, Dalk. EH22 57 BX24
Woodburn Gdns, Dalk. EH22 57 BY24
Woodburn Gro, Dalk. EH22 57 BY25
Woodburn Ln, Dalk. EH22 57 BY24
Woodburn Medway, Dalk.
  EH22 57 BY25
Woodburn Pk, Dalk. EH22 57 BY24
Woodburn Pl EH10 42 BD16
Woodburn Pl, Dalk. EH22 57 BY25
Woodburn Prim Sch EH22 57 BY24
Woodburn Rd, Dalk. EH22 57 BX24
Woodburn St, Dalk. EH22 57 BY24
Woodburn Ter EH10 42 BD16
Woodburn Ter, Dalk. EH22 57 BZ25
Woodburn Vw, Dalk. EH22 57 BY25
Woodend Pk, Ros. EH25 67 BH32
Woodfield Av EH13 50 AV21
Woodfield Pk EH13 50 AV21
Woodfield Pk (Bils.),
  Ros. EH25 61 BF29
WOODHALL 50 AU21
Woodhall Av, Jun. Grn EH14 50 AT21
Woodhall Bk EH13 50 AV22
Woodhall Dr, Jun. Grn EH14 50 AT21
Woodhall Gro EH13 50 AV22
Woodhall Millbrae, Jun. Grn
  EH14 50 AU21
Woodhall Rd EH13 51 AW21
Woodhall Ter, Jun. Grn EH14 50 AT21
Woodlands Gro EH15 29 BN14
Woodrow, Gore. EH23 70 BY34
Woods Ct, Bonny. EH19 3 63 BR28
Woodside Dr, Pen. EH26 69 BB38
Woodside Gdns, Muss. EH21 32 CA13
Woodside Ter EH15 30 BS12
Woodstock Pl EH16 44 BK18
Woodville Ter EH6 16 BJ8
Woolmet Cres (Dand.),
  Dalk. EH22 45 BR19
Wright's Hos EH10 42 BD14
Writers' Mus (Lady Stairs Ho)
  EH1 5 7 BF11
Wyvern Pk EH9 43 BF15
Wyvis Pk, Pen. EH26 69 BC36

Y

Yardheads EH6 15 BH6
Yarrow Ct, Pen. EH26 69 BC36
Yeaman La EH11 26 BB13
Yeaman Pl EH11 26 BB13
Yewlands Cres EH16 44 BK20
Yewlands Gdns EH16 44 BK20
York Bldgs EH2 7 7 BF10
York La EH1 7 BF10
York Pl EH1 7 BF10
York Rd EH5 15 BE5
Young Av, Tran. EH33 35 CM14
Young St EH2 6 BD11
Young St La N EH2 6 BD11
Young St La S EH2 6 BD11

Z

Zetland Pl EH5 14 BD5